ONE LAND,
TWO PEOPLES

DILEMMAS IN WORLD POLITICS

Series Editor

George A. Lopez, University of Notre Dame

Dilemmas in World Politics offers teachers and students of international relations a series of quality books on critical issues, trends, and regions in international politics. Each text examines a "real world" dilemma and is structured to cover the historical, theoretical, practical, and projected dimensions of its subject.

EDITORIAL BOARD

FORTHCOMING TITLES

Gareth Porter and Janet Welsh Brown
Global Environmental Politics, second edition

□ □ □

Bruce E. Moon
International Trade in the 1990s

□ □ □

Karen Mingst and Margaret P. Karns
The United Nations in the Post–Cold War Era

SECOND EDITION

ONE LAND, TWO PEOPLES

■ ■ ■

The Conflict over Palestine

Deborah J. Gerner

UNIVERSITY OF KANSAS

Westview Press

BOULDER □ SAN FRANCISCO □ OXFORD

Dilemmas in World Politics Series

Copyright © 1991, 1994 by Westview Press, Inc.

Published in 1994 in the United States of America by Westview Press, Inc., 5500 Central Avenue, Boulder, Colorado 80301-2877, and in the United Kingdom by Westview Press, 36 Lonsdale Road, Summertown, Oxford OX2 7EW

Library of Congress Cataloging-in-Publication Data
Gerner, Deborah J.
   One land, two peoples: the conflict over Palestine / Deborah J. Gerner. — 2nd. ed.
      p.   cm.—(Dilemmas in world politics)
   Includes bibliographical references and index.
   ISBN 0-8133-2179-4. ISBN 0-8133-2180-8 (pbk.)
   1. Jewish-Arab relations—1949–   .   2. Israel-Arab conflicts.
I. Title.   II. Series.
DS119.7.G425   1994
956.9405—dc20
                                                                                94-16016
                                                                                CIP

Printed and bound in the United States of America

⊗ The paper used in this publication meets the requirements
   of the American National Standard for Permanence of Paper
   for Printed Library Materials Z39.48-1984.

10   9   8   7   6   5   4

Contents

□ □ □

Tables and Illustrations

Tables

Maps

Photos

□ □ □

Acknowledgments

This book has benefited enormously from the involvement of numerous individuals over the past five years. Conversations with George Lopez, editor of the Dilemmas in World Politics Series, and Miriam Gilbert of Westview Press about our shared commitment to undergraduate education persuaded me to take on the challenge of textbook writing. For this I thank them. Louise Cainkar, Ann M. Lesch, and Karen Mingst critiqued the draft manuscript of the first edition with tremendous care and precision. Their suggestions were superb. Ronald Francisco, Alex Mintz, Jamal Nassar, Julia Pitner, Michael Suleiman, and Antony Sullivan each read sections of the original text and offered valuable insights; Martin Sampson contributed to the initial framing of the manuscript.

In preparing the second edition, I was aided by the illuminating comments of those individuals who reviewed the book in print as well as faculty, students, and other readers who passed along to me their reactions and suggestions. These include Hisham H. Ahmed, Nasir Aruri, Ralph Carter, Lenny Chernilla, Walter C. Clemens, Jr., Ray L. Cleveland, Bryan R. Daves, Peter Hahn, Jamil E. Jreisat, Amal Kawar, Fred J. Khouri, Roy E. Licklider, Philip Mattar, Don Peretz, Abdol-Latif Rayan, Robin Roosevelt, Cheryl Rubenberg, Kenneth W. Stein, M. S. Stern, Ann Lesch's students at Villanova University who wrote perceptive book reviews, my own students at the University of Kansas, and members of the Dilemmas in World Politics editorial board. Shannon Davis, Jamie Hubbard, and Jon Pevehouse provided essential research assistance; Peter Lems and Julia Pitner were valuable sources of information on human rights issues and the evolution of the peace negotiations. In the Middle East, Ibrahim Abu-Lughod, Jan Abu-Shakrah, Reyad Agha, Terry Boulatta, Kahlil Tufukji, Anita Vitullo, and Michael Warshawski were particularly helpful. The National Council on U.S.-Arab Relations provided me the opportunity to meet with high-level Syrian government officials to whom I would not otherwise have had access. Finally, Philip Schrodt served as my sounding board as this book evolved and read multiple drafts of the manuscript. His incisive comments improved it considerably.

At Westview Press, Jennifer Knerr has offered a keen editorial eye and cheerful encouragement throughout the process; her assistant Eric W. Wright was consistently helpful. Ida May B. Norton's copy editing was clear and sensitive to nuances; Jane Raese carefully guided the second edition through the final production process.

To all these people—students and mentors, friends and colleagues—I express my appreciation, along with the inevitable but essential caveat that none of them should be held responsible for any flaws that remain despite their generous assistance. This text is dedicated to all who are working for self-determination and peaceful coexistence for both Palestinians and Israeli Jews, with the hope that the final decade of the twentieth century will bring a just solution to the long-standing conflict over Palestine.

Deborah J. Gerner

□　□　□

A Note on Transliteration

Neither Arabic nor Hebrew transliterates easily into English. As a result, there are a number of different systems of transliteration with varying degrees of linguistic accuracy. Because this is an introductory text, I have chosen to use conventional English-language forms for common personal names and place-names, even though these may be less linguistically pure, and have dropped the "al-" from most names. I have also omitted diacritical marks, including the Arabic ayn and hamza, feeling that this would be less confusing. To those who are familiar with Arabic or Hebrew and are offended by this practical solution, my apologies.

D.J.G.

□ □ □

Acronyms

ADP	Arab Democratic party
AHC	Arab Higher Committee for Palestine
AIPAC	American-Israel Public Affairs Committee
ALF	Arab Liberation Front
ANM	Arab National Movement
BCE	Before Common Era
CCP	Conciliation Commission for Palestine
CE	Common Era
CIA	U.S. Central Intelligence Agency
CRM	Citizens' Rights Movement
DFLP	Democratic Front for the Liberation of Palestine
EC	European Community
HAMAS	Islamic Resistance Movement
ICIPP	Israeli Council for Israeli-Palestinian Peace
IDF	Israeli Defense Forces
IRO	International Refugee Organization
LF	Lebanese Front
LNM	Lebanese Nationalist Movement
NGC	National Guidance Committee
NRP	National Religious party
OAPEC	Organization of Arab Petroleum Exporting Countries
OPEC	Organization of Petroleum Exporting Countries
PCP	Palestine Communist party
PFLP	Popular Front for the Liberation of Palestine
PFLP-GC	Popular Front for the Liberation of Palestine–General Command
PISGA	Palestinian Interim Self-Governing Authority
PLA	Palestine Liberation Army
PLF	Palestine Liberation Front
PLO	Palestine Liberation Organization
PLP	Progressive List for Peace
PNC	Palestine National Council
PNF	Palestinian National Front

PPP	Palestine People's Party
PPSF	Popular Palestinian Struggle Front
UN	United Nations
UNEF	United Nations Emergency Force
UNIFIL	United Nations Interim Force in Lebanon
UNL	Unified National Leadership of the Palestinian Uprising
UNRRA	United Nations Relief and Rehabilitation Administration
UNRWA	United Nations Relief and Works Agency for Palestine Refugees

The Modern Middle East

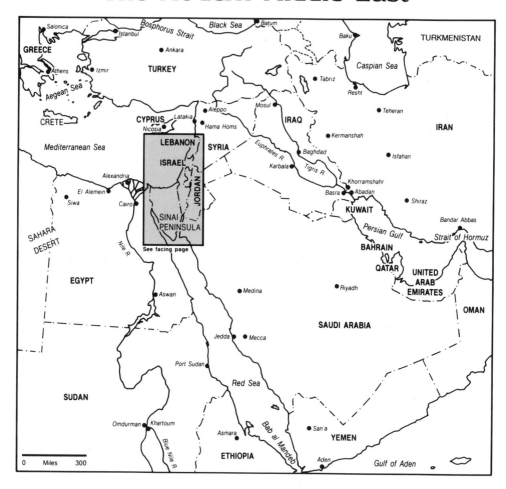

Enlargement of area outlined
in map on facing page

□ □ □

Introduction

On 30 December 1989, more than 20,000 people—Israelis, Palestinians, Europeans, and Americans—joined hands in a two-and-a-half-mile long circle around the Old City of Jerusalem, sang songs, waved olive branches, and called for peace in the Holy Land. The participants in this demonstration, which was the culmination of a three-day program called "1990—Time for Peace," included Jews, Christians, and Muslims; they represented hundreds of international and regional nongovernmental organizations and spanned the political spectrum. Members of the Israeli parliament and Palestinian political leaders also participated in the event, which was jointly organized by Israeli and Palestinian peace activists. It was the largest peace demonstration in Jerusalem since the 1982 Israeli war in Lebanon and indicated, in the words of one participant, that "we can put aside our dreams and our nightmares, shake each other's hands, and work for peace."[1] It was a hopeful beginning for the last decade in a century that has seen almost continual hostility between Zionists and Palestinians.

Nearly four years later, on 13 September 1993, Israeli Prime Minister Yitzhak Rabin and Yasir Arafat, leader of the Palestine Liberation Organization (PLO), met in Washington, D.C., for the signing of a historic document: "Israeli-PLO Declaration of Principles on Interim Self-Government Arrangements." The official endorsement of the Oslo Accords, as the agreement was quickly dubbed because it was negotiated secretly in Oslo, Norway, was executed by Mahmoud Abbas, chief of the political directorate of the PLO, and Israeli Foreign Minister Shimon Peres. In the speeches that preceded the signing ceremony, both Arafat and Rabin stressed the momentous nature of the occasion and their hopes for peace.

We who have fought against you, the Palestinians, we say to you today, in a loud and clear voice, enough of blood and tears. Enough. ... We, like you,

1

By Signe Wilkinson. Reprinted by permission of Cartoonists & Writers Syndicate.

are a people—a people who want to build a home. To plant a tree. To love—live side by side with you. In dignity. In empathy. As human beings.

—*Yitzhak Rabin*

We will need more courage and determination to continue the course of building co-existence and peace between us. This is possible. ... The battle for peace is the most difficult battle of our lives. It deserves our utmost efforts because the land of peace, the land of peace yearns for a just and comprehensive peace.

—*Yasir Arafat*[2]

Many Palestinians and Israelis hailed the Oslo Accords, and the exchange of letters of mutual recognition between Rabin and Arafat that occurred the previous week, with jubilation; others, however, greeted the events with despair. Whatever their reaction, few people disagreed that the Oslo Accords (and subsequent Cairo Agreements) represented a critical turning point in Israeli-Palestinian relations.

The conflict over Israel/Palestine is one of the most significant—and most difficult—dilemmas facing the international community today. It is a conflict full of complexities and subtle nuances and seems to lack simple or easy solutions. For that reason, many people feel overwhelmed by the issue and become convinced the Palestinian-Israeli conflict is too convoluted to understand and too intractable to solve. This short text is designed to alleviate those feelings of confusion and helplessness. Although it is not intended to be a fully comprehensive analysis of the conflict, the book does provide the necessary contemporary and historical background for readers to understand why the issue has been such a difficult one for the international community and for them to begin to formulate their own assessment of what will be needed to achieve a just solution to the conflict.

The Israeli-Palestinian conflict is interesting not only as a case study but also because it provides the opportunity to examine a host of concepts important to international relations at the end of the twentieth century: national identity and self-determination, the increasing importance of nonstate actors, the role of natural resources and strategic location in determining the "political significance" of a country, Great Power involvement in the Third World, the role of religion in international politics, global militarization, the relative impotence of international law and international organizations such as the United Nations (UN) in dealing with very complicated conflicts, and forms of violent and nonviolent conflict resolution. By examining a specific contemporary dilemma in international relations, it is possible to see how these general issues and concepts are expressed in the "real world."

Several themes will be important in the analysis. The first is that this conflict is the result of the search for national identity and self-determination by two peoples—the Palestinians and the Jews—in the context of nineteenth-century European imperialism and twentieth-century decolonization. It is a contemporary struggle, one that comes out of evolving international understandings of statehood and nationalism. This raises a number of interesting questions, such as whether nationalism results from possession of territory or shared history or common religion or self-identification or some combination of these. This is also a conflict rooted in its own reality. In other words, although the conflict is affected by the international environment in significant ways, it is not fundamentally a function of external phenomena such as the U.S.-Soviet competition of the 1950s through 1980s. The cold war has ended, but the Israeli-Palestinian conflict remains.

The second organizing motif is the historical and contemporary attempts of superpowers and European states to manipulate and control the conflict in order to enhance their perceived national interests. Examples of this type of involvement are Britain's concern to protect other parts of its empire—such as India and Egypt—in the early part of the twentieth century, the United States' desire to maintain regional stability and access to petroleum in the post–World War II period, and heightened Soviet strategic interests in the Middle East since the 1950s. Of particular interest are the ways in which the policies of states and other actors external to the conflict have frequently exacerbated tensions between the principal participants.

The third theme that will be addressed is the importance of looking inside the black box of state policy in order to understand how and why particular foreign policy positions are developed or maintained. The policies of each of the principal parties to the Israeli-Palestinian conflict as well as of the secondary/external actors are affected by a range of domestic factors such as the structures of their governments, changes in public opinion, vocal interest groups, and specific political leaders. For example, in Israel the role of religious political parties in the formation of government coalitions is crucial; within the Palestinian national movement, conflicts between groups help explain Palestine Liberation Organization policy decisions; in the United States, public opinion, especially in an election year, may determine the parameters of acceptable foreign policy action. The concept that state and nonstate actors are not monolithic entities is an important one.

Finally, efforts of international organizations to mediate the conflict over Palestine/Israel, and the relevance of the guidelines of international law, will be examined at a number of points. This is an intriguing issue. Much of our understanding of the right to self-determination and our concept of state sovereignty is drawn from the precepts of international law, and the very existence of the State of Israel was specified by a UN Resolution in 1947 that also called for the establishment of a Palestinian state. The United Nations has passed numerous additional resolutions regarding the conflict over Israel/Palestine, and UN peacekeeping forces have been sent to the region on several occasions. Yet scholars and political observers suggest that international law is often ignored in this conflict and that international organizations have been unsuccessful in solving the basic problem.

One Land, Two Peoples traces the evolution of the Palestinian-Israeli conflict since its inception in the nineteenth century and presents the issues that will need to be addressed in order to resolve this critical dilemma in world politics. The treatment of the topic is more historical than is common in political science texts because the Israeli-Palestinian conflict is fundamentally embedded in history and the differing interpretations of that history by the principal actors.

For many Zionists, the Jewish claim to the land of Palestine is based on the history of the Hebrew tribes who intermittently lived in and occasionally ruled this land from the second millennium B.C.E. (before common era, that is, prior to the birth of Jesus, from which Western countries commonly mark their calendar) until their expulsion from Jerusalem by the Romans in 135 C.E. (common era). Furthermore, some Jews and Christians believe this land was promised to the Hebrew people and their descendants by their tribal god, Yahweh, in a covenant with the Prophet Abraham in the seventeenth century B.C.E. As reported in *Genesis* 15:18, Yahweh told the Hebrew people: "To your descendants I give this land, from the river of Egypt to the great river, the river Euphrates." For many Zionists, these ancient religious-historical ties still carry tremendous emotional weight, as well as religious and political legitimacy in the modern era.

Palestinians' claims are similarly grounded in history, including their continuous occupation of the land at least since the seventh century C.E. Although Palestinians do not dispute the existence of ancient Hebrew kingdoms in Palestine, they challenge the idea that this justifies the establishment of a Jewish state in Palestine in the twentieth century. Many question the use of a religious text such as the Bible to justify a political, secular claim. Finally, Palestinians point out that it was Europe that persecuted and ultimately massacred the Jewish people and argue that the people of Europe and the United States had no right to salve their consciences over the Shoah (or Holocaust) by creating a state for the Jewish people in the midst of the Arab world.

In the 1990s, references to past historical injustices in Palestine, in Europe, and elsewhere in the world continue to influence discussions about possible proposals for structuring a resolution to the conflict. Thus, it may be unrealistic to say, "Why not forget the past? Let's start over and figure out how to deal with the conflict as it exists today without worrying about who did what to whom in 1921 or 1936 or 1948 or 1990." For many Israelis and Palestinians, this is extremely difficult: For them, the past is alive in the present. Differing interpretations of Jewish-Palestinian relations over time fundamentally affect the current situation and prospects for future peaceful coexistence.

For this reason, *One Land, Two Peoples* explores the regional and international dimensions of the Israeli-Palestinian conflict through its historical development. Chapter One, "Competition over the Land," examines the growth of nationalist sentiments among Palestinian Arabs and European Jews in the 1800s and describes how these came to be expressed in the 1900s as a conflict over the Ottoman-controlled region known for hundreds of years as Palestine. It also discusses the involvement of a variety of international actors in the nationalist struggles, most significantly Britain and the League of Nations prior to World War II and the United States and the United Nations after 1945. This chapter ends with the decision by the United Nations in November 1947 to partition Palestine into Jewish and Arab states.

Chapter Two, "Clashes and Coalescence: Jewish State, Palestinian Nation," opens with discussion of the Palestine War that followed the United Nations' action, the establishment of the State of Israel in 1948, and the resulting dispersion of the Palestinian people. The chapter then examines the evolution of the Israeli and Palestinian political systems and analyzes the variety of perspectives on the Israeli-Palestinian conflict represented in the decisionmaking bodies of the two national groups, the Israeli Knesset and the Palestine National Council (PNC). The Israeli military presence in the West Bank and Gaza Strip (often referred to as the Occupied Territories), Israeli settlement policies, and the Palestinian uprising (*intifada*) are also described with an eye toward understanding how they affect peace prospects.

In its description of "The Crowded Stage," Chapter Three considers some of the global dimensions that need to be addressed in order to mediate successfully the conflict over Palestine. The bulk of the chapter is an examination of the numerous Arab-Israeli wars, as well as the 1990–1991 Gulf War, and the ways in which these armed conflicts have changed the parameters of the Israeli-Palestinian relationship. Other important international aspects of the conflict include U.S. and Soviet (now Russian) foreign policy involvement; the off-and-on U.S. dialogue with the PLO that began in December 1988; the role of the United Nations and the European countries throughout the past five decades; and international concern about militarization and terrorism in the Middle East.

The last chapter asks whether the future will see "Conflict, Compromise, or Conciliation" between Israelis and Palestinians. The first section outlines the options facing the two groups and summarizes the stages of the peace process, from defining the problem and developing a commitment to negotiate through arranging and conducting negotiations and implementing the agreements reached. The chapter also examines specific issues that will need to be resolved, such as state boundaries, citizenship rights, and the status of Jerusalem. The chapter ends with a discussion of the Madrid conference, the bilateral negotiations of 1991–1993, the Oslo Accords, and the 1994 Cairo Agreement.

ONE

□ □ □

Competition over the Land

The contemporary structure of the global system, with its division of
territory into autonomous nation-states, is a relatively recent phenomenon. Most international relations scholars date its beginning to 1648,
when the Treaty of Westphalia concluded the Thirty Years' War between
Protestants and Catholics and signaled the end of the preeminent rule of
the Holy Roman Empire in Europe. This was a turning point for Europe,
as individual loyalties began to shift from the established church to centralized political units with control over a fixed territory and population.
These political units came to be known as **states.** At the same time, the
concept of **sovereignty** developed, with its emphasis on the territorial integrity of states, the right of states to conduct foreign policy relations however they desired, and the freedom of states from external interference in
their domestic affairs.

This transition to a world of states was neither quick nor painless. It involved the destruction of old social structures, the dislocation of communities, and the breakdown of long-standing patterns of interaction. Although nationalism and state-building served to unite people within the
new political units, the process also constructed economic, social, and political barriers where none had existed before. As recently as the beginning of World War I, significant portions of the world were still part of
large empires, such as the disparate British Empire, with its colonial territories around the world, or the smaller Austro-Hungarian Empire in Europe. In the case of the vast Ottoman Empire, the people were united by a
shared culture and a widespread commitment to pluralism that to a large
extent transcended their ethnic and religious diversity.

Eighty years later, after two world wars and numerous wars of independence against colonial rule, the old political empires are gone. Today,
every inch of inhabitable land on earth is claimed by one or more states.
The majority of the 179 countries that hold membership in the UN did not
exist as distinct political units prior to 1945. Virtually every person in the
world is now identified as a citizen of one and, generally speaking, only

7

one state; this may not, however, correspond to their self-identification. (One notable exception is the significant number of Palestinians who have no citizenship in any country.) Other loyalties—to a religious group, a local community, a clan, an ethnic group, or a broad region of the world—may be at least as compelling as a state-based commitment, although these are often mistakenly viewed as less significant.

There is an important distinction between a "state" and a "nation," which is often ignored in casual conversation. Many of the earliest areas to establish an autonomous political existence, such as England, France, Persia, and Japan, were composed of a relatively homogeneous population with a common language, a shared history and culture, and a corporate sense of identity as a people. This group sense of oneness and of belief in a common destiny is what distinguishes a **nation.** Thus, nationality is primarily a sociological rather than a political concept; it reflects how people characterize themselves in relation to others and who is defined as "we" or "they." When people who have this common sense of self are located together in a self-governing, fixed territory, the resulting political entity is called a nation-state. Not all modern political units are nation-states. Some states contain more than one national group, as does Israel with its Jewish and Palestinian communities. Similarly, a single national group can be spread throughout more than one state, as are the Kurds of Turkey, Iran, and Iraq.

Nonetheless, in the twentieth century the assumption developed among many people that the members of a single nation will make up a single state. Thus, as the concept of nationalism developed, it was necessary to determine who was part of "the group." Was ethnicity more important than shared history or common language? Could people of different religions be part of a single nation? Conversely, were people who shared a religious belief but little else part of the same nation? Should every nation have a separate state?

The answers were not obvious, but a consensus evolved among political scientists that any group of people that has at least some of the attributes of a nation and that thinks of itself as a nation *is* a nation. In other words, a judgment about whether the sense of common destiny and oneness that identifies a nation exists can be made only by the participants within the group, not by an outsider. National identity might be shaped by forces outside the group, but the initial creation and continuing development of such identity is fundamentally a matter of personal (or corporate) choice. This approach to identifying a nation does not, however, resolve the issue of whether every nation, of whatever size and wherever located, should be constituted as a fully autonomous political unit. That question remains unsolved at present. In practical terms, the nations able to establish themselves as states in the modern world are those that had sufficient military power to impose their desires or the support of an already established state willing to act on their behalf. This is not common; there have been many efforts to establish autonomous nation-states that have not succeeded, such as Biafra's attempt to secede from Nigeria or the secessionist efforts of the Katanga province in the Congo (now Zaire). The breakup of the Soviet Union in the early 1990s led to the creation of a number of new states, but many contain multiple national groups and are internally unstable.

These issues about nationality and statehood are reflected in the hundred years of struggle over the lands that—by international consensus—are currently referred to as Israel and Palestine, where Israel is understood to include the boundaries of the state prior to the June 1967 War and Palestine is understood to include the West Bank and the Gaza Strip. This chapter looks at the creation and development of national identity for Jews and Palestinians in the nineteenth and twentieth centuries and the conflict that arose over the expression of this national identity in Palestine prior to the declaration of the State of Israel in 1948.

PALESTINE IN 1900

At the beginning of the twentieth century, the land that came to be known as the Mandate of Palestine was part of the Ottoman Empire, which had ruled Western Asia since 1516. The people who lived in the area referred to it as *Filastin,* or by the Arabic phrase *al-Ard al-Muqadassa* (the Holy Land), reflecting its great importance to Islam, Christianity, and Judaism. Palestine was an area filled with hundreds of small villages and a few large towns. The population was spread across the hilly interior, which includes the Galilee region, Nablus, Hebron, Bethlehem, and Jerusalem; the fertile coastal plain, with the cities of Jaffa, Haifa, and Gaza; the Jordan Valley/Dead Sea region, where Jericho is located; and the Negev Desert, populated mostly by bedouin tribes. The population was ethnically diverse, the legacy of migrations by Greeks, Romans, Turks, Persians, and Jews during the previous two millenniums. As each group passed through, members were assimilated into the existing community, adding to its diversity but never displacing the Arabs who had settled there in the 600s. From the seventh century through the mid-twentieth century, Palestine was predominantly a Muslim area, although Christian Arab and Jewish communities also shared this small region.

Most of the people of Palestine made their living through subsistence agriculture or the export of produce such as olives, grain, sesame products, and oranges, which were sent to Europe through the ports at Jaffa, Gaza, and Acre. Small-scale industries—glass-blowing, cotton cloth weaving, and soap making—also existed, and religious tourism provided

The brightly colored Dome of the Rock, located on al-Haram al-Sharif (Temple Mount to Jews) in Jerusalem, is considered one of the most beautiful mosques in the world. Next to it stands al-Aqsa mosque, the third holiest site in Islam.

a livelihood for some. Finally, there was a small group of powerful families whose members had traditionally been involved in education, religious observances, or politics. Palestine was a localized world, one in which most people rarely traveled more than a day's walk from their home village and a family might live on the same land for hundreds of years.

Within the Ottoman Empire, Palestine was roughly divided into three administrative regions: the Jerusalem *sanjak* (province), which included the territory south of Jerusalem as well as the city itself; and the districts of Nablus and Acre. Representatives from these districts were elected to the short-lived Ottoman parliament in the 1870s, but for the most part the Ottoman rulers were far away and uninvolved in the day-to-day administration of local affairs. Political loyalties were community-based and significant power was held by the heads of prominent families and the religious leaders in each town or region. The Ottoman rulers' use of the *millet* **system** of governance allowed the Christian and Jewish populations a great deal of autonomy: They were granted communal jurisdiction for their own religious, social, cultural, and even legal affairs. For example, the Christian Greek Orthodox patriarch in Jerusalem was responsible for maintaining and protecting the Christian religious sites. There was a relatively high degree of religious tolerance and an acceptance of peaceful coexistence that was at variance with the situation in many other parts of the world.

It is impossible to say for certain how many people lived in Palestine during the first decades of the twentieth century. A Turkish census of 1914 counted 690,000 people, and the British census of 1922 identified more than three-quarters of a million inhabitants, but both numbers are now thought to understate the true population. Of those counted by the 1922 British census, 78 percent were Arab Muslims, 11 percent were identified as Jewish, and nearly 10 percent were Christians (primarily Arabs, but also some Europeans).[1] Virtually all the Christians and Muslims had been born in Palestine. Of the Jews, perhaps two-thirds were immigrants who had come to Palestine in the previous forty years; the remainder were part of a long-standing, culturally and linguistically assimilated community of primarily Orthodox Jews who saw their presence in the Holy Land as fulfilling a religious obligation rather than expressing a national political claim.

EMERGENCE OF JEWISH
AND ARAB NATIONALISM

The transformation of the Levant—Syria, Jordan, Lebanon, Israel, and the Palestinian West Bank and Gaza Strip—from part of the Ottoman Empire to a group of modern states was swift, occurring over a period of less than thirty years. Although the process of building a sense of national identity was more difficult, it too was accomplished relatively rapidly. In 1850 neither Jews nor Arabs viewed themselves as members of an ethnically, culturally, linguistically homogeneous, territorially based nation in the modern sense of the word. Less than a century later, both had developed such identities. In the history of how this occurred are found the modern roots of the Israeli-Palestinian conflict.

Nineteenth-Century Jewry

In the 1800s the Jewish people could be found on every inhabited continent. By far the largest group lived in Eastern and Southern Europe (nearly 75 percent of the total Jewish population in 1880); an additional 14 percent were in Western and Central Europe. About 3 percent of all Jews lived in the United States, a figure that had jumped to over 11 percent by 1900. In addition, there were smaller Jewish communities in the Arab Middle East—Yemen, Iraq, Morocco, Tunisia, Egypt—and elsewhere in Africa, Asia, and Latin America.[2]

The political, economic, and social situation for Jews varied. During several centuries of Ottoman rule, Jews in Arab lands in the Middle East and North Africa experienced favorable conditions and a high degree of toleration by the Muslim leaders. As "people of the book," that is, as one of the monotheistic traditions with which Islam shared a common religious heritage, Jews (along with Christians) had a higher status in Islamic society than nonbelievers or people who followed a polytheistic faith. Like Christians, they were not considered quite equal to Muslims; they shared many social and cultural attributes with their Muslim neighbors, however, and did not experience the widespread persecution that characterized Jewish life in Europe.

In Western Europe periods of religious tolerance of non-Christians alternated with times of severe discrimination and persecution, such as the expulsion or forced conversion of Jews in Spain in 1492. After the French Revolution of 1789, with its emphasis on the equality of all people, the status of Jews in Western Europe began to change for the better. By the 1860s the economic, political, and legal situation of Jews in Western Europe had improved sufficiently to give many hope that Jews could be accepted as equal citizens of the countries in which they resided. Although the situation for Jews in Russia and Eastern Europe was never as favorable, under the reformist movement of Tsar Alexander II (1855–1881) the prospects for increased equality seemed promising.

At the same time, the ideas that had stimulated nationalist sentiment among the general population also had an impact on the Jews of Europe, Russia, and later the United States and raised questions within the Jewish community about what it meant to be a Jew. Was Judaism a religion only? Should Jews retain their separate language, their kosher dietary laws, and their distinctive identity as a social community? Should Jews fight for their state even if it meant fighting against other Jews? The debate hinged on whether or not Jews constituted a distinct *national* group and, if the answer to that question was "yes," whether they should remain in Europe or establish a new state elsewhere. The answers were not straightforward, but initially European Jews began to move toward greater acculturation, even assimilation, and away from a separate identity as Jews.

The widespread optimism of Jews throughout Europe was shattered by the shock of the violent Russian **pogroms** in 1881–1882, during which the government sanctioned the massacre of Jews, and the 1894 Dreyfus affair, in which a Jewish French army captain was unjustly convicted of treason. Symptomatic of the general rise in hostility and persecution against European and Russian Jews during the last two decades of the nineteenth century, both events were of critical importance in convincing many Jews that anti-Jewish sentiment (whether based on religious or "racial" grounds) was unlikely to disappear, and that complete Jewish assimilation was impossible. Thousands of Jews left Russia for the United States in response to this shift in attitude. Others concluded that only in a separate homeland could Jewish national identity be fully expressed and Jews feel secure.

Leon Pinsker represented the latter school of thought. A Russian Jew, Pinsker was convinced that Jews were immutably alien in a gentile (non-Jewish) society, and that Jewish emancipation by Gentiles in the context of Western liberalism could never succeed. Jews had to emancipate themselves, he argued in his pamphlet *Auto-Emancipation!* published in September 1882. Although Pinsker was not initially an adherent to the view that Jews must move to Palestine, he became involved in, and eventually headed, an organization called Hovevei Tsion (Lovers of Zion), whose goal was to promote and finance such emigration.

The first modern wave (*aliyah;* plural *aliyot*) of Jewish immigrants to Palestine (1882–1903) was composed almost entirely of Russian and Polish Jews.[3] Many came from Orthodox religious backgrounds and were attracted to Palestine, which they called Eretz Yisrael, as the biblical homeland, but a significant number of the first immigrants were secular Jews. The majority of people settled in the towns—Jaffa, Hebron, Haifa, Jerusalem—while a much more limited number set up agricultural communities supported by Jewish philanthropists like Baron Edmond de Rothschild. Most of these early settlers, who joined a small existing Jewish community in Palestine (known as the **Yishuv**), had few political ambitions; their desire was to rejuvenate Judaism morally and spiritually so that it could serve as a "light unto the nations." Asher Ginsberg (Ahad HaAm) is representative of this group of cultural Zionists who tried to promote cooperation between the new immigrants and the indigenous people of Palestine.

Zionism

Distinctly political **Zionism**—Jewish nationalism—dates its beginning from the efforts of a secular, Viennese Jew named Theodor Herzl, an author and journalist whose short book *The State of the Jews: An Attempt at a Modern Solution to the Jewish Question,* published in 1896, became a manifesto for the new movement. In this volume, Herzl presented the argument that Jews "are a *people—one* people," and as such entitled to a separate state. This thesis was consistent with European Enlightenment ideas about nationalism that had gained popularity during the 1800s. "Let the sovereignty be granted us over a portion of the globe large enough to satisfy the rightful requirements of a nation; the rest we shall manage for ourselves," Herzl wrote. Unlike the Lovers of Zion, who stressed self-help activities, Herzl intended to bring about Jewish migration and the creation of the Jewish state through Jewish philanthropic activities and with the assistance and involvement of the major European powers.

An initial step was the First Zionist Congress, held in late August 1897 in Basel, Switzerland, and attended by some 200 delegates, virtually all of whom were Russian and Eastern European members of the Lovers of

Zion. Among the statements to come out of the congress was a resolution that began: "Zionism aims at the creation of a home for the Jewish people in Palestine to be secured by public law." After the congress had ended, Herzl confided in his diary that this marked the creation of the Jewish state: "Were I to sum up the Basle Congress in a word—which I shall guard against pronouncing publicly—it would be this: at Basle I founded the Jewish state. ... If I said this out loud today, I would be answered by universal laughter. Perhaps in five years and certainly in fifty everyone will know."[4]

Herzl was not initially committed to Palestine as the only possible conceivable site for the new Jewish state. Other locations, such as Argentina, where large-scale Jewish agricultural colonization had already begun, the Sinai Peninsula, and Uganda, were also considered viable options. Ultimately, however, the majority of delegates voted in favor of Palestine, arguing that only the idea of a return to the biblical Land of Zion could evoke the emotional response necessary to make Zionist dreams a reality. At the same time, the World Zionist Organization was established in order to facilitate the spread of Zionist ideas and the migration of Jews to Palestine. In its early years, the movement remained circumspect on the eventual goal of creating an independent Jewish state, focusing instead on the less radical-sounding idea of a Jewish homeland.

The First Zionist Congress was tremendously important for the establishment of modern Jewish nationalism. It provided a locus for activism on behalf of Jewish nationalism, a means to institutionalize and gain loyalty on behalf of the still small movement, and a forum in which to discuss specific policy options. It also established the principle of bringing together in a single organization the diverse strands of Zionism. Five years after the Basel conference, Theodor Herzl was dead. But his activities created a political movement that was to have consequences far beyond what he had imagined.

Zionism and European Colonialism

At this point, it is necessary to examine the political environment that made the idea of establishing a Jewish home in Palestine acceptable or even attractive to large numbers of people. First, the concept of Jewish return to the Promised Land had been embedded in the religious expressions of Jews—their liturgy and their traditions—ever since the Romans' destruction of the Jewish synagogue in Jerusalem in 70 c.e. and the expulsion of the Jews from Jerusalem in the second century c.e. The subsequent persecution Jews experienced reinforced the idea that only with a return to the Promised Land would life again be good for the Jewish people. For most of the period after the destruction of the Second Temple, there was a tiny community of religious Jews—composed largely of individuals who moved to Palestine late in life in order to end their days with a spiritual commitment to the Holy Land—living in and around the cities of Jerusalem, Hebron, Tiberias, and Safed. In short, the religious and spiritual tie of Jews to Jerusalem and the surrounding area was strong.

The spiritual importance of Jerusalem to Judaism was recognized by European and U.S. Christian religious and political leaders, many of whom believed they would be participating in a religiously significant task by helping the Jewish people settle in Palestine. It was a form of debt repayment to the people whose heritage was the historical basis of Christianity. Not coincidentally, it was also a way to address the "Jewish problem" domestically. According to some prejudiced people, if Jews all moved to Palestine, they would no longer serve as irritants in their current countries of residency. At the same time, these European Jews could be expected to remain favorably inclined toward the policies of the European states. A Jewish homeland would therefore serve to protect Western interests in the region by adopting foreign policies similar to those of Europe and the United States.

In addition, the European attitude toward colonialism in the late 1800s and early 1900s conveyed the clear message that Africa, Asia, and the Middle East were the property of any European who wished to settle there, "bring civilization to the masses," and tap its natural resources. In 1900 Britain and France in particular but also Belgium, Spain, the Netherlands, Portugal, and Italy maintained direct or indirect political and economic control over colonies around the world. **Imperialism**—the establishment by force or coercion of political and economic control by a state or empire over foreign territories—was viewed as an honorable activity, with little recognition of the exploitation accompanying it. Europeans who settled in Africa or Asia or the Middle East were often romanticized and glorified as pioneers spreading civilization to the non-Western world. The notion of European-Jewish colonization of Palestine was therefore consistent with similar European activities elsewhere.

That Palestine had an existing population, with its own history and aspirations, was no more relevant to early Zionists than was Kenyan history to the British or Algerian society to the French. In describing the attitudes of the early Zionists who participated in the Basel conference, Israeli politician and journalist Uri Avnery wrote, "Except for a handful, these more or less self-appointed delegates of the Jewish people had never been to Palestine, had no idea what it was like and took little interest in its realities. Reality did not bother them. They were out to build a new world, only half imagined. The only reality they knew was one they wanted to get away from—the reality of Eastern Europe, with its pogroms, its discrimination, its forebodings of greater catastrophes to come."[5] Thus, many early Zionists operated under a set of illusions about Palestine that blinded them to the true situation: the illusion that Palestine was an almost empty land that could easily accommodate their dreams and aspirations, the illusion that the people already in Palestine would welcome Zionist colonization, and especially the illusion that any resistance to Zionism could be blamed on Arab politicians or anti-Jewish prejudice rather than on broad-based sentiment against the European immigration.

Jewish Immigration to Palestine

Prior to the First Zionist Congress, the numbers of people moving to Palestine were not great—about 25,000 between 1881 and 1900—and their impact was limited. Even after the Basel conference, the movement remained small for another two decades. As had been true of earlier immigrants, nearly two-thirds of those in the second (1904–1914) and third (1919–1923) *aliyot* were from Poland and the Soviet Union, with the remainder coming almost entirely from other Eastern European countries such as Romania. There was, however, a shift in ideology from the cultural and spiritual Zionism of the 1800s to the political, state-building Zionism of the twentieth century.

The new immigrants, who like those before them came to Palestine to escape pogroms and discrimination, were frequently socialists, committed to Jewish communal living on **kibbutzim** (agricultural settlements with collective ownership; singular *kibbutz*) and **moshavim** (cooperative agricultural settlements on government lands with private economic activities; singular *moshav*). Because of their ethic of egalitarianism within the community and a desire to strengthen the Jewish people through physical activity, the settlers insisted that only Jewish labor could be used on lands owned by Jews. This policy led to tensions with Palestinian peasants who lost their traditional right to sharecrop the land when it was sold to Zionist immigrants by absentee owners and were then unable to find work among the new immigrant communities.

The immigrants from the second and third *aliyot* eventually formed the backbone of the Jewish peasant and working classes in Palestine and served as the foundation of the Jewish Labor movement. They were explicitly interested in establishing a *Jewish* state rather than living as a part of the existing Arab communities; in fact, many of Israel's first political leaders came from this group. This put them in direct conflict with the existing Jewish population, which was more fully integrated into the indigenous Palestinian community.

At this point, the total number of Jewish immigrants was still limited, and many who came to Palestine did not remain. (Between 1915 and 1920 there was actually a net loss of 15,000 Jews from Palestine as a result of wartime conditions.) The pattern changed dramatically with the fourth (1924–1928) and fifth (1929–1939) waves of immigration. The Jews who arrived in the fourth *aliyah* were more middle-class and less leftist than the Yishuv as a whole. Many of these immigrants were disappointed with the weak and stagnant economy they found in Palestine and soon left for the Americas, where economic conditions were more favorable.

As the situation for Jews in Central Europe grew worse—particularly with Hitler's rise to power in Germany in 1933, the passage of the discriminatory Nuremberg Laws in 1935, and Germany's annexation of Austria and Czechoslovakia in 1938—immigration to Palestine from Germany and German-controlled territories increased dramatically. Whereas between 1919 and 1924 a total of only 35,000 Jews had moved to Palestine, between 1924 and 1939 an average of about 16,000 Jews immigrated each year, with the bulk arriving between 1931 and 1935. Immigration peaked in 1935. This massive influx was one of the main factors that triggered the 1936–1939 Arab Revolt in Palestine.

By 1939, Jews made up 31 percent of the population of Palestine, a dramatic increase from 17 percent in 1931, less than 10 percent in 1919, and perhaps 6 percent prior to the first *aliyah*.[6] Often these new settlers, particularly those of the fifth *aliyah* who arrived after the economic collapses of the early 1930s, were hostile to the egalitarian socialism of the earlier colonists.

Equally important as the increase in the number of Jews immigrating to Palestine in the 1920s and 1930s was that many of these later immigrants, particularly those from Germany, brought with them significant financial resources to invest in industries and shops, thus strengthening the economic base of the Yishuv. Even Jews who lacked financial resources (or who were forced to leave their wealth behind when they came to Palestine) were encouraged to immigrate, however. Thus, several groups were established to assist the new settlers. The most important of these was the **Jewish National Fund,** founded in 1901 at the Fifth Zionist Congress, which was responsible for the purchase, afforestation, reclamation, and development of land in the name of the Jewish people. Land obtained by the fund became the inalienable property of the Jewish people and was never to be resold to a non-Jew. A second early organization, Keren Hayesod (the Jewish Foundation Fund), which financed agricultural and other settlement activities, was created after World War I. The **Jewish Agency** was established in 1929 to manage the governance of the Jewish community in Palestine, encourage immigration, and raise money for settlements. Other groups included Hadassah (the Women's Zionist Organization of America), which founded numerous health institutions in Palestine, and the United Jewish Appeal, created in 1939 to raise funds in the United States on behalf of Jews in Palestine.

18

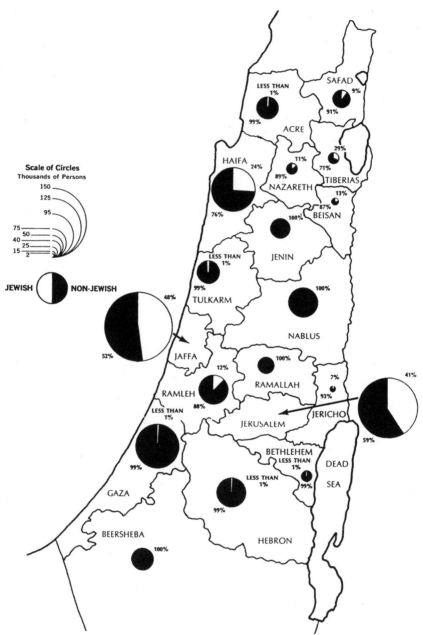

MAP 1.1 Population of Palestine by subdistricts, 1931. *Source:* Ibrahim Abu-Lughod, ed., *The Transformation of Palestine: Essays on the Origin and Development of the Arab-Israeli Conflict* (Evanston, IL: Northwestern University Press, 1971), p. 148. Copyright © 1971 by Ibrahim Abu-Lughod. Reprinted by permission.

At this point, the Jewish population in Palestine was heavily concentrated, the vast majority settling in the Jaffa, Jerusalem, Haifa, and Ramleh subdistricts (see Map 1.1). In these areas, modern Hebrew was spoken and there was an emphasis on establishing separate Jewish social and cultural institutions: schools and universities, hospitals, banks, civil courts, the General Federation of Labor (known as the **Histadrut**), and defense forces (the **Haganah**). Decisionmaking regarding the Jewish community in Palestine was exercised through the National Council, a body elected by the various Jewish groups through their representatives to the Assembly of the Elected. The British, who controlled the area after the breakup of the Ottoman Empire at the end of World War I, condoned and even encouraged these state-building activities, particularly as they were funded with contributions from abroad.

Divisions Within the Zionist Movement

From the beginning, there were serious cleavages within the Zionist movement, cleavages reflected even today in the debates within the Israeli polity. Spiritual or cultural Zionism has already been mentioned as a nonnationalistic form of Zionism. Its adherents were small in number and their voices were quickly drowned out in the debates between two other groups: the mainstream Labor Zionists, and the Revisionists.

The leader of the **Revisionist movement** was journalist Vladimir Ze'ev Jabotinsky, born in Odessa, Russia, in 1880. From its inception as a party in 1925, Revisionist Zionism was maximalist—it called for a Jewish state in all of historic Israel at its furthest boundaries: from the Litani River in the north to the Negev Desert in the south, and from the Nile River to well beyond the east side of the Jordan River. Jabotinsky was harsh in his attitude toward the existing Palestinian population. He proposed that an "iron wall" of Jewish military power be built around Palestine to secure the land for the Jewish people, and he demanded that within this wall a state be created immediately, without concern regarding compensation for the people currently living in the area. Initially, Jabotinsky was supportive of the British presence in Palestine and expected the new Jewish state to become part of the British Commonwealth. As Britain's actions failed to live up to Revisionist expectations, however, the Revisionists turned against Britain.

Labor Zionism was the Zionism of Israel's first prime minister, David Ben-Gurion, and reflected the democratic socialist ideology of the second and third *aliyot*; its bases were the *kibbutz* movement, the Haganah defense forces, and the Histadrut labor movement. For Labor Zionists, there was an essential link between political power and economic infrastructures. Labor leaders such as Ben-Gurion felt that the Jewish state had to be created from the ground up, rather than imposed militarily before a firm foundation existed. This foundation would be built through the physical labor of Jews in Palestine, thus the name Labor Zionism.

Although many of the long-term goals of Labor Zionism were the same as those of the Revisionists, two major differences existed: Both the socialism and the step-by-step approach to state-building characteristic of Labor Zionism were anathema to the Revisionists. Eventually the contradictory orientation of these two approaches became so great that the Revisionists withdrew from the World Zionist Organization and in 1935 established the New Zionist Organization. They also split from the Haganah and formed the National Military Organization (**Irgun Zvai Leumi**), in which Menachem Begin, Israeli prime minister from 1977 until 1983, played a leading role after his arrival in Palestine in May 1942. Irgun itself then split over the issue of Zionist relations with the British. The new group, the Fighters for the Freedom of Israel (Lohamei Herut Israeli, also known by the acronym Lehi or the name **Stern Gang,** after its founder Avraham Stern), was disinclined to cooperate with the British even against the Palestinians (a position Irgun eventually adopted as well). After the British capture and murder of Avraham Stern, Yitzhak Shamir (Israel's prime minister from 1983 until 1984, and again from October 1986 until June 1992) reorganized and rejuvenated Lehi and led the group until it was incorporated into the Israeli Defense Forces (IDF) in 1948.

A third group within political Zionism, much smaller and less influential, held some of the same underlying beliefs as did the cultural Zionists. In particular, these Zionists believed that Palestine was the land of two national peoples, Palestinian Arabs and Jews, and that therefore it was necessary to discover a way to accommodate the national aspirations of both peoples. Brith Shalom, created in the 1920s by Jewish theologian Martin Buber and Hebrew University President Judah L. Magnes, among others, was representative of this school of thought. Its founding statute, published in English, Arabic, and Hebrew, read in part: "The object of the Association is to arrive at an understanding between Jews and Arabs as to the form of their mutual social relations in Palestine on the basis of absolute political equality of two culturally autonomous peoples, and to determine the lines of their co-operation for the development of the country."[7] This perspective was rejected by the overwhelming majority of Zionists, however, and faded in importance.

Not all Jews shared the enthusiasm for Zionism. In fact, prior to World War II, many strongly opposed the political expression of Jewish identity, believing it to be a form of religious heresy. For Orthodox Jews, the effort to establish a state in Palestine was an attempt to force the hand of God, since only God could return the Jews to the Promised Land. In Palestine, this perspective was represented by the Agudat Yisrael movement. Other anti-Zionists felt that Judaism was a religion, not an ethnicity or a nationality, and that efforts to define the Jews as a separate people would only increase prejudice against them in their current homes. The fear was that if Jews were given special rights in Palestine, Christians could argue that Christians should have special rights in European countries and the United States. A third group believed that the Jewish mission of bringing high ethical standards to the world could best be undertaken in the **diaspora** (in exile; the places outside of Palestine to which Jews were scattered). Each of these disagreements with political Zionism continued to be strongly voiced, particularly in the United States, throughout the first four decades of the twentieth century.

Arab and Palestinian Nationalism

At the same time that some Jews in Europe were dreaming of and planning for a Zionist state to serve as an expression of their national identity, throughout the Arab world the seeds of nationalism had been scattered. In the **Levant** (the eastern Mediterranean region), these ideas found a fertile ground and took root. In many ways, the development of Arab nationalism was more straightforward than that experienced by the early Zionist movement. The Arabs already had a shared language, culture, and history; they were in place, on the land, as they had been for hundreds of years. There was no need to *create* a sense of community—to a large extent it already existed.

Several factors led this general sense of shared identity to be expressed in more explicitly nationalistic form. First was the contact with Western nationalist ideas. European and U.S. missionaries to the Levant brought with them the concepts of nationality and statehood that were causing ferment in Europe. Arab intellectuals studying abroad returned with new ideas of giving political allegiance to a territorially based entity. The arrogance of Ottoman pan-Turanianism, which argued for the superiority of the Turks over the Arabs, added fuel to the fire that was to become Arab nationalism, as did the Zionist movement and the perceived threat of increasing Jewish migration to Palestine.

Initially, Arab nationalism was expressed primarily as a desire to replace Turkish Ottoman rule with local Arab political control. Although a sense of local identity existed, it was taken for granted and was deemphasized in favor of pan-Arabism. As early as 1868, Arabs at a secret meeting of the Syrian Scientific Society were challenged in a poem by Ibrahim Yazeji to throw off Ottoman rule: "Arise, ye Arabs, and awake." By 1880 there was the beginning of a movement, based in Damascus and

Beirut, demanding the independence of the Levantine Arabs from the Turks. A placard from December 1880 indicated the outlines of its political agenda:

(1.) the grant of independence to Syria in union with Lebanon;
(2.) the recognition of Arabic as an official language in the country;
(3.) the removal of the censorship and other restrictions on the freedom of expression and the diffusion of knowledge;
(4.) the employment of locally recruited units on local military service only.[8]

To accomplish these goals was not a simple matter, however. The Turkish Sultan, Abdel Hamid, recognized that the nationalist spirit sweeping Europe and spreading to the Middle East had the potential to destroy the Ottoman Empire, and he suppressed any public expression of Arab nationalism as well as any efforts at local autonomy. During his rule, therefore, the growth of Arab nationalism was slow. After the coup d'état against Abdel Hamid in Istanbul in 1908, there was a brief period of greater political openness, but soon the Young Turks, whose actions had led to a new constitution and other changes in the structure of governance over the Ottoman Empire, clamped down on all non-Turkish nationalist activities, much as the sultan had done. Nonetheless, Arab nationalism had taken hold and remained quietly active, not only in Beirut and Damascus but in Baghdad and elsewhere in the region, waiting for fuller expression as the Ottoman Empire fell apart.

Palestinian, as distinct from Arab, nationalism developed somewhat later. During most of the 1800s, the political identity of the people of Palestine was of several overlapping types: a commitment to local Arab leadership; awareness of the distant rule of the Ottoman Turks; and a growing but still diffuse sense of connection with the larger Arab community. For Muslim Palestinians, there was also a sense of belonging to the Islamic *millet,* but because the Ottoman Turks were also Muslims, this did not serve to differentiate the Palestinian Arabs as a national group. Initially, Palestinians were part of the general movement of Arab nationalism that engulfed the Levant. With the breakup of the Ottoman Empire and the division of the Levant into areas of French and British control, Arab hopes of a Greater Syria encompassing the entire Levant region were quashed, and a separate Palestinian national identity, which was already present, began to flourish.

The initial lack of explicit Palestinian nationalism did not mean, however, that Palestinians simply acquiesced to European Jewish immigration in the years prior to 1918. At first their actions took the form of unorganized and spontaneous resistance to their eviction, after its sale by absentee landowners, from the land on which they had lived and worked for generations. As early as 1890, a group of influential Palestinians protested to the Ottoman rulers against these land sales and against Zionist immigration to Palestine and other Arab territories under Ottoman control. They also objected to the appointment of a pro-Zionist governor for Jerusalem. These protests had little effect. Officially, Ottoman policy was that Jewish immigrants could settle "as scattered groups throughout the Ottoman Empire, excluding Palestine," but in practice this restriction could be circumvented quite easily and did not serve to limit significantly Jewish migration to Palestine. After the overthrow of the Ottoman sultan in 1908, anti-Zionist sentiments were more widely expressed and began to be explicitly linked with Arab and Palestinian nationalism.

Palestinian Political Expression

In the period immediately following the end of World War I, Palestinians were faced with an unclear political future. Ottoman rule had been replaced by British control, and independence seemed no closer than it had been under the Turks. If anything, the prospects appeared worse, for Britain's pro-Zionist policy threatened Palestinian nationalist aspirations. Furthermore, there was disagreement regarding the political entity through which Palestinian national aspirations should be expressed. Should Palestine stand alone as a separate state or be part of an independent Greater Syria that would also include Lebanon and possibly Iraq? Although the majority of Palestinians were committed to local autonomy, the proponents of a Greater Syria were outspoken and gained significant attention.

There were other issues about which there was no debate among Palestinians, however, such as their resistance to Zionism and their desire to be free of British authority. Palestinian leaders attempted to make this clear whenever and wherever possible. By the end of 1920, it was evident that Palestine and Lebanon were not going to be included in a Greater Syria. It was equally significant, as Palestinians began to recognize, that despite the pan-Arab rhetoric of Syrian and Iraqi leaders, protection of Palestinian national rights was a lower priority for them than assuring their own local interests. For this reason, many scholars believe that a separate Palestinian national movement would have developed after World War I even without the incentive provided by Zionism, because the perceived need for an independent political identity existed as a discrete issue.

With the collapse of the Greater Syria option, Palestinians focused attention on appealing for independence from British control, resisting the implications of the **Balfour Declaration** (a letter by British Foreign Secretary Arthur James Balfour and endorsed by the British government that called for the establishment of a Jewish homeland in Palestine), and demanding an end to Jewish immigration until the status of Palestine was clarified. Their preferences were clearly articulated in the December 1920 statement of the Third Palestinian Arab Congress to the British high commissioner, and further elaborated in a letter sent to the British colonial secretary in October 1921. The British refused to recognize these and subsequent statements, letters, and petitions from Palestinian political leaders, ostensibly because the leaders, although widely regarded to reflect Palestinian views, had not been elected by the general population. This set a standard for determining the legitimacy of indigenous leadership that could not be met by virtually any colonized people, as elections were not generally held in such situations.

The Third Congress also resulted in the creation of the Arab Executive, a group elected to conduct political activities on behalf of the congress between its meetings. The original nine-member Christian-Muslim Arab Executive was headed by Musa Kazim Husseini, and the Husseini family continued to have a dominant role in the Arab Executive and the Arab Congress, as well as the newly formed Supreme Muslim Council, throughout the first half of the 1920s. Political opposition to the Husseini family was represented primarily by the Nashashibi family, which in November 1923 launched the Palestine Arab National party. The party was slow to gain supporters, but it eventually became the rallying point for opponents of the political views presented by the Arab Executive. During the 1920s and 1930s, the Nashashibi faction, which included a number of large landowners and wealthy businesspeople, called for a "positive policy" vis-à-vis the British, by which they meant cooperation even with proposals calling for less than full independence.

The Palestinian Arab Congress held meetings in 1921, 1922, and 1923. After a lapse of five years, the Seventh Congress convened in June 1928. In political composition, this was a very different congress than those of the early 1920s. The delegates represented both the Husseini and Nashashibi political movements, and the newly expanded Arab Executive also reflected the increased power of the Nashashibi opposition forces. This coalition held for several years and allowed the Palestinians to deal as a unified body with the British. At the Seventh Congress, a number of permanent committees were established and a resolution was passed that called for the establishment of parliamentary government and a representative council to govern Palestine. In March 1930 a delegation representing the congress was sent to London. The delegation, which included Musa Kazim Husseini and the younger Amin Husseini, stressed both economic and political issues in its meeting with the British, reflecting its recognition of the need for multiple avenues of argumentation.

Meanwhile, the Zionist movement and immigration to Palestine was gaining momentum. Palestinian fears and frustration grew in direct response to Zionist immigration. In the eyes of the Palestinian community, the European immigrants were exclusivist and arrogant in their political and economic ideas, too Western, too modern, too aggressive, and in general a corrupting influence. More important, Palestinians quickly recognized that Zionism would be detrimental to nascent Palestinian nationalist aspirations. These reactions were strengthened as the numbers of immigrants increased in the early 1920s. Zionism and Palestinian nationalism were on a collision course, and the question was when, rather than whether, the first major confrontation between these two communities would occur.

The answer was not long in coming. First in April 1920 in Jerusalem, then in Tel Aviv, Jaffa, and the surrounding areas beginning on 1 May 1921, in Jerusalem again in 1929 and repeatedly in the 1930s, Zionists and Palestinians clashed violently. In some cases Zionists' actions were the precipitating cause; in other instances Palestinians started the confrontations. Each hostile act increased the fears of the other group; each incident was used by partisans as evidence of the aggressive and hostile intent of their opponents.

Among the best-known disturbances are those that began 23 August 1929 and are referred to as the Wailing Wall riots. Although the underlying cause of the riots was the high level of distrust and fear between the two groups, the immediate trigger was the issue of access to the Western (Wailing) Wall in the Old City of Jerusalem. For Muslims, the wall is part of al-Haram al-Sharif, the third holiest site in Islam and the location of the Dome of the Rock and al-Aqsa mosque. For Jews, it is equally sacred as part of the ancient wall that surrounds the area on which Solomon and Herod built their temples. Under the Ottoman Empire, Jews were allowed to pray at the wall, but were not permitted to bring in chairs or other semipermanent items. The British continued this policy when they gained responsibility for Palestine. In 1928 some members of the Jewish community tried to extend their jurisdiction over the wall by bringing in chairs and screens, and at one point proposed buying the wall outright to create an exclusive claim. The Supreme Muslim Council responded by staging a confrontation in an effort to force the British to restore the status quo, that is, no benches or chairs and no partitions or screens allowed. In November 1928 the British produced a government policy statement (known as a white paper) that supported the Muslim position on the basis that the wall was legally the property of the Muslim community.

This ruling did not settle the issue, however, and by 1929 the dispute regarding control of the wall had come to symbolize not only religious differences but political power. When the issue finally broke open on 23

August, the resulting riots were more violent than either group had likely expected. In Jerusalem, 38 Arabs and 29 Jews died; the spread of violence into Hebron and Safed during the following week left a final toll of 120 Jews and 87 Palestinians dead.[9] Most detrimental to the image of the Palestinian national movement was that many of the Jews killed in Safed and Hebron were Orthodox Jews who were not Zionists but were linked in the minds of Palestinians with the Jerusalem Jews whose actions had led to the original problems.

Arab Revolt of 1936–1939

The process of Palestinian political and national development accelerated in the first half of the 1930s. By 1935 there were six political parties vying for support. These included the National Defense party of the Nashashibis (which was a descendant of the Palestine Arab National party); the Palestine Arab party of the Husseini family; the Youth Congress, organized by Muslim Palestinians in 1932; Istiqlal, a branch of the pan-Arab Independence party that was supported primarily by young professional elites and called for the independence of all Arab countries; and two locally based parties: the Reform party of Husseini Khalidi, which was allied with the Palestine Arab party, and the National Bloc of Abdal-Latif Saleh, a rival of the Husseini family. This tendency of political parties to identify with specific elite families was a legacy of the Ottoman policy of local autonomy. Under the Ottoman system, authority was vested in community religious and political leaders who developed rudimentary political structures around themselves. When the Ottoman Empire was forced to withdraw from the region and the British took control, these nascent political institutions formed the obvious nucleus for further political organization.

There were tremendous pressures on these political parties by the Palestinian population. The 1930s were hard years for the Palestinian community, particularly the peasants. Jewish immigration had increased greatly, the Histadrut was engaged in militant anti-Palestinian labor activities, and efforts to convince Britain to drop support for the Balfour Declaration had seemingly reached a dead end. As a result of economic difficulties, large numbers of Palestinians were forced to sell their land, thus exacerbating the trend of Zionist land acquisition begun by the absentee landowners. This drove Palestinian peasants to the urban areas, where they were often unsuccessful in their efforts to find work. It also contributed to the fragmentation of traditional Palestinian society and increased hostility toward the Zionists, who were identified as the cause of these problems. The policy of exclusive Hebrew labor, which was fundamental to Zionist socialism as a way to provide a broad base of workers for the new Jewish society and to put all immigrants on an equal footing, also meant no Palestinian labor and minimal economic interactions with Palestinians. This affected the peasants, who not only lost their land but could not be hired to farm it, and the urban population, which found that the Jewish immigrants would not buy from their shops, use their sea port, or hire them as workers.

In 1936 the Palestinian population took matters into its own hands. The **Arab Revolt of 1936–1939** was the longest sustained protest against Jewish national aspirations in Palestine prior to Israel's establishment as a state. This grassroots response to continuing Jewish immigration had both violent and nonviolent dimensions. It began in April 1936 with widespread riots, but the main thrust of the first stage of the revolt was a six-month period of strikes, nonpayment of taxes, and other forms of civil disobedience, coordinated by local committees and by the newly formed Arab Higher Committee for Palestine (AHC) headed by Amin Husseini. The first period of the revolt was terminated at the request of Arab leaders who encouraged Palestinians to wait for the outcome of deliberations by the Palestine Royal Commission (Peel Commission) set up by Britain to investigate the situation.

The second stage of the revolt began in the fall of 1937. It was sparked by the announcement of the **Peel Commission report** proposing to partition Palestine into two states in recognition of the competing claims of the two national groups. By 1938 the region was in complete turmoil, with Zionist, Palestinian, and British forces fighting for control. In large portions of Palestine, the British civil authorities lost all ability to manage the day-to-day affairs of the population as the Palestinians established many elements of an autonomous government, including a separate court system. The reaction to the Peel Commission report was particularly intense in the Galilee region (in what is now northern Israel), for under the partition proposal the Palestinian population living there was to be forcibly removed to make way for the Jewish state.

In order to restore their position of control, the British sent in more than 20,000 troops; imposed emergency regulations (which were later incorporated into Israeli law and used against Palestinians); dissolved the AHC and expelled virtually all the significant Palestinian leaders, including Amin Husseini; demolished homes of suspected activists; and imposed collective fines against villages that rebelled against British rule. By spring 1939 the Palestinian leadership was in jail or in exile, the population was demoralized, and the revolt had been crushed. The cost in lives was enormous: 101 British soldiers, 463 Jews, and at least 3,073 (and probably closer to 5,000) Palestinians had been killed.[10] At the same time, the Palestinian revolt had achieved one of its main objectives, although only for the short run: Britain scrapped the 1937 partition plan.

Although Palestinian resistance to partition and to the establishment of a Zionist state in Palestine continued, the core of the Palestinian national movement had been temporarily eliminated. The Arab Higher Committee was reconstituted in 1945, but it was again dominated by the Husseini family and was unable to gain the support of other political parties, which resented the Husseinis' control. By the late 1940s, the Nashashibis, for instance, had allied themselves with the Hashemite Kingdom of Jordan. Without a unified political organization able to speak on behalf of the Palestinian movement, the Palestinians were at a decided disadvantage in presenting their case to the international community. The Zionists were also divided, but they had greater financial resources, better contacts with British, European, and U.S. politicians, and more experience dealing with the Western political system. Given this, and in the absence of a strong counterweight to Britain's pro-Zionist sentiments, the rest of the world went along with Britain's interpretation of the situation in Palestine and did not support Palestinian desires for self-determination.

INTERNATIONAL INVOLVEMENT IN PALESTINE

With the Allies' defeat of the Ottoman Empire in 1918, Palestine came under the direct control of the British Military Administration, and in July 1920 the British established a Civil Administration for the region. Britain's **mandate,** that is, its commission to administer the political affairs of the area and prepare it for independence, was confirmed by the League of Nations in July 1922 and officially began in September 1923. Even prior to 1918, however, Britain had already made three conflicting commitments regarding the future of Palestine. These commitments reflected British war interests as well as British-French competition in the Middle East and domestic politics rather than concern for the inhabitants of Palestine. Nonetheless, their impact on the region was profound. The agreements were followed in the 1920s and 1930s by a series of proposals and British white papers designed to reconcile the contradictory promises made to Palestinian Arabs and to Zionists. These efforts were unsuccessful, and Britain eventually turned over the decision about the future of Palestine to the newly created United Nations.

Britain's Wartime Promises

The **Hussein-McMahon correspondence** between Sharif Hussein of Mecca, governor of the Hijaz province of Arabia, and Sir Henry McMahon, the British high commissioner to Egypt, represents one of the most controversial aspects of British involvement in the Middle East. In a series of eight letters written between 14 July 1915 and 30 January 1916, the two men negotiated the terms under which Hussein would encourage the Arabs to revolt against the Ottoman Empire and enter World War I on the side of the Allies. In particular, Hussein demanded British recognition of the independence of the Arab areas of the Ottoman Empire now known as Syria, Iraq, Jordan, Israel, the West Bank and Gaza, and Saudi Arabia.

Under the assumption of British support for Arab independence as discussed in the letters, Hussein led the Arab revolt against the Ottoman Empire that began on 5 June 1916. The Arabs faced disappointment once the war ended, however, when McMahon and Hussein disagreed on what areas had been included in the territory to be granted independence. In particular, McMahon later claimed he never meant to guarantee the independence of Palestine, while Hussein believed Palestine was included in the commitment. The letters themselves, which were kept secret for a number of years, are ambiguous, and their interpretation has been a subject of great controversy.

A second and conflicting commitment regarding Palestine and other areas in the Levant was made in the 1916 **Sykes-Picot Agreement.** This was a deal worked out between Sir Mark Sykes, a member of Parliament and secretary to the British Cabinet, and French diplomat Charles Georges-Picot (with the knowledge and consent of the Russians and the Italians) to divide the Levant into territories of direct control and indirect influence by Britain and France after World War I had ended. France was to govern the areas that became Lebanon and Syria; Britain would take responsibility for Iraq and Jordan. Because of its religious status, and to avoid a fight for control among the Triple Entente states, Palestine was to be placed under an undefined "international administration" (see Map 1.2). Originally intended to be kept secret, the pact was made public by the Bolsheviks in November 1917. It is clear from this agreement that Britain had no intention of fulfilling its commitment to support Arab independence in the Levant at the end of the war, whatever might have been promised in the Hussein-McMahon correspondence. At the same time, those promises of Arab independence could be used as a tool to strengthen Britain's position vis-à-vis the French by denying France the possibility of claiming colonial or mandatory control over the areas.

Balfour Declaration

The third promise made by the British regarding Palestine during World War I was the Balfour Declaration. It provided international sanction to the Zionist movement and gave the Zionists the necessary Great Power backing for increased immigration into Palestine. Although the Balfour Declaration was a far vaguer statement than Zionists hoped for, it

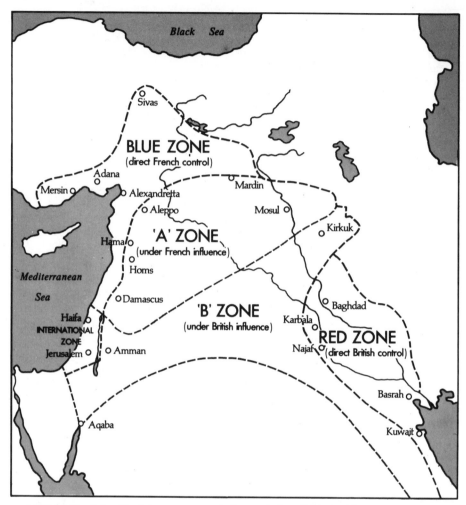

MAP 1.2 The Sykes-Picot Agreement, 1916. *Source:* Arthur Goldschmidt, Jr., *A Concise History of the Middle East*, 3d ed., revised and updated (Boulder, CO: Westview Press, 1988), p. 196. Original cartography by Don Kunze.

was eventually used to argue in favor of the establishment of a Jewish state. The declaration that was to change the course of Palestinian history was short and in the form of a letter from British Foreign Secretary Arthur James Balfour to Jewish philanthropist and Zionist supporter Baron Lionel Walter Rothschild, dated 2 November 1917:

> I have much pleasure in conveying to you, on behalf of His Majesty's Government, the following declaration of sympathy with Jewish Zionist aspirations, which has been submitted to, and approved by, the Cabinet:

"His Majesty's Government view with favour the establishment in Palestine of a national Home for the Jewish people, and will use their best endeavours to facilitate the achievement of this object, it being clearly understood that nothing shall be done which may prejudice the civil and religious rights of existing non-Jewish communities in Palestine, or the rights and political status enjoyed by Jews in any other country."

I should be grateful if you would bring this declaration to the knowledge of the Zionist Federation.[11]

The Balfour Declaration served a number of important interests for the British. First, it allowed Britain to maintain a friendly presence in Palestine from which it could protect the Suez Canal from the east. At the same time, by claiming that Palestine was to become a national home for the Jewish people, rather than just another British colony, Britain could resist French demands that Palestine be internationalized, as was called for in the Sykes-Picot Agreement. In addition, the Balfour Declaration was intended to encourage the United States to join the war effort, to motivate Russian Jews to pressure their government to remain in the war, and to preempt a similar statement Germany was rumored to be considering. It also, however, committed the British to irreconcilable obligations. It quickly became clear, as should have been evident even in 1917, that it was impossible to create a Jewish Zionist state in Palestine (which is what was obviously meant by Zionists when they spoke of a national home) without prejudicing the rights of the Christian and Muslim Palestinians who at the time constituted nearly 90 percent of the population. Nonetheless, the declaration gained the endorsement of U.S. and European leaders as well as the Vatican and was included in the League of Nations statement regarding the mandate over Palestine. In the years that followed, the Balfour Declaration stood as a symbol of the Great Power commitment to Zionism over Arab nationalism in Palestine.

Although the Balfour Declaration was proclaimed loudly in Europe and the United States, information about this new British promise was not made public in the Middle East until 1919. Palestinian Arabs responded to the Balfour Declaration with a mixture of anger and bewilderment. Ever since the new migration of Jews from Europe to Palestine had begun in the 1880s, Palestinian Arabs had been worried about its implications. The willingness of absentee landlords to sell land to the Zionists had been of particular concern. Now there was a new concern. With the Balfour Declaration, it appeared that Britain was going to turn over control of Palestine entirely to the Jewish European immigrants. To the Zionists, this represented a return to sovereignty over the land of their ancestors after 2,000 years of exile. But to the Palestinians, it was a case of a colonial settler community being granted preference over the rights of the indigenous population.

Initially, Palestinians attempted to have Britain renounce the Balfour Declaration and instead agree to establish representative government in Palestine. Because at this point Zionists were still very much in the minority, the Palestinians reasoned that self-government would mean the Zionists would be unable to create a Jewish state in Palestine, for this would be against the will of the majority of the people. They were unsuccessful in this approach.

Post–World War I International Setting

At the end of World War I, the political borders of Europe and the Middle East shifted significantly. The Ottoman and Austro-Hungarian empires were demolished, their territories reduced and their power diminished. This left a power vacuum, particularly in the Middle East, which Britain and France were eager to fill. Both already had colonial ties to the region: France was involved in North Africa, whereas Britain claimed Egypt, Sudan, and the coasts of the Arabian Peninsula as part of its colonial empire. Britain was particularly interested in increasing its control over the Levant because of its central location near the essential Suez Canal and along the trade route between Britain and India. There was also the historical appeal of the holy city of Jerusalem. France saw the collapse of the Ottoman Empire as an opportunity to expand in a new direction, as its colonies were virtually all in north and west Africa.

Even as European imperialism spread to the Levant, competing political ideals were gaining strength in other parts of the world. Popular support for national self-determination, international law, and restrictions in the arms trade grew as people tried to identify and analyze the causes of the war. Political **idealism** developed as the dominant ideology in the United States and much of Europe, in striking contrast to the preeminent position that political **realism** had held prior to World War I and which it regained after World War II. Realists viewed humans as flawed, power-seeking, sinful creatures, whereas idealists believed that human nature was essentially good. For an idealist, wars were the result not of evil people but of evil institutions and structures that motivated people to act selfishly rather than altruistically. As a result, wars could be eliminated only through global structural changes and a system of collective security.

Many of the beliefs of idealism were articulated by U.S. President Woodrow Wilson in his Fourteen Points speech to the Congress in 1918. In this speech Wilson indicated a number of ways in which an idealist perspective could be implemented, including "open covenants openly arrived at," free trade relations, reductions in armaments, and self-determination for Europe as well as for colonized areas. Wilson also called for the establishment of "a general association of nations" and was a leading force in the 1919 creation of the League of Nations (although the Senate rejected U.S. membership in the organization). The league had as its primary purpose the preservation of global peace and security through international law. Although ultimately it failed in that ambitious goal, during the interwar period the League of Nations addressed a number of other issues, including the establishment of colonial mandates over former Ottoman territories, with varying degrees of success.

A third aspect of the interwar period, in addition to the rise of political idealism and the extension of European imperialism into the Levant, was the Russian Revolution of 1917, which overthrew the tsarist government and ultimately led to the establishment of the Union of Soviet Socialist Republics. The USSR was the first state to be based on Marxist socialism; its ideology eventually put it on a collision course with the United States. During the period of Stalinist rule, from the late 1920s until Stalin's death in 1953, the USSR was not directly involved with the Arab Middle East. Nonetheless, the revolutionary rhetoric of the new Soviet state caused concern among the industrialized capitalist countries and provided an additional justification for increased European presence in the Levant. Instability in the Soviet Union was also one of the many factors leading to increased Jewish migration to Palestine.

British Mandate over Palestine

In the years immediately following World War I, there were several opportunities for Palestinians to express their desire for independence rather than rule from abroad. For example, in 1919 President Wilson appointed the **King-Crane Commission** to ascertain the political preferences of the people of Greater Syria, Palestine, and Mesopotamia and to make recommendations to the Paris Peace Conference. After meeting with a variety of groups in June, July, and early August, the commission reported that there was strong Arab support for independence, consistent with the promises of the Hussein-McMahon correspondence. On the other hand, there was tremendous resistance to the possibility of the French being granted a mandate over the region. The United States or Britain was preferred as the mandatory power if independence was to be denied. The commission also addressed the issue of Zionism in Palestine:

We recommend ... serious modification of the extreme Zionist Program for Palestine of unlimited immigration of Jews, looking finally to making Palestine distinctly a Jewish state. ...
The Commission recognized also that definite encouragement had been given to the Zionists by the Allies in Mr. Balfour's often quoted statement, in its approval by other representatives of the Allies. If, however, the strict terms of the Balfour Statement are adhered to ... it can hardly be doubted

that the extreme Zionist Program must be greatly modified. For "a national home for the Jewish people" is not equivalent to making Palestine into a Jewish State; nor can the erection of such a Jewish State be accomplished without the gravest trespass upon the "civil and religious rights of existing non-Jewish communities in Palestine." The fact came out repeatedly in the Commission's conference with Jewish representatives, that the Zionists looked forward to a practically complete dispossession of the present non-Jewish inhabitants of Palestine, by various forms of purchase . ... In view of all these considerations, and with a deep sense of sympathy for the Jewish cause, the Commissioners feel bound to recommend that only a greatly reduced Zionist program be attempted by the Peace Conference and even that, only very gradually initiated. This would have to mean that Jewish immigration should be definitely limited, and that the project for making Palestine distinctly a Jewish commonwealth should be given up.[12]

These recommendations, however, were not made in time to be considered by the Paris Peace Conference, nor do they appear to have carried weight when the San Remo Conference of April 1920 met to finalize a settlement with Turkey and to allocate mandatory responsibility in the Levant. To the contrary, the San Remo Conference endorsed the idea of the Jewish homeland and instructed the British administration in Palestine to "facilitate Jewish immigration under suitable conditions and ... [to encourage] close settlement by Jews on the land."[13] Despite this statement of support, the conference did not accept the World Zionist Organization's recommendation for a state of Israel in all of Palestine as well as parts of Jordan and Lebanon (see Map 1.3). In making their decision, the European powers were motivated less by overwhelming support of Jewish nationalism on its own merits than by an awareness of how such a Western enclave could be valuable to European interests.

Although sections of the San Remo document, which was confirmed by the League of Nations in July 1922, stressed the equal treatment of Jews, Muslims, and Christians in Palestine, the significance of these directives paled before the decision to support Zionist aspirations in Palestine. This was greeted with enthusiasm by Zionist supporters and with dismay by Palestinians who were aware of Zionist leader (and later the first president of Israel) Chaim Weizmann's statement to the Paris Peace Conference in February 1919 that he hoped "Palestine would ultimately become as Jewish as England is English."[14] The reaction of the Muslim Christian Society of Nablus was typical of the concerns expressed: "The Allies have declared that they have actually fought to avoid war and establish peace, and restore scattered people to their countries. Is it therefore admissible for them under right and justice to create in the Arabic country a national home for foreigners causing the country terrible material and moral inju-

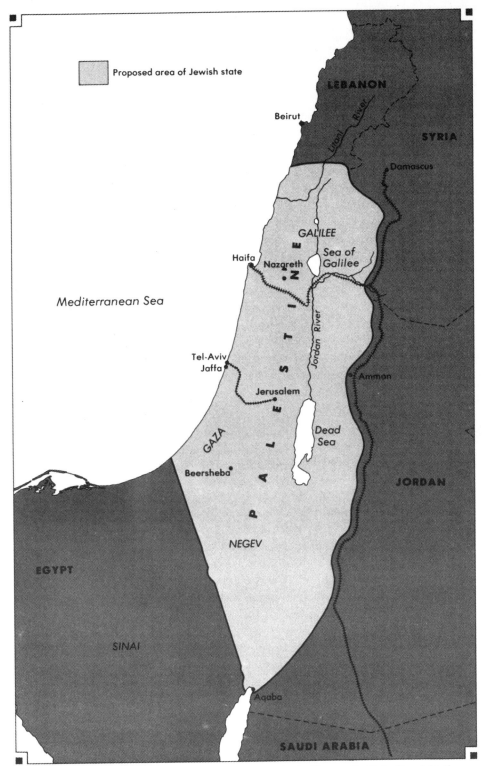

MAP 1.3 The Zionist plan for Palestine, 1919. *Source:* Simha Flapan, *The Birth of Israel: Myths and Realities* (New York: Pantheon Books, 1987), p. 17. Copyright © 1987 by Simha Flapan. Reprinted by permission of Pantheon Books, a division of Random House, Inc., and by permission of the heirs of Simha Flapan.

ries, and to increase the number of a strange nation in the country they intend to destroy the inhabitants thereof?"[15]

Also given little attention by Western leaders at the League of Nations was the Haycraft Commission report, which resulted from an official British inquiry, headed by the chief justice of Palestine, into the Jaffa riots of May 1921. In its October 1921 report, the commission indicated that the underlying cause of the violence, which had left 120 Palestinians and nearly 200 Jews wounded or dead, was Palestinian distrust of the movement of an alien community into the area. Palestinians might have been willing to accommodate this foreign immigration except for one crucial point. The Zionists did not want to become a part of the existing society of Palestine—they wanted to replace it with their own political, economic, and cultural structures. This, said the commission, was the root of the problem. To the Zionists, however, the Jaffa riots provided a different message: They were seen as additional evidence of the need for an exclusively Jewish state.

The concerns raised in the Haycraft report were reflected in the June 1922 **Churchill White Paper.** In this document, Britain indicated that it was not its intention that an exclusively Jewish state be created in Palestine, nor was there to be any subordination of Arab population, language, or culture to Jewish nationalist aspirations. The white paper also established the idea of treating Jewish immigration as an economic issue rather than a strictly political one through a focus on the economic absorptive capacity of the region: "This [Jewish] immigration cannot be so great in volume as to exceed whatever may be the economic capacity of the country at the time to absorb new arrivals. It is essential to ensure that the immigrants should not be a burden upon the people of Palestine as a whole, and that they should not deprive any section of the present population of their employment."[16] This approach was to characterize British immigration policy from 1922 until 1939. In addition, the Churchill White Paper proposed a constitution for Palestine and a legislative council, to be composed of eight Palestinian Muslims, two Palestinian Christians, two Jews, and eleven officials to be appointed by the British. The elections never occurred. Most Palestinians rejected this proposal, fearing it would produce a permanent majority in favor of British government policies hostile to Palestinian interests.

The early 1930s saw a number of additional commission reports, white papers, and private letters, all designed to clarify the British role in Palestine and the balance between Palestinian and Zionist claims. For example, the Shaw and Hope-Simpson reports, written in response to the 1929 riots, condemned the Jewish policy of excluding Palestinian labor from Jewish lands and suggested that the principal causes of the riots and other disturbances were Palestinian fears of continuing Jewish immigration, concerns about their economic future, and disillusionment at the failure of Britain to support Palestinian national aspirations.

Less than a year later, the 1930 Passfield White Paper recommended a halt in Jewish immigration and restrictions on land sales to Jews if these actions were believed necessary to protect Palestinian employment. The Passfield White Paper also reiterated Britain's interest in the establishment of some type of legislative council to govern Palestine, a proposal already made in the Churchill White Paper of 1922. In February 1931 many of the ideas expressed in the Passfield White Paper were undercut by an open letter from British Prime Minister J. Ramsay MacDonald to Chaim Weizmann that reinterpreted the white paper in a way far more favorable to the Zionist cause. The lack of agreement within British governing circles about the appropriate policy toward Palestine is clearly reflected in this constantly changing public stance, characteristic of the entire period of the British mandate.

Peel Commission Report

Throughout the 1930s, British-Palestinian, British-Zionist, and Zionist-Palestinian tensions continued to mount. In 1936 the Peel Commission was sent to Palestine to assess the options available to the British to deal with this increasingly intractable situation. In its report, issued 7 July 1937, the commission acknowledged that the political as well as economic dimensions of Jewish immigration to Palestine had to be addressed. This was a direct contradiction of the British approach since 1922. The Peel Commission concluded the mandate was unworkable in its present form:

> To foster Jewish immigration in the hope that it might ultimately lead to the creation of a Jewish majority and the establishment of a Jewish state with the consent or at least the acquiescence of the Arabs was one thing. It was quite another to contemplate, however remotely, the forcible conversion of Palestine into a Jewish State against the will of the Arabs. For that would clearly violate the spirit and intention of the Mandate System. It would mean that national self-determination had been withheld when the Arabs were a majority in Palestine and only conceded when the Jews were a majority. ... [T]he international recognition of the right of the Jews to return to their old homeland did not involve the recognition of the right of the Jews to govern the Arabs in it against their will.[17]

This constituted an acknowledgment by Britain that the achievement of Jewish nationalist aspirations in Palestine was of necessity prejudicial to the rights of the indigenous Palestinian population. The commission recommended the partition of Palestine into a Jewish state and a Palestinian area to be merged with Jordan. This was precisely the solution Palestinians had feared all along, and this report set off the second stage of the Arab Revolt in the fall of 1937. The Zionist Congress meeting of 1937 also rejected the partition plan as presented. Zionists argued that the proposed Jewish state was too small, that Jews had an inalienable right to settle anywhere in Palestine, and that Britain should pay for the transfer of all Palestinians from the territory of the new Jewish state to the Jordan Valley and the Beersheba district.

The fundamental issues that had led to the Arab Revolt were not resolved by the Peel Commission's proposals. Thus, Britain decided to invite representatives of the Jewish Agency, the Arab countries, and the Palestinians to a round-table conference in London to be held in March 1939. The purpose of the conference was to develop a position on Palestine acceptable to all parties. The involvement of the Arab states reflected the increasing internationalization of the Palestine conflict. The conference was a failure, however, because of the incompatibility of the goals of Zionists and Arabs. When it became clear the conference was deadlocked, Britain issued its own policy statement, the 17 May 1939 **MacDonald White Paper,** which concluded that the partition plan proposed by the Peel Commission and by a 1938 Partition Commission was also unworkable.

Several points were made in this document. First, Britain reiterated its policy as expressed in the 1922 Churchill White Paper that although Palestine was not included in the area promised to the Arabs by Henry McMahon during World War I, it also was not British policy or intent that Palestine should become a Jewish state or that there would be "the subordination of the Arabic population, language or culture in Palestine." The paper recommended that after a five-year period, during which a total of 75,000 Jews would be allowed to enter Palestine (consistent with what was judged to be the absorptive capacity of the area), Jewish immigration would be limited by the approval of local residents of Palestine. Land sales were also to be restricted and regulated in some parts of Palestine in order to assure that Jewish immigration did not lead to the creation of a landless Palestinian population. Finally, self-governing institutions were to be established with a view toward independence, within ten years, of a Palestinian state "in which the two peoples in Palestine, Arabs and Jews, share authority in such a way as to ensure that the essential interests of each are secured."[18]

Just as the Palestinians had been tremendously upset by the Peel Commission report, the Zionists were furious at the recommendations of the MacDonald White Paper. British policy was branded as "treacherous," "a breach of faith," and a surrender to Arab violence,[19] and the limitations on immigration to Palestine were later blamed for hundreds of thousands of Jewish deaths at the hands of the Nazis. Radicalized, Zionist activists of the Yishuv initiated a campaign of terror and sabotage directed at the Brit-

ish and the Palestinians alike, beginning a period Avnery described as
"gun Zionism."[20] Some Palestinians were also hostile to the 1939 white
paper, in part because it was vague on the establishment of a legislative
council, but others supported it, recognizing that at this stage no solution
proposed was likely to be completely acceptable.

THE PARTITION OF PALESTINE

World War I had destroyed empires and redrawn state boundaries. The
results of World War II were still more widespread. These included:

- [ ] the near destruction through genocide of the Jewish community in
  Europe
- [ ] the replacement of the League of Nations by the United Nations, in
  which the United States was heavily involved
- [ ] the development and use by the United States of nuclear weapons
  with previously unimagined explosive power
- [ ] the decline of Europe and the rise of the United States as the pre-
  dominant Western political, economic, and military power
- [ ] the establishment of a bipolar world in which the United States and
  the USSR faced off in a cold war, the effects of which were felt
  throughout the world

Each of these changes in the international arena had implications for the
Arab-Zionist conflict over Palestine, although not all were immediately
obvious.

World War II Period

During the war, the Zionist movement continued its campaign to gain
international support for Jewish control of Palestine. In May 1942 the
World Zionist Congress met at the Biltmore Hotel in New York City for
what was arguably its most important session since the founding of the
congress in 1897. Six hundred delegates from the United States, Europe,
and Palestine attended the congress, which passed a series of declarations
known as the Biltmore Program. Among the most significant acts was a
resolution that Jews should demand that Palestine be established as a Jewish state as part of the new world order to be constructed at the end of the
war. According to the declarations, the Yishuv should be allowed to have
its own army and its own flag, and there should be unrestricted Jewish
immigration to Palestine under the auspices of the Jewish Agency. The
congress also declared that the word "homeland," as used in the Balfour
Declaration, implied a nation, and that a nation meant a state. Only in this

way, according to the congress, could the "age-old wrong to the Jewish people be righted."

The Biltmore Program was a triumph for the Revisionist faction of the Zionist movement. It meant a public declaration of the position long held privately among Zionists that their final goal was a Jewish political entity in all of Palestine. It also ended any official Zionist efforts to find a compromise with Palestinian leaders. Although the program was temporarily abandoned in August 1946, when the Jewish Agency decided that partition and control over part of Palestine was better than no state at all, the strength of the Revisionist position tilted the balance within the Zionist movement in ways that still have ramifications today.

In the early to mid-1940s, most attention in Palestine was directed to the course of the war. Compared to the 1930s, there was relatively little Zionist-Palestinian violence. Clashes between the Zionists and the British continued, however, and once the German threat to the Middle East was ended in 1942 these increased. Violent attacks were made by the Palmach (an elite branch of the Haganah) against railways, bridges, and communication lines; bombings, hostage-taking, and other terrorist and paramilitary activity became common. Two particularly dramatic actions against the British, both undertaken by paramilitary groups rather than the Haganah itself, were Lehi's assassination of Lord Moyne, the British minister-resident in Cairo, on 6 November 1944, and Irgun's destruction on 24 July 1946 of the King David Hotel, which housed the senior members of the British Administration for Palestine. Britain's response to such attacks was harsh, as was its treatment of Jewish immigrants fleeing Europe who were caught trying to enter Palestine illegally.

With the victory of the Allies in Europe in May 1945, the full horror of Germany's Nazi regime became known to the world. Hitler's plan for the final solution of the Jewish question had been the extermination of the Jewish people. To facilitate this goal, Jews were rounded up and sent to transit, concentration, and forced labor camps—such as Gurs, Dachau, Buchenwald, and Bergen-Belsen—throughout Germany and the German-occupied territories. Prisoners in the camps were compelled to perform hard physical labor; many were forced to participate in sadistic, inhumane "medical experiments." The conditions were appalling, and a large proportion of those confined died of disease, malnutrition, and mistreatment. As the war dragged on, increasing numbers of Jews were transferred to the death camps—Chelmno, Belzec, Sobibor, Majdanek, Treblinka, and Auschwitz-Birkenau—where millions were systematically killed in the gas chambers. By the time Germany surrendered to the Allied Forces, an estimated six million European and Soviet Jews had been murdered in the Shoah. Communists and Social Democrats, many but not all of whom were Jews, as well as gypsies, homosexuals, disabled persons, and others deemed "undesirable" by the Nazis were also annihilated by Hitler's forces.

As realization of the near destruction of the Jewish people of Europe spread, the Zionist movement in the United States, the country that now contained the largest Jewish community in the world, gained a tremendous measure of support. It was inconceivable to most U.S. citizens, regardless of their religious beliefs, that they could fail to support Jewish aspirations for a safe place where Jews could never again be slaughtered. In the process, the reality of Palestine and its indigenous people was ignored.

The UN Vote on Partition

The United Nations (UN) officially came into existence as an international organization with the signing and ratification of its founding charter in 1945 by a number of countries, including the United States and the Soviet Union. According to its charter, the goals of the United Nations include the maintenance of international peace and security and the development of cooperative relations among states to facilitate the solving of global economic, social, cultural, and humanitarian problems. The charter also specifies that the principal organs of the UN are the General Assembly (which includes a representative of each member state), the Security Council, the International Court of Justice, the Economic and Social Council, the Trusteeship Council, and the Secretariat.

Among the first challenges facing the newly formed international organization were the unresolved conflict over Palestine and the European refugee problem. In April 1946 the Anglo-American Commission of Inquiry recommended that a UN trusteeship, along the lines of the League of Nations mandates, be temporarily established over Palestine. Once the population was judged ready for self-government, the trusteeship would be replaced by establishment of a single binational state as proposed in the 1939 MacDonald White Paper. The commission also endorsed the admission of 100,000 Jewish refugees from Europe into Palestine, demanded that the Zionists disband their illegal militias, and indicated that the United States and other countries would need to accept a large number of European Jewish refugees as there was not room for them all to go to Palestine. This last point was not popular in the United States, and was even opposed by some U.S. Jews who felt that a large influx of poor Jewish refugees would damage their carefully won position of relative equality and status in the United States.

In the post–World War II concern for European Jewry, many aspects of the commission's report, such as the plan for a unified binational state in Palestine, were simply ignored. Furthermore, the efforts of British and

U.S. government officials, notably Henry F. Grady and Herbert S. Morrison, to implement the full range of proposals were rejected. Instead, all public attention was focused on the recommendation to admit 100,000 Jews into Palestine. President Harry Truman also favored this idea and mentioned it frequently in his campaign activities on behalf of Democratic congressional candidates in 1946.

In a final effort to deal with the intractable problem of Palestinian sovereignty, Britain attempted to hold a conference in London at which the Arab Higher Committee, the Arab governments, and the Jewish Agency were invited to present their views. The first session began in September 1946, with a second round scheduled for 1947. Only the Arab states sent representatives; for different reasons both the Jewish Agency and the Arab Higher Committee refused to participate, and the conference was judged a failure. By this point, the British recognized that they had lost all ability to mediate the increasingly complex conflict, and on 2 April 1947 they turned their responsibility over to the United Nations.

The UN set up an eleven-member Special Committee on Palestine, which presented two alternative proposals to the General Assembly. Each called for a rapid end to the British mandate. The principal proposal, supported by a majority of the committee, was for the United Nations to facilitate the establishment of two separate political entities in Palestine to be joined economically. The minority proposal argued that because most residents of Palestine opposed partition, a single federal state containing autonomous Jewish and Palestinian areas should be created. Only the former proposal was acceptable to Zionist supporters, who insisted that the "Jewish homeland" must be distinctively Jewish rather than religiously or ethnically pluralist. Even as they endorsed the partition plan, with reservations, Zionist leaders continued to state their belief that all of Palestine should eventually come under Jewish control. The partitioned portion of Palestine would serve as a steppingstone to achieving this larger state.

From the Palestinian point of view, the partition plan meant the illegal and illegitimate division of Palestine and the expulsion or "transfer" of local residents. Thus, the Arab Higher Committee and the Arab League, which had been formed in 1945, rejected both the idea of partition and the federal state model, and instead called for a single, unified state in Palestine that would be democratic and secular, with equal rights for all its citizens. The Arab restriction that only Jewish immigrants and their descendants who had arrived prior to the Balfour Declaration would be considered citizens of this state was only one of the factors that made this unacceptable to Zionists.

At first it appeared that the proposal to partition Palestine would fall short of the necessary two-thirds majority in the UN General Assembly. Zionist supporters were able to obtain a brief recess of forty-eight hours in order to lobby undecided or wavering countries. Under heavy pressure, seven states changed their positions during the crucial recess, and on 29 November 1947 the General Assembly voted in favor of **UN Resolution 181**, which called for the creation of a Jewish state and an Arab state within a partitioned Palestine. The British mandate over the area was to end 15 May 1948, and the two states were to be established by 1 July 1948. Jerusalem and Bethlehem were to become a *corpus separatum* under UN jurisdiction.

In the years immediately following the Shoah, sympathy for the Jewish people was high. For this reason, it is perhaps not surprising that the UN proposal for partition was far from equitable. The plan for partition gave the new Jewish state 57 percent of Palestine, including the fertile coastal region, although at the time Jews represented only abut 33 percent of the population and owned only 7 percent of the land. United Nations' estimates suggested that this division would give the Jewish state economic revenues three times as great as those accruing to the Palestinian state. Furthermore, as designed by the UN, the new Jewish state was to have, at least initially, as many or more Palestinians as Jews.

Establishment of the Jewish State

Internal turmoil in Palestine increased between 29 November 1947 and 14 May 1948, and violence against civilians was used by all parties. During this period, well-organized and well-equipped Zionist military forces systematically extended their control beyond the areas specified by UN Resolution 181 to include additional parts of Palestine that they judged essential to the security and economic success of the still-to-be-declared State of Israel. As the situation in Palestine deteriorated, neither Britain nor the United Nations seemed able to control the escalating tensions. After a report by the U.S. Central Intelligence Agency (CIA) in February 1948 indicated that partition could not be successfully implemented without the use of force and could cause irreparable damage to U.S.-Arab relations, many in the U.S. government called for a reassessment of the partition plan and its replacement by a temporary UN trusteeship.

The United Nations met in mid-April to consider the U.S. proposal, but in the weeks that followed the United States was unable to persuade the necessary two-thirds majority of member states to overturn the partition resolution. The General Assembly did, however, vote to appoint a mediator to coordinate the development of essential public services, assure the protection of the religious sites, and promote "a peaceful adjustment of the future situation of Palestine." The person chosen was Count Folke Bernadotte of Sweden, who was known for his previous humanitarian activities, including his efforts to gain the release of thousands of prisoners from Nazi concentration camps before the end of World War II.

The State of Israel declared its independence on 14 May 1948; the five surrounding Arab states immediately responded by attacking the new state, converting the situation from widespread civil strife to an all-out international war. During the war, none of the Arab fighting units was able to develop an effective offensive strategy. In the case of Jordan, recent scholarship has revealed that there was an explicit decision not to fight aggressively against Israel, as part of a tacit deal between the Zionist leadership and King Abdullah that their two countries would split Palestine between them. Still, the war was long and resulted in the loss of thousands of Israeli and Arab lives.

Shortly after the war broke out, Bernadotte traveled to the Middle East to begin the immense tasks to which he had been appointed. Unfortunately, Bernadotte's successes were limited to arranging two short ceasefire agreements in June and July. Although he also made specific proposals for changing the final boundaries of Israel and permitting Palestinian refugees to return home, these were not accepted. Whether he might have accomplished more remains unknown. On 17 September 1948 he was assassinated by members of the Zionist paramilitary Stern Gang, thus ending the first UN-sponsored mediation effort in the Middle East.

Fighting continued sporadically throughout 1948 and into the following year. When the armistice agreements were finally signed in 1949, the Mandate of Palestine had been divided, but not, as the United Nations had intended, into a Jewish state and a Palestinian state. Instead, Israel had expanded its control over Palestine to include 77 percent of the area, including significant portions not originally allocated to it. The Gaza region was occupied by Egypt, and Jordan had taken control of the central hills that became known as the West Bank. Hundreds of thousands of Palestinians had been displaced and had lost their homes, their lands, and their livelihoods. The name "Palestine" was wiped off the political map of the world (see Map 1.4).

CONCLUSION

The Introduction to this book pointed out that the conflict over Palestine represents in part the search for national identity and self-determination by two peoples—Jews and Palestinians—as well as the clash between a colonial settler community and an indigenous population. For both groups, the nationalist and state-building movement in Europe was one of the factors that prompted the development of an explicit nationalist identity among peoples who had previously been held together by other bonds, such as religion, geography, language, or culture. Palestinians, more than Jews, were also affected by political developments within the Ottoman Empire. In 1850 neither Jews nor Palestinians saw themselves as

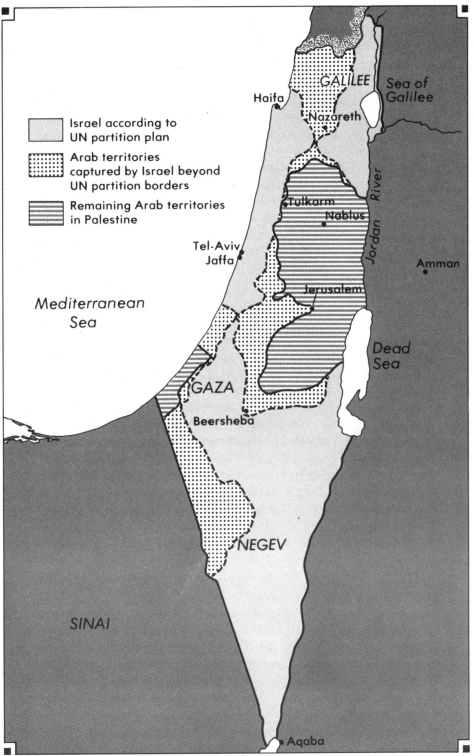

MAP 1.4 Territories captured by Israel in 1948 and 1949. *Source:* Simha Flapan, *The Birth of Israel: Myths and Realities* (New York: Pantheon Books, 1987), p. 51. Copyright © 1987 by Simha Flapan. Reprinted by permission of Pantheon Books, a division of Random House, Inc., and by permission of the heirs of Simha Flapan.

constituting a separate political entity. One hundred years later, each had developed the corporate sense of oneness characteristic of a national people. One group—the Jews—had achieved statehood through the establishment of Israel. The other group—the Palestinians—had been denied that expression of self-determination and was forced into exile.

The role of outside actors in this process is clear. Countries like Britain and the United States; intergovernmental agencies, including the League of Nations and later the United Nations; and nongovernmental international groups such as the World Zionist Organization all had important roles to play in the eventual partition of Palestine. In many cases, decisions about the Mandate of Palestine were made for reasons other than what was best for that region. Britain's conflicting promises during World War I, for example, paid little heed to the needs and desires of the people of Palestine but were motivated instead by wartime strategies. The votes of individual countries on the UN partition plan were subject to pressures from the United States, which itself was under pressure from U.S. Zionist supporters, both Jewish and Christian. As a result, the majority of people in Palestine were denied the right of self-determination.

This early history of the conflict also illustrates the internal disagreements present within states and nonstate actors that are often dealt with as though they were unified entities. The pre–World War II debate within the Jewish community around the world over the appropriateness of Zionism, and the differences within the Zionist movement regarding the strategies and eventual aims of the movement, provide examples. Similarly, the establishment in Palestine in the 1920s and 1930s of political parties reflecting alternative approaches to dealing with British colonialism and Zionist immigration indicate that the Palestinian national movement, like the Zionist movement, was not (and is not) a monolithic whole.

So much space has been devoted to the history of Zionist and Palestinian nationalism and international involvement in Palestine prior to 1948 because, in the eyes of all the parties to the conflict, that history is as potent and vital a force today as it was half a century ago and forms the foundation of the contemporary situation. The reference points for current debates are found in the period before Israel was established as a state; the issues raised then and the political positions developed are reflected clearly in the arguments made in the 1990s. For this reason, it is impossible to discuss the contemporary Israeli-Palestinian conflict without an understanding of its deep and complex roots. This account is continued in Chapter Two with an examination of the ongoing relationship between the State of Israel and the Palestinian nation and a discussion of the key actors within each political entity.

TWO

□ □ □

Clashes and Coalescence:
Jewish State, Palestinian Nation

Prior to 1948, the conflict over Palestine was waged by two nascent, nonstate national groups—Zionists and Palestinians—with involvement by Britain and, to a far lesser extent, the Arab countries. Once the British had withdrawn militarily and the State of Israel had been proclaimed, the principal actors and the forms of the conflict took on clear international dimensions. Although Palestinians were greatly affected by the subsequent wars, and in the 1982 War in Lebanon were a major target of the fighting, the battles were fought primarily by the military forces of sovereign states such as Israel, Egypt, Jordan, Syria, Lebanon, and, in 1956, France and Britain.

The years since the establishment of the State of Israel can be divided into three separate phases: May 1948 to June 1967, June 1967 to December 1987, and December 1987 to the present. During the first nineteen years of Israel's existence, Palestinian nationalism was muted and resistance to Israel was expressed almost entirely by the surrounding Arab states. This changed dramatically with the June 1967 War and the subsequent Israeli occupation of the West Bank and Gaza Strip, among other territories. At this point, the conflict again took on elements of a Palestinian-Israeli nationalist clash without losing the interstate character that had developed since 1948. Palestinian political and military groups were established during the subsequent twenty years and Palestinian nationalist expression regained its past vigor and in fact increased in strength.

This trend was accentuated with the beginning of the Palestinian uprising, or *intifada,* in December 1987. The popular protests of the *intifada* were seen by Palestinians and some Israelis as part of a nationalist war of resistance or liberation by Palestinians against Israel's military occupation of the West Bank, including East Jerusalem, and the Gaza Strip. Although international aspects to the conflict with Israel remain, the *intifada* refocused global attention on the basic conflict between Zionists and Palestinians: Which nation or nations will control the territory known as both Palestine and Israel, and what civil, political, social, economic, and cultural rights do those who live in the area have under whatever government rules the land? The pre-1948 competition between two nonstate national groups became a highly uneven contest between a major military power and a predominantly unarmed civilian population.

This chapter examines what happened to Palestinians and Zionists after the 1947 UN vote in favor the partition of Palestine. It discusses the dispersion of Palestinians and the ingathering of the Jews, the structure of the newly formed Jewish state and its current policies, and the Palestinian national movement, including the creation of the Palestine Liberation Organization. The chapter ends with a brief description of the Israeli occupation of the West Bank and Gaza Strip and of the *intifada* in those territories.

DISPERSION OF THE PALESTINIANS

Of the total Palestinian population of approximately 900,000 people, only 150,000 remained in what became Israel after the Palestine War (also referred to as the Israeli War of Independence or the 1948 War). These Palestinians, who lived mostly in the Galilee, the Little Triangle region, and the Negev, were viewed by Zionist leaders as a threat to the internal security of Israel and as a hindrance to the achievement of a fully Jewish state. Although they were residents and legal citizens of Israel, the day-to-day existence of Palestinians was precarious. Until military law was abolished on 1 December 1966, Palestinians could be arbitrarily jailed or deported, their economic activities were limited, and their freedom of movement was restricted, all under the guise of Israeli security concerns. Furthermore, these Palestinians were isolated from the rest of the Arab world. Just fifty years earlier they had been part of the vast Ottoman Empire; now they found themselves strangers in their own homeland, surrounded by a culture and a political system not their own.

A second, much larger group of Palestinians were refugees and exiles in the West Bank and Gaza Strip, in nearby Arab countries (particularly Egypt, Jordan, Lebanon, Syria, and Iraq), or in the Arab Gulf states, Europe, or the United States. Members of this group were torn between their desire to return to their homes and their lands and the need to create new lives for themselves. Those with no means of livelihood—and this represented the vast majority—had to depend on assistance from the governments of the host states, from the United Nations Relief and Works Agency (UNRWA) that was created to deal with Palestinian refugees, or from voluntary organizations. There were a few Palestinians, generally upper-class, who left on their own initiative immediately after the UN partition vote instead of being forced out of their homes. Many of these were able to join family members already living abroad and found it economically easier to rebuild their lives. But they were still exiles.

Finally, there were a significant number of Palestinians who had been and remained residents in the parts of Palestine not taken over by Israel: the West Bank (under Jordanian control between 1948 and 1967) and the Gaza Strip (which between 1948 and 1967 was under Egyptian military rule in a kind of legal limbo). These people also had divided emotions. On the one hand, there was a desire to regain Palestinian control of the rest of the Mandate of Palestine in order to reunite the Palestinian people socially, economically, and politically. This goal was in tension, however, with the fear that further conflict with Israel would result in additional loss of territory and possibly their own expulsion from their homes.

The political activism shown by the Palestinians prior to the establishment of Israel was greatly diminished in the 1950s and 1960s. Palestinians were shattered by the events of 1947–1949: the creation of Israel, the failure of the Arab armies to maintain control even of the lands allotted to the Palestinians in the UN partition resolution, the Jordanian and Egyptian occupation of part of the territory that was to become the Palestinian state, and the dispersion of the Palestinian community. The efforts of various Arab regimes to co-opt the Palestinian movement for their own purposes also contributed to this decline and to the fragmentation and disorganization of the Palestinian people. With their leadership in exile and the economic and social basis of Palestinian society all but destroyed, the Palestinian national movement entered nearly two decades of relative quietude. During this period numerous institutions were created that came to characterize the Palestinian diaspora (such as the General Union of Palestine Students, founded in 1959, and the General Union of Palestine Workers, begun in 1963), but to a large extent Palestinians put their faith in the Arab states to assist in their return to their homeland. Ultimately, this faith proved misplaced.

Displaced and Refugee Populations

Among the most controversial aspects of the 1947–1949 period is the exodus of an estimated 750,000 Palestinians from their ancestral homes. The areas originally allocated by the UN to Israel and the territories conquered by Israel between December 1947 and early 1949 contained numerous Palestinian communities. By the end of 1949, hundreds of these towns and villages had been destroyed or taken over by the Israeli government; their residents had fled or been forced to leave. It was, at minimum, a great convenience for Israeli leaders, "a miraculous clearing of the land," as Chaim Weizmann put it.[1] Had the exodus not occurred, the new State of Israel would have contained a greater number of Palestinians than

This woman and child are residents of Gaza's Bureij camp, one of twenty-seven crowded refugee camps in the West Bank and Gaza Strip that are home to approximately 360,000 displaced Palestinians.

Jews, undercutting Zionist efforts to create a Jewish state. The massive dispersion of Palestinians not only reduced the Palestinian presence significantly; it also meant that entire villages, complete with terraced agricultural lands and personal property, were empty and could thus be used by the thousands of Jewish immigrants who came to Israel in the years immediately after its declaration of independence.

Traditional Israeli history has presented the Palestinian exodus as the responsibility of Arab leaders who ordered the Palestinians to flee, promising that they could soon return to their homes as conquering heroes, whereas Israeli leaders encouraged them to stay in their homes and villages. Recent research by historians and political scientists, including Israeli scholar and journalist Benny Morris, reveals that this image is a myth on several grounds. First, there was no widespread or coordinated effort by Arab leaders to encourage Palestinians to leave the area, although on a few occasions individual local elites did give such orders. To the contrary, as early as March and April 1948, radio broadcasts by the Arab Higher Committee unsuccessfully urged, and even ordered, Palestinians to stay in their homes. Second, although thousands of Palestinians, mostly from the middle and upper classes, did voluntarily leave the area allocated by the United Nations to Israel, many thousands more were driven out by Jewish military forces or fled in terror. Using newly available British, Israeli, and U.S. archival materials, Morris provides the following list of reasons Palestinians abandoned some 369 villages throughout the territory that became Israel:

- ☐ expulsion by Jewish military forces
- ☐ fear of Jewish attack or of being caught up in the fighting
- ☐ military assault on the settlement by Jewish troops
- ☐ abandonment on orders of local Arab notables
- ☐ Haganah/IDF "whispering" campaigns (psychological warfare)
- ☐ influence of the fall of, or exodus from, a neighboring town

The vast majority of Palestinians, according to Morris, was expelled by the Israeli Defense Forces or fled because of terrorist attacks by Jewish military forces, whether Haganah, IDF, Irgun, or Lehi.[2] Direct expulsion became more common after July 1948, but there were also cases prior to the 15 May declaration of the State of Israel. The official justification for the actions by Jewish regular and irregular forces was "security"; however, the Zionist political leadership was certainly cognizant of the multiple benefits of these actions and did nothing to discourage the military from extending its jurisdiction as far as possible.

A significant component of Zionist plans was **Plan Dalet,** which officially went into effect when Israel declared its independence but which was actually put into operation two months earlier. This military blueprint gave details on the "expulsion over the borders of the local Arab population in the event of opposition to our attacks, and the defense of contiguous Jewish settlement in Arab areas, including the 'temporary' capture of Arab bases on the other side of the border."[3] The idea behind the plan was to secure Zionist control over the areas allocated for the new Jewish state, expand control beyond these territories, and reduce the Palestinian presence through the depopulation and destruction of Arab villages. Under Plan Dalet, the towns of Haifa, Jaffa, Tiberias, Safed, Acre, Lydda, and Ramleh, among others, were cleared of most of their Palestinian populations. Those expelled were allowed to take with them only what they could carry; many had their valuables stolen by Israeli soldiers as they passed military checkpoints. Once the areas had been evacuated, soldiers looted or destroyed most of the property the residents had been forced to leave behind. The towns were then settled by recent Jewish immigrants.

By 1949, roughly 280,000 Palestinians were living as refugees in the West Bank, joining 440,000 Palestinians whose original homes were in the area. An additional 70,000 people had fled to the East Bank of the Jordan River. The economic demands this placed on Jordan, which had taken control of the West Bank during the Palestine War and illegally annexed it in 1950, were tremendous. But they paled in comparison to the situation in the Gaza Strip region, where 190,000 refugees joined an original community of 88,500 residents, all crammed into a tiny stretch of land 28 miles long and between 4 and 8 miles wide, surrounded by Israel, the Sinai Desert, and the Mediterranean Sea. Gaza's rural, nonindustrialized economy was completely unprepared to deal with this influx of refugees, and conditions were extremely poor. Another 100,000 Palestinians ended up in Lebanon; 75,000 went to Syria; 7,000 traveled to Egypt; and 4,000 fled to Iraq.[4]

The Arab states, which of necessity accepted the Palestinian refugees, had neither the economic resources nor the political will to facilitate their integration into existing communities. Nor, in most cases, did the Palestinians desire full integration. Even though they might have preferred greater economic opportunities and the option to apply for citizenship (only Jordan granted citizenship to a significant number of Palestinians), their main desire was to return to their homes in Palestine.

Israeli Response to Palestinian Exile

As the number of refugees and exiles increased, the international community began to pressure Israel to allow their repatriation to their homes. Prior to his assassination in September 1948, the UN-appointed mediator, Swedish Count Bernadotte, was among those expressing dismay over the plight of the refugees, but he was unsuccessful in his efforts to convince Israel to allow their return. The Israeli argument was, first, that a significant Palestinian presence would be harmful to Israel's internal security; second, that with all the Jews coming to Israel there was no room to allow the Palestinians back in; and third, because the Palestinians left "voluntarily," they had given up any rights they might have had to live in Israel.

In light of the joyful Zionist reaction to the Palestinian exodus, the Israeli position was not surprising. For many years there had been consensus within the mainstream Zionist movement that an all-Jewish Palestine was the preferred situation. In 1937 the Jewish Agency passed a formal resolution demanding the compulsory transfer of Palestinians from Palestine, and many of the leaders of the Yishuv, including David Ben-Gurion, supported this idea. Another Zionist leader, Yosef Weitz, wrote in his diary on 20 December 1940:

> Between ourselves it must be clear that there is no room in the country for both peoples. ... We shall not achieve our goal of being an independent people with the Arabs in this small country. The only solution [after the end of World War II] is a Land of Israel, at least a western Land of Israel [that is, Palestine], without Arabs. There is no room here for compromises. ... There is no way but to transfer the Arabs from here to the neighboring countries, to transfer all of them, save perhaps for [the Arabs of] Bethlehem, Nazareth and old Jerusalem. Not one village must be left, not one tribe. ... And only after this transfer will the country be able to absorb millions of our brothers and the Jewish problem will cease to exist. There is no other solution.[5]

Whether by political design or military necessity, something close to such a situation existed after 1949, and the Israeli leadership had no intention of allowing a return to the 1947 status quo.

Nor did the Palestinians have much success in receiving compensation for property left behind, despite the existence of an absentee property office Israel set up to address such claims. In general, the Israeli position was that such property now belonged to Israel, to make up for property left in Arab countries by Jews when they immigrated to Israel. This formulation was not widely accepted by the international community, but, as with the issue of repatriation, Israel held the upper hand and ultimately had its way.

Palestinian Refugees as an International Issue

The Palestinian refugees represented a challenge to the rest of the world, which only recently had begun to be concerned about refugees in general. Prior to the twentieth century, the international community made few systematic attempts to address the problem of refugee populations created by war or persecution. After World War I, however, the same impulse that led to the formation of the League of Nations also resulted in the development of international organizations to assist Russian refugees from the 1917 Revolution, Armenian and Greek refugees from Turkey, and other groups displaced during the political shuffles of the interwar years. This commitment to collective, global responsibility for refugees remained in the post–World War II period, although other aspects of political idealism lost popular support.

In the midst of World War II, a group of countries joined together as the United Nations Relief and Rehabilitation Administration (UNRRA) to provide aid to some eight million displaced persons from Czechoslovakia, Greece, Italy, Poland, Yugoslavia, and elsewhere. As areas were recon-

quered from the German-Italian Axis forces, the UNRRA repatriated virtually all the refugees to their countries of origin. About a million people
were unwilling to return to their home countries, which at the end of the
war were under the control of Communist governments. These people
were helped to resettle in other European countries. In 1946 the UNRRA
was joined in its work by the International Refugee Organization (IRO);
three years later the UNRRA discontinued its operations. The IRO, which
among other responsibilities dealt with the refugees created by the 1947
partition of the Indian subcontinent into the states of India and Pakistan,
was replaced by the Office of the United Nations High Commissioner for
Refugees in 1951. The latter was given the responsibility to seek a permanent solution to the refugee problem, to offer international protection to
refugees under its mandate, to coordinate the activities of voluntary agencies working on behalf of refugees, and to assist the most needy refugee
groups. The underlying assumption was that refugees would be helped to
return to their homes if this is what they desired. Otherwise they should
be assisted in establishing new lives in alternative countries of residence.
In no case was it anticipated that a refugee situation would remain unresolved indefinitely.

This changed with the Palestinians. Palestinian refugees were dealt
with through a separate UN agency rather than being placed under the
Office of the United Nations High Commissioner for Refugees or its predecessors. Initially, this entity was the United Nations Relief for Palestine
Refugees. In 1948 UN General Assembly Resolution 194 (III) set up the
three-state Conciliation Commission for Palestine (CCP). The mandate
given to the CCP was "to facilitate the repatriation, resettlement and economic and social rehabilitation of the [Palestinian] refugees and the pay-
ment of compensation." Representatives from France, Turkey, and the
United States quickly ran into a basic conflict. The Arab and international
position was that the issues of compensation and repatriation were the
first priority. Israel, however, was unwilling to allow more than a trivial
number of refugees to return, and these only in the context of a general
peace settlement. Furthermore, Israel said the Palestinians would be unable to return to their original homes, as these had either been destroyed
or were now inhabited by Jewish immigrants. In light of this deadlock, the
CCP soon turned its attention to designing alternative solutions for the
Palestinian refugees.

In August 1949 the CCP sent to the region a survey mission that was instructed to find an economic solution for what was essentially a political
problem. This mission recommended the establishment of the United Nations Relief and Works Agency for Palestine Refugees. UNRWA was
founded in 1949, taking over most tasks of the United Nations Relief for
Palestine Refugees, which had been caring for the refugees until they

could be repatriated. UNRWA's initial responsibilities included the creation of schemes for integrating the refugees into their hosts' economies and providing emergency assistance. As the political issues between Israel and the Palestinians remained unsolved, what had been expected to be a short-term problem—as had been the case with the European refugees—was converted into a long-standing condition, with hundreds of thousands of Palestinians relying on UNRWA for food, housing, and education. This remains the situation.

THE ISRAELI STATE

The Zionists also faced tremendous challenges after 1948, but these were the positive challenges of a people who had used both diplomatic and military means to gain control of a land for themselves. While the Palestinians experienced despair and diaspora, the new Jewish Israelis began to construct a Western-style state in the middle of the Arab world. All the skills and financial resources of the wider Jewish community were directed toward creating an Israel that would serve as a home for Jews and would allow Jews to live without fear of prejudice or persecution.

Israel was not the only new state created in the years following World War II. Virtually the entire continent of Africa gained independence in the 1950s and 1960s, as did parts of the Middle East and Asia. All these new states faced similar tasks: developing a sense of national unity, creating a solid economic foundation, building political institutions and a political leadership, and establishing beneficial foreign relations with a variety of countries. Israel had several advantages not available to most other new states, however. These included a population that was to a large extent well educated, skilled, highly motivated and politically sophisticated, and extensive financial support from the Jewish community abroad. In addition, after 1967 Israel was the recipient of extensive military and economic assistance from the U.S. government. Israel also faced unique challenges. The most obvious of these were the absorption and integration of hundreds of thousands of Jews from diverse backgrounds, the development of an appropriate policy toward the Palestinians within its boundaries, and the establishment of peaceful relations with the surrounding states. The first two of these are discussed here; the third is addressed in Chapter Three.

Ingathering of the Jews

One of the first tasks facing the new state, consistent with the Zionist dream that all Jews should return to the Land of Zion, was to "ingather" Jews to Israel—not just the remnant of European Jewry who had survived

This Jewish Israeli farmer is among the 6 percent of the Israeli labor force involved in the agricultural activities that remain an important element of the Israeli economy (photo courtesy of Israeli Embassy).

Hitler's slaughter but also Jews from around the world. With the passage by the **Knesset**—the parliament of Israel—of the Law of Return on 5 July 1950, Israel formalized the policy, in place since 1948, of essentially unrestricted immigration by Jews. During its first ten years, Israel admitted over 900,000 immigrants. Initially, the largest number came from refugee camps in Europe, but this soon changed: Between 1950 and 1956 more than 50 percent—and up to 87 percent—of the immigrants each year came from North Africa or Asia.[6] Among the most dramatic immigrations was Operation Magic Carpet, which was responsible for bringing to Israel about 45,000 Jews from Yemen in 1949. In 1950 virtually the entire Iraqi Jewish community—123,000 people—fled to Israel, motivated by numerous anti-Jewish attacks. At the time, it was widely assumed these attacks were perpetrated by hostile Iraqis, but recent scholarship indicates the actions were undertaken by overly zealous Zionists who wanted to create an atmosphere of fear that would convince the Iraqi Jews to move to Israel.[7]

By the time the major postindependence immigrations were complete (and significant numbers of Palestinians had fled or been forced out of the area), Israel's population structure had changed radically from what it had been in May 1948. In 1948 virtually the entire Yishuv was composed of European, or **Ashkenazi,** Jews, and there was still a significant Palestinian population. Ten years later, about 90 percent of the population of Israel was Jewish, and although the Ashkenazi community still dominated politically, socially, and economically, a third of the Jews were of **Sephardic** backgrounds (that is, they came from Spain or from Middle Eastern countries).

In general, the post-1948 immigrants from Europe were better educated and more highly skilled than those from North Africa and Asia. Thus, they were able to fit easily into the existing structure of the society created by the Ashkenazi community during the previous fifty years. The situation was more difficult for the Sephardic Jews, who were expected to discard their past in order to be assimilated. Their cultural backgrounds and value systems were different, they spoke Arabic rather than Yiddish or another European language, they ate different foods, and they had different social structures. And whereas most European Jews were secular, the Sephardic communities were more often deeply and traditionally religious, with a belief in the intimate connection between religion and politics. This followed from the fact that, unlike Jews in Europe, Jews living in Arab countries were frequently allowed to be fully Jewish because of the autonomy given to non-Islamic communities under Muslim rule.

Ironically, in many ways the Sephardic immigrants had more in common culturally with the Christian and Muslim Palestinians who had remained in Israel than with the Ashkenazim with whom they shared an identity as Jews, but little else. Many Sephardim, however, have worked hard to differentiate themselves from Christian and Muslim Palestinians, accepting, or perhaps reacting defensively against, the Ashkenazim's negative stereotyping of all Arabs. Sephardic Jews have also benefited since 1967 by the Palestinians' of the West Bank and Gaza Strip taking the lowest-level menial work within Israel, allowing the Sephardim to move up a step on the socioeconomic ladder. Not surprisingly, these factors complicated the challenge of nation-building within the new state, and the Sephardic-Ashkenazi split continues to have political implications today.

Policies Toward Palestinians Within Israel

The Palestinians who remained in Israel after the Palestine War were considered a problem by the Jewish state. On the one hand, they stood in the way of Israel's becoming an exclusively Jewish state, as many Zionists desired. Furthermore, they were perceived as a security risk. At the same time, Israel's position in the world community depended in part on its image as an outpost of democracy in a nondemocratic Arab world. Israel's solution was to grant citizenship to the remaining Palestinian population, but then to place under military control most of the towns and villages in which Palestinians lived. These areas were ruled primarily by the British Defense Regulations of 1945, which the British originally used against the Jews while Britain still controlled Palestine. Under these regulations, Palestinians had to obtain permission to travel in or out of a security area, their economic activities were restricted, their property could be seized, and they were subject to arrest or even expulsion for political reasons. The justification for these regulations was "national security," an ambiguous term that left a great deal of latitude for interpretation. The Israeli policy also served to isolate the Palestinian citizens from the rest of the Arab world.

In addition, the Israeli government passed new rules that further constricted the economic and political position of Palestinians. The 1950 Law for the Acquisition of Absentee Property, for example, said that any person who had left his or her usual place of residence at any time between 29 November 1947 and 1 September 1948 for any place outside of Jewish control was considered an absentee person whose property could be confiscated and placed under the control of the Custodian of Absentee Property. This was true even if the person had left home only for a short period of time to avoid the fighting, had returned immediately thereafter, and was a legal resident of the state (a "present absentee"). Furthermore, once property was declared absentee property, this status remained in force, even if it could later be proved that the property had been incorrectly classified.

A second set of regulations, known as the Emergency Articles for the Exploitation of Uncultivated Areas, was often used in connection with the Absentee Property Law. The emergency articles allowed the agriculture minister to take over any land not cultivated for the previous three years. A common tactic was to declare an area farmed by Palestinians a closed military zone so that no Palestinian was allowed to enter it. After the three-year period had elapsed, the land could then be declared uncultivated and could be confiscated and turned over to the Department of Agriculture. In addition, the finance minister had the authority to confiscate land "for public purposes." Finally, for a variety of reasons a portion of the land traditionally farmed by Palestinians was registered in the name of the Ottoman Empire or the British high commissioner. Customary law dictated that tenants of state land could continue to live on and work the land indefinitely. After 1948, however, the new Israeli government took over this land, saying it belonged to "the State of Israel." The Palestinian tenants were expelled and the land turned over to Jewish settlements.

At first, Palestinians inside Israel, as with Palestinians in the West Bank, Gaza Strip, Jordan, and elsewhere in the region, were in a state of shock over the loss of control over Palestine, the land confiscations, and their restricted status. Once they began to recover and to attempt to organize themselves, their efforts were suppressed by the Israeli military administration that controlled every facet of Palestinian life. When an Arab nationalist movement called al-Ard (the Land), founded in 1958, was outlawed in the 1960s because, according to the Israeli High Court, "there is no place for an Arab organization which is not based on recognition of the State of Israel as a state of the Jews," the only legal avenue of non-Zionist political expression available to Palestinians was the frequently harassed but never banned Israeli Communist party. Throughout the 1960s, Palestinians protested the military administration, which was finally abolished in 1966. This did not mean, however, that Palestinians were fully equal citizens of Israel. There were and remain significant differences in the educational and social service funding for Palestinian villages; many employment possibilities, particularly in the leading sectors of the economy such as the military-industrial complex, are closed to Palestinians; and as non-Jews who do not serve in the military, numerous benefits available only to those with military service or religious exemption are denied to them. Since 1967 the Palestinians of Israel have been reunited on some levels with Palestinians of the West Bank and Gaza Strip, although the legal position of the two groups is quite different.

Getting Inside the Black Box

Foreign policy analysts often discuss the choices and activities of states and other international actors as though these actors were monolithic entities that operate as rational, efficient decisionmakers carefully analyzing how the interests of the entity can best be achieved. There are some significant advantages to this **rational actor model,** not the least of which is that it makes the discussion of foreign policy relatively straightforward: Figure out what the objective interests of the state or nonstate actor are, assume that the individuals making decisions on behalf of the actor have these interests in mind when they calculate the costs and benefits of each option, and assess how successful the actor is in meeting its interests. Often this can provide a good picture of the foreign policy process, and foreign policy decisionmaking has been discussed in precisely that way throughout this text.

It is essential, however, to keep in mind that this model of decisionmaking is a simplification and in many cases does not reflect the actual processes that occur as foreign policy choices are made. States and nonstate actors are *not* monolithic entities with clearly defined and agreed-upon objective interests. Instead, their interests are often multidimensional and subjective, with tremendous internal debate regarding policy preferences and appropriate goals. In addition, a variety of constraints make rational decisionmaking difficult or impossible. These include the psychological and intellectual limits of human beings, their desire to simplify the world, their tendency to take shortcuts in thinking that violate formal logic, and their inability to hold a complex set of variables in their minds simultaneously; moreover, time and resource constraints mean that all options, consequences, and probabilities in a given situation cannot be known to the decisionmakers as would be required for fully rational decisionmaking.

In order to address these weaknesses in the rational actor model of foreign policy decisionmaking, scholars have developed a range of alternative conceptualizations. Some focus on the individual or idiosyncratic attributes of the decisionmakers—their perceptions, predispositions, personalities, and prejudices—and the cognitive processes that operate within each person. Other scholars examine the collective or bureaucratic dimensions of foreign policy formulation, looking at how individuals and departments within the foreign policy structure work to protect their own institutional interests, and how group dynamics may influence the choices made. A third approach emphasizes that foreign policy decisions are made in a particular domestic context with the possible influence of public opinion, interest groups, and the structural attributes of the actor. In each of these approaches, the goal of the foreign policy analyst is to get inside the black box of foreign policy in order to better understand the factors that affect the choices individuals make on behalf of states or nonstate actors.

To present a full analysis of the decisionmaking process for each of the significant actors involved in the Israeli-Palestinian conflict would be a massive undertaking, involving an assessment of the leaders, bureaucratic structures, societal settings, and so on for a dozen different actors. The goal here is more modest: to provide a few pieces of the puzzle by describing the diverse views on the conflict reflected by the political parties and interest groups within Israel and also within the Palestinian national movement.

Israeli Political System

When the State of Israel was established in May 1948, a provisional government was formed to rule until elections could be held the following year. The transition from Yishuv to state was not as major as it might at first appear. Many of the components of a government had already been established during the British mandate; thus, all that was necessary was to convert these prestate structures, such as the Haganah, into the formal framework of the new State of Israel.

Israel was set up as a republic with a weak president, a strong cabinet headed by the prime minister, and a strong parliament—a system similar in many ways to the French Fourth Republic. Chaim Weizmann became the first president; David Ben-Gurion was chosen as the first prime minister, a position he held until 1963. The Knesset, a 120-person unicameral (single chamber) body, was established as the main decisionmaking institution within Israel. There are no geographically based districts, as in the United States or Great Britain. Instead, the entire country is treated as a single unit, and citizens vote for their preferred political party rather than for an individual candidate. Any party that receives at least 1.5 percent of the popular vote gains representation in the Knesset. This leads to a situation in which a number of small and frequently changing political parties hold seats, although none has challenged the dominance of the two main parties, **Labor** and **Likud.** On the positive side, this allows for the expression of a wide variety of viewpoints. But it does make coalition building difficult and often results in minority groups' having disproportional influence on decisionmaking within the Knesset. It also means individual Knesset members are not accountable to a specific group of citizens, as is the case when a legislator is elected to represent a district.

The Knesset elects the president, who can serve for no longer than two five-year terms. The position, held since 1993 by Ezer Weitzmann, is largely honorary, but the president can engage in agenda-setting activities on some occasions. The legislative and policy leader of Israel is the prime minister. This individual, in consultation with others, picks the members of his or her Cabinet and assigns their portfolios (that is, their responsibilities within the government). Cabinet members need not be members of the Knesset, nor is there a set number of Cabinet members.

From 1948 through 1992, the leader whose party gained a plurality of votes in the election was given the first opportunity to negotiate with other party leaders to create a ruling coalition. If successful, that person became the prime minister; if not, the president would turn to the party with the second highest number of votes and give that leader the same chance to form a government. In March 1992, the Knesset voted to institute direct election of the prime minister beginning in 1996. The intention is to give the prime minister somewhat greater autonomy and to allow citizens to split their vote by choosing a member of one party for prime minister and of another for the Knesset. Israelis hope this change will eliminate—or at least minimize—the problem of fragile coalition governments that has plagued Israel in recent years.

One of the earliest decisions made by the new leaders of Israel was not to create a written constitution. This allowed Israelis to put off making difficult decisions about the nature of the Jewish state that might have alienated some portions of the population, such as the official role of religion in the country, the rights of non-Jews, and the final official boundaries of the state. Instead, when the Constituent Assembly met in February 1949, it enacted the Transition Law, sometimes called the "Small Constitution," which dealt with the structure of government. Over the years, the Transition Law has been supplemented by a series of "Basic Laws" that address issues such as the military, the economy, the status of Jerusalem, and the judicial branch of government. In some ways these substitute for a constitution, but because they are legislative decisions they can be modified at any time and thus are more likely to be affected by temporal political concerns than a constitution would be.

Two other aspects of the political structure should be mentioned. First, Israel's judicial system is different from that of most Western countries in that it has both civil and religious branches. This structure, which derives from the old Ottoman *millet* system (no longer used in modern-day Turkey), assigns all matters of personal status to the religious courts. All persons, even if they have no religious beliefs, are legally placed in one of the existing religious-legal categories for purposes of marriage, divorce, child custody, treatment at death, inheritance, and so forth. The civil courts deal only with civil and criminal concerns. As Israel is explicitly a Jewish state, there are also civil laws based on Judaism that affect all Israelis, whether Jewish or not. Examples include the prohibition against public transportation running on the Sabbath, the recent law that bans the importation of non-kosher meat into Israel, the nonrecognition by the Interior Ministry of civil marriage ceremonies conducted in Israel, and the 1986 law that forbids bread to be sold during Passover, except in areas where "the majority of the inhabitants ... are non-Jews." A crucial concern for ultra-Orthodox groups in the past several elections has been the extent to which new Israeli laws will be passed to institutionalize Jewish religious precepts as part of the civil code of Israel.

Second, the role of the military in Israeli society is also of tremendous importance in understanding Israeli politics. Israel has almost universal military service. Jewish men, with the exception of ultra-Orthodox Jews, and the majority of Jewish women are required to serve in the Israeli Defense Forces. Most Israeli Palestinians, with the exception of the Druze and the bedouin communities, are neither required nor encouraged to serve in the military. Jewish Israeli men remain part of the military reserves until they are fifty-five years old and must serve a period of active reserve duty, from thirty to sixty days, each year. Since 1967, military service in Israel has often meant an individual must participate not only in a defensive capacity but also as part of an occupation army involved in political and legal affairs as well as military- or security-related activities in the Occupied Territories. The ways in which individuals react to this experience frequently affect their political views once they return to civilian life. In addition, although officers are forbidden to engage in political activities while on active duty, the involvement of senior reserve officers in the higher levels of government has been growing steadily since the 1960s. So important is the military experience in Israel that high military ranking—and combat experience in one or more of Israel's many wars—is an important attribute for success in the political arena.

For Jewish citizens, Israel, with its complex and ever-changing party structure, is one of the most open political systems in the Middle East. Although it is common to try to place the numerous parties on some kind of unidimensional continuum, cross-cutting cleavages make this difficult. At least five sets of issues have to be taken into account in classifying any party's political position: economic policies, ranging from center-right to socialist; religious-secular issues; class and ethnicity, particularly the Sephardic-Ashkenazi division; Zionist versus non-Zionist or anti-Zionist beliefs; and views on security and foreign policy, that is, attitudes regarding the occupation and Israel's relations within the region. Although all are significant, the last is most salient for this discussion. Thus, political parties will be identified as annexationist, endorsing the concept of Greater Israel and no withdrawal from the West Bank and Gaza; mainstream, favoring some sort of "land-for-peace" agreement but not complete withdrawal from the Occupied Territories or acceptance of a Palestinian state; or accommodationist, supporting Palestinian self-determination and complete Israeli withdrawal from the West Bank and Gaza.

Labor, Likud, and Their Allies

The two principal political parties in Israel are the Labor party, representing the center-left economically, and the Likud coalition, representing the center-right (see Table 2.1). The Labor party was created in 1968 through the merger of three separate parties, including the once-dominant Mapai that had existed since before the State of Israel was created. The predominantly Ashkenazi, socialist-Zionist movement controlled Israeli politics from 1948 until the 1977 elections when for the first time Likud won a plurality of the votes and formed the government with Begin as prime minister. In the past decade, Labor has moved somewhat away from the socialist policies that characterized its predecessor parties.

Traditionally, Labor supporters and leaders have been secular rather than religious in orientation. In recent years this has harmed its efforts to form a ruling coalition, although in the past the religious parties did align themselves with Labor. In terms of the Palestinian issue, Labor's policies have been mixed. Although it is generally perceived to be more moderate and willing to compromise than Likud, in the years after the June 1967 War Labor strongly supported Jewish settlements in the Occupied Territories, and Labor Prime Minister Yitzhak Rabin, who served as defense min-

TABLE 2.1 Israeli Political Parties

	Seats in the Knesset				Key Leader(s)
	1992	1988	1984	1981	
Likud	32	40	41	48	Benjamin Netanyahu, David Levy, Ariel Sharon, Benny Begin
Tehiya	0	3	5	3	Yuval Neeman, Geula Cohen
Tzomet[a]	8	2	part of Tehiya		Rafael Eitan
Moledet	3	2	–	–	Rehavam Zeevi
Labor	44	39	44	47	Yitzhak Rabin, Shimon Peres, Avraham Burg
Meretz[b]	12	–	–	–	
Citizens' Rights Movement	–	5	3	1	Shulamit Aloni, Yossi Sarid, Dedi Zucker
Mapam	–	3	part of Labor Alignment		Yair Tzaban
Shinui	–	2	3		Amnon Rubenstein
Shas	6	6	4	–	Arye Deri, Yitzhak Peretz
National Religious party	6	5	4	6	Avner Shaki, Zvulun Hammer
United Torah Judaism[c]	4	–	–	–	
Agudat Yisrael	–	5	2	4	Zeev Feldman, Avraham Verdiger
Degel Hatorah	–	2	part of Agudat Yisrael		Avraham Ravitz
Hadash	3	4	4	4	Tawfiq Zayyad
Progressive List for Peace	0	1	2	–	Mohammed Miari, Matti Peled
Arab Democratic party	2	1	part of Labor Alignment		Abdal Wahhab Darawsha
Other Parties	0	0	8	7	

[a] In February 1994, three Knesset members split from Tzomet and formed a new faction, Yaad.
[b] Meretz is an electoral list composed of the Citizens' Rights Movement, Mapam, and Shinui.
[c] United Torah Judaism is an electoral list composed of Agudat Yisrael, Degel Hatorah, and a third small religious party.

Sources: 1981–1988 election results adapted from Don Peretz and Sammy Smooha, "Israel's Twelfth Knesset Election: An All-Loser Game," *Middle East Journal* 43:3 (Summer 1989), p. 390. 1992 election results and key leaders compiled by the author.

Yitzhak Rabin has served as prime minister of Israel since 1992 (photo courtesy of Israeli Embassy).

ister during the 1984–1990 Israeli government, has been tough in his dealing with the *intifada*. Labor officially supports a "land-for-peace" formula that would involve withdrawing from parts of the West Bank and Gaza in exchange for a peace treaty with the Arab states. In the spring of 1994, Israel began to implement such a plan with the partial withdrawal of its troops from Gaza and Jericho. But Labor leaders have also said they will not accept the formation of an independent Palestinian state and have consistently refused to join a coalition government with parties that favor such a state.

In 1992, three smaller Zionist parties generally aligned with the Labor party—Mapam, Citizens' Rights Movement (Ratz), and Shinui—combined as a single electoral list called Meretz (Energy), running on the campaign slogan "We are going to energize Rabin." Mapam (United Workers) is an ideologically socialist, *kibbutz*-based party. Prior to 1948, it supported the idea of a binational state in Palestine, and it is the only Zionist party to have full-fledged Israeli Palestinian members. Mapam became part of the Labor alignment in 1969 but withdrew in 1984 when Labor agreed to form a unity government with Likud; Mapam claimed that Labor had sold out to join the ruling coalition. It remains close to Labor, however, on a variety of issues. Ratz was founded in 1973 as a Zionist, anti-Orthodox party supportive of national rights for Palestinians as well as for Israeli Jews. Its supporters tend to be liberal Ashkenazi intellectuals, many of whom were alienated by the positions its leaders took after joining the Labor-led government in June 1992. Shinui, whose name means "change," was formed as a protest movement after the October 1973 War. It was originally part of Labor and, like Mapam, remains politically close to it. Shinui is more conservative economically than its partners in Meretz, which has caused tensions within the coalition. Historically, all three parties were more willing than Labor to consider Israeli negotiations with the PLO, complete Israeli withdrawal from the West Bank and Gaza, and Palestinian self-determination.

The Likud coalition is the result of the 1973 merger of several political parties, including Begin's nationalist Herut party, whose roots date back to Jabotinsky's Revisionist movement, and the once-powerful right-of-center Liberal party. Benjamin Netanyahu has led Likud since March 1993 when he won an unexpectedly strong victory in Likud's first elections for party leadership. His position has been weakened, however, by frequent sniping from colleagues David Levy and Ariel Sharon. Likud is more conservative economically and religiously than Labor and also takes a more hardline stance on the Palestinian issue. The Likud coalition claims Jewish sovereignty over the West Bank, including East Jerusalem, the Golan Heights, and the Gaza Strip and seeks their eventual de jure incorporation into Israel. Because Likud sees these areas as a part of the inseparable "Great Land of Israel," it does not accept the international position that they are occupied territories. Likud officially opposes the 1993 Oslo Accords and subsequent agreements and has vowed to resist their implementation, although some individuals have broken ranks with the Likud leadership on this issue.

In the 1992 election, three militantly nationalistic parties were clearly allied with Likud: Tehiya, Tzomet, and Moledet. Tehiya was formed in 1978 in opposition to the **Camp David Accords,** the Israeli-Egyptian Peace Treaty, and the return of the Sinai to Egypt. It calls for formal annexation of and massive Jewish settlement in the Occupied Territories. Despite holding five seats during the previous legislative session, Tehiya (Renaissance) failed to gain sufficient votes to be represented in the 1992 Knesset, in part due to its failure to develop distinctive positions on issues other than the Arab-Israeli conflict. Tzomet (Crossroads), which was created before the 1988 elections, appeals to politically conservative, middle-class secularists concerned about security issues, electoral reform, and efficient government. It benefited significantly from Tehiya's decline, capturing eight seats in the 1992 Knesset (up from only two seats in 1988). The third party, Moledet (Homeland), is religiously, economically, socially, and politically right-wing; in 1988 it campaigned on the slogan "Them or Us." Both Tzomet and Moledet have publicly supported the idea of "population transfer," that is, forcing or strongly encouraging Palestinians to leave all parts of "Greater Israel," although Tzomet deemphasized this in the 1992 campaign. Tehiya's platform did not explicitly endorse "population transfer," but that is the logical extension of its Jewish settlement policies.

Religious Parties

The religious parties originally emerged in direct response to the development of political Zionism at the end of the nineteenth century and have become highly significant in the formation of a ruling coalition after each election. Unlike Labor, Likud, and their allies, the religious parties are not uniformly Zionist. Some deny the validity of Zionism completely on the grounds that it created a secular Jewish state rather than waiting for the Messiah to create a religious state; others feel Jews should settle in the Holy Land as a way of fulfilling religious obligation but that Zionism should not be seen as a secular nationalism. Still other religious Jews view the creation of Israel as the first stage in the messianic process and are supportive of political Zionism.

Historically Israel's most powerful religious party has been the National Religious party (NRP). This strongly Zionist, religiously Orthodox party follows a liberal economic policy, and its members tend to be active participants in the mainstream of Israeli political life. In recent years, the NRP has become an increasingly outspoken advocate for the annexation of the West Bank and Gaza, and its members were among the founders of the settlement movement **Gush Emunim** (Bloc of the Faithful).

For the 1992 election, three ultra-Orthodox religious parties joined together in a single list known as Yahadut Hatorah (United Torah Judaism). The largest group, Agudat Yisrael, was established in the early part of the century, long before the State of Israel was declared. Its supporters, primarily Russian and Polish Jews, believe that the community of Jews should live in accordance with the teachings of the Torah and that this should be institutionalized in the laws of the State of Israel. Unlike supporters of the National Religious party, members of Agudat Yisrael live in autonomous neighborhoods, educate their children separately, and are exempt from compulsory military service. Although the party was originally strongly anti-Zionist, since 1948 it has participated in the political life of the state to a limited extent, and it appears to have accepted Zionism as a feature in the Israeli political scene. Nonetheless, members of Agudat Yisrael refuse to pledge allegiance to the Israeli national institutions and the flag of Israel, indicating their continued opposition to the secular state. Agudat Yisrael is divided in terms of its policies toward the West Bank and Gaza but in general has been less strongly annexationist than the NRP.

The other members of Yahadut Hatorah are Moriah, a new party that was not represented in the 1988 Knesset, and Degel Hatorah (Torah Flag). Degel Hatorah is a small party that originally split off from Agudat Yisrael over religious and personality differences. Like other ultra-Orthodox parties, the Ashkenazi-dominated Degel Hatorah argues in favor of a Jewish state based purely on *Halakah* (Jewish religious law). Degel Hatorah is non-Zionist and supports the possibility of territorial compromise regarding the West Bank and Gaza Strip.

Another ultra-Orthodox, non-Zionist religious party is Shas, which was established in 1984 in a split from Agudat Yisrael. Shas has special appeal for the economically and socially disadvantaged Sephardic community for which it serves as an organized form of political expression. Shas has been more interested in religious legislation than in political matters, but its rulings on the inferior position to be given to non-Jews in Israel have clear political implications. At the same time, its position on territorial issues such as Israeli control of the West Bank and Gaza Strip has been more moderate than that of some of the other religious parties. Shas's spiritual leader, Chief Rabbi Ovadiyah Yosef, has said that "the sanctity of human life is paramount" and that therefore territorial compromises are acceptable in order to save lives.

Accommodationist Political Parties

Two parties represented in the 1992 Knesset appeal primarily to Palestinian citizens of Israel and to non-Zionist or anti-Zionist secular Jews. The attitude of non-Zionist Jews toward Judaism and toward Israel is dramatically different from that of most Zionists. As one non-Zionist Israeli Jew explains:

> A Non-Zionist believes in the multicentrality of Jewish life, world-wide, rather than in the unicentrality of Jewish life around Israel.
>
> A Non-Zionist does not oppose the existence of the State of Israel, and is, indeed, concerned for its inhabitants, Jewish and Arab. He does, however, refuse the Israelis' self-assumed pretention to speak for him, or to deny him the right to speak up in a different voice from theirs.
>
> A Non-Zionist believes there is such a thing as Jewish morals, both secular and religious; and that the state of Israel and most of its inhabitants do not adhere to them. ...
>
> A Non-Zionist recognizes the Israeli-Palestinian conflict has dragged all Jews into it, willy-nilly, but does not feel the need to identify with this strug-

gle simply because he is a Jew; even less so to side with the official policy of Israel. ...

As long as the Israeli establishment holds on to the immigration of all Jews to Israel as one of its goals, and gives Jewish immigrants prerogatives over the state's Arab citizens, there is a need for a Non-Zionist stance among Israeli Jews.[8]

Many of these views are reflected in the political platforms of the accommodationist parties.

The Democratic Front for Peace and Equality (Hadash), an anti-Zionist party associated with the Israeli Communist party, has been in existence since 1977. Hadash supporters believe that there will be no freedom or security for the Israeli people as long as Palestinians are denied freedom, security, and self-determination. In the 1992 election, Hadash received 23 percent of the votes cast by Israeli Palestinians, a decline from 34.5 percent in 1988. In 1988, Abdal Wahhab Darawsha left the Labor party over disagreements with its policies in the West Bank and Gaza Strip and founded the Arab Democratic party (ADP). The ADP received about 15 percent of the votes of Palestinian citizens of Israel in the 1992 election, up from its 11 percent in 1988. A third accommodationist party, the secular, anti-Zionist Progressive List for Peace (PLP), was part of the Knesset in 1984 and 1988 but failed to reach the 1.5 percent vote threshold needed for representation in the 1992 Knesset. Like Hadash, the PLP involves both Jews and Palestinians in its political activities. Members support full equality of civil and national rights for Jewish and Palestinian citizens of Israel within its pre-1967 boundaries, Israeli withdrawal from the West Bank and Gaza Strip, and the "right of return" for Palestinians.

Interpretation of Recent Elections

The results of the past three Israeli elections have been inconclusive, reflecting the fundamental divisions within the polity regarding how best to deal with massive economic problems, the role of religion in Israel, and, most crucially, the Occupied Territories. In 1984, Labor won a plurality of the seats but was unable to muster sufficient support from smaller parties to achieve the necessary sixty-one votes, in part because they were unwilling to include any of the accommodationist parties such as Hadash or the PLP. Likud was also unable to put together a winning coalition. This led to the creation of a National Unity government. For the first two years of the four-year term, the prime minister's position was held by Labor leader Shimon Peres and the foreign minister's position by Likud leader Yitzhak Shamir. In the second two years of the government this was reversed.

A similarly indecisive outcome after the 1988 election resulted in the formation of a second National Unity government. By then, however, the balance of power had shifted just enough that Likud was able to gain absolute control of a number of the important Cabinet portfolios, including the positions of prime minister and foreign minister. Labor lost votes to the Left and to Likud; Likud lost votes to the religious parties but compensated with the new votes from former Labor supporters. Likud was reluctant to share power with Labor and for several weeks pursued the possibility of a narrow coalition including the religious and the far-right parties before deciding on the broader-based Unity government. Some in Labor felt they compromised their ability to critique Likud by being inside the government rather than serving as the loyal opposition, but in the end both parties concluded that their uneasy marriage was preferable to a Likud-led government that rested on the support of the religious parties, with their unpopular demands for strict religious laws. Furthermore, there was widespread sentiment that Israel needed a broadly based government in place to deal with changes in U.S. foreign policy, such as the U.S. decision to open a dialogue with the PLO. Finally, a second Unity government was preferred by U.S. Jews, who denounced the demands of the religious parties that would have challenged the religious status of Reform and Conservative Jews.

In terms of Israel's policy toward the *intifada* and the Arab-Israeli conflict, the 1988 election results provided no clear mandate from the Israeli citizenry. In the fifteen months the Unity government was in existence, there were constant disagreements between Labor and Likud regarding how Israel should deal with the long-term issues of Jewish settlements throughout lands controlled by Israel and of peace negotiations with the Palestinians. In March 1990 the coalition collapsed after Shamir's government received a vote of no-confidence by the Knesset. The religious parties proved pivotal in the vote: Agudat Yisrael voted against the Shamir government and five members of Shas abstained, thus bringing down the government for the first time in Israel's history.

As leader of the Labor party, Peres was given the first opportunity to create a new government, but despite extensive negotiations with the religious parties and individual members of Likud, he was unable to put together a working majority. The mandate then passed to Shamir, who under Israeli law remained acting prime minister of a caretaker government. At the last possible moment, Shamir was able to assemble a sixty-two-person coalition that included the members of Likud, Tehiya, Tzomet, Moledet, NRP, Shas, and Degel Hatorah as well as one defector each from Agudat Yisrael (which had pledged to support Labor) and from Labor. The government was approved by the Knesset on 11 June 1990.

The political paralysis that resulted from the difficulties Peres and Shamir experienced as each attempted to form a governing coalition increased demands for reform of the national electoral system and was one of the factors leading to the change in how the prime minister is chosen. Half a million Israelis—representing 22 percent of the country's voters—signed a petition calling for some form of restructuring to make it easier for one of the large parties to win enough seats to govern by itself. Many suggested some form of direct, constituent election of legislators; another proposal would increase the percentage of votes needed for a party to gain representation in the Knesset.

In the months preceding the 1992 elections, Israelis remained divided in their opinions about the future direction of their country. In January 1992, Tehiya and Moledet defected from the ruling coalition to protest Israel's participation in the peace negotiations begun in Madrid, Spain, the previous October. This left the Likud-led government with control of only fifty-nine seats in the Knesset and forced Prime Minister Shamir to call for new Knesset elections on 23 June rather than waiting until November as he had originally intended. The election pitted Shamir against Labor leader Yitzhak Rabin, who defeated Shimon Peres in a U.S.-style primary election within the Labor party by arguing that Labor was more likely to regain control of the Knesset under his leadership.

As in previous elections, key issues included the faltering economy, the impact of continuing mass settlement activities on U.S.-Israeli relations, protection of Israel's security (an issue of increased importance after the 1990–1991 Gulf War), questions about whether and how to negotiate with the Palestinians and the Arab states in the post-Madrid period, and relations between religious and secular Jews. Charges of corruption against Likud and Shas leaders also played a role, as did severe infighting among Likud Knesset members. Labor benefited from Likud's difficulties, and the switch from Peres to Rabin strengthened Labor's popularity with moderates who saw Rabin as closer to the political center than Peres.

The results of the 23 June election put Labor (with 44 Knesset seats) in a strong position to put together a majority coalition. Rabin originally hoped to form a broad-based Cabinet including Meretz (with 12 seats), the religious parties (with 16 seats among them), and Tzomet (which had captured 8 seats). The advantage of such a coalition, from Labor's perspective, was that it would not be excessively dependent on the votes of the left-wing Meretz. Radical differences among these parties made such an alliance impossible, however, and Rabin eventually settled for a government composed of Labor, Meretz, and Shas (for 62 seats), with the electoral support of the 5 seats held by Hadash and the Arab Democratic party. This coalition held until fall 1993 when Shas withdrew from the government in protest over corruption charges against its leader. This left Rabin with a minority government of 56 seats that had to rely on the 5 Arab votes to defeat motions of no-confidence by Likud and its allies.

Shas rejoined the government in spring 1994 after the Knesset passed religious legislation important to Shas.

Other Israeli Political Actors

Outside the government are several organizations or groups that play a significant role in Israel's political system. Among the most important of these is the Histadrut, founded in 1920. As initially envisioned, the Histadrut made no provision for the involvement of Palestinians; its goal was a Jewish, socialist society in Palestine in which all work was to be done by Jews. In 1959 the policy of Hebrew-only labor was dropped, and Israeli Palestinians were allowed to join the Histadrut, albeit without all the benefits accruing to the Jewish members. Palestinians from the West Bank and Gaza, however, are not permitted to become members, although their labor has become an essential part of the Israeli economy.

The Histadrut is generally described as a trade union federation, but it is more like a social movement. Virtually all trade unions are part of the Histadrut, but so are some employers. More important, the organization is itself an employer, second only to the government in size; its enterprises include a bank, a major health insurance program, sports clubs, stores, bus companies, and a wide range of other economic, social, and cultural activities. Thus, the influence of this Labor-dominated body, to which a majority of adult Israelis belong, has been tremendous, and election results in the Histadrut are often used as an indirect indicator of the relative strength of various political parties in the country as a whole. In recent years, the power of the Histadrut has declined dramatically. Tens of thousands of members have withdrawn from the organization amid accusations of financial mismanagement and abuse by the leadership. There have been calls for increased openness, elimination of the traditional ties between the Histadrut and the Labor party, and other reforms. Such changes could radically alter the role of this historically critical organization.

A wide variety of nongovernmental organizations formed in the past fifteen years also express discontent of all types with Israeli domestic policies toward Palestinian citizens or with Israel's stance vis-à-vis the occupation, Lebanon, and so forth. Only a few of the most influential are mentioned here. On the annexationist side, one of the most outspoken groups is Gush Emunim, an extremist nationalist-religious organization founded in 1974 and headed by Moshe Levinger. Loosely associated with the National Religious party, Gush Emunim promotes the construction of Jewish settlements throughout the land of Eretz Yisrael, including in areas densely populated by Palestinians (such as Kiryat Arba, located just outside of Hebron). Its supporters see themselves as the new Israeli pioneers in the tradition of the *kibbutzniks* of the prestate period. They are opposed to Israeli withdrawal from any part of the West Bank or Gaza Strip, basing their claim to the land on nationalist and religious grounds, and have stated repeatedly that if such withdrawal is the price of peace, then peace is not worth it.

On the other side are a number of groups opposed to expansionist Israeli government policy. These range from the relatively mainstream Peace Now, founded in 1978 in response to Egyptian president Sadat's peace initiative and politically close to the Labor party, to the leftist Jewish-Palestinian group known as the Peace Block, established in April 1993 to provide a political alternative to Meretz. Peace Now is probably the best-known group outside of Israel because of its strength in mobilizing large numbers of people for demonstrations against the war in Lebanon and against brutal policies in the West Bank and Gaza Strip. Peace Now recognizes the principle of Palestinian self-determination and is opposed to the occupation but does not advocate a complete return to the pre-1967 borders. It is a loosely organized group that for a number of years resisted specifying a detailed political program in order to avoid alienating any of its diverse supporters. Similar in political ideology to Peace Now, but much smaller, is Hamizrach El Hashalom (East for Peace), a group composed of Sephardic Jews who felt alienated from the predominantly Ashkenazi Peace Now. East for Peace supporters are proud of their Arab ethnic background as well as their Jewish religious beliefs and try to serve as a bridge between Ashkenazi Jews and Christian and Muslim Palestinians. The organization was formed after the 1978 Israeli invasion of Lebanon.

The mainstream approaches of Peace Now and East for Peace contrast with another small Zionist group, the Israeli Council for Israeli-Palestinian Peace (ICIPP), organized in 1976. ICIPP believes dialogue with the PLO is both possible and essential. It calls for mutual recognition by the two nations and supports the establishment of a Palestinian state in the West Bank, including East Jerusalem, and the Gaza Strip. West Jerusalem would serve as the Israeli capital, East Jerusalem as the capital of the Palestinian state. Members of ICIPP met with supporters and members of the PLO, including Yasir Arafat, long before it was legal to do so and have been involved in a range of protest actions against Israeli government policies.

One of the most controversial groups within Israel is Yesh Gvul (There Is a Limit), which gained prominence during 1982 when 2,500 Israeli reservists signed a petition asking that they not be sent to fight in Lebanon. After the beginning of the *intifada*, a similar petition was circulated that indicated that its signers refused to serve in the West Bank or Gaza Strip. Yesh Gvul is concerned with the philosophical question of the general limits of obedience to the state and the military and provides support for those who feel compelled to engage in civil disobedience regarding military service. In a few highly publicized cases, Yesh Gvul members have been jailed for their refusal to serve outside the 1967 borders of Israel, and the more mainstream groups have shunned association with them.

Since the *intifada*, a number of Israeli women's organizations—Women Against the Occupation, Women for Women Political Prisoners, Women in Black, and others—have organized international conferences, demonstrations, peace marches, and other activities in opposition to the occupation. In addition, there has been a significant increase in political dissent by professional organizations, including those of mental health workers, physicians, lawyers, architects, academics, journalists and other writers, and artists of all types. All of the groups mentioned, from Gush Emunim to Yesh Gvul, reflect the broad range of political opinion and activism within the Jewish Israeli public regarding Israel's future borders and its relations with the Palestinian people. Few people in Israel are neutral about these issues. At the same time, the overall level of mobilization and political expression remains lower than might be expected from the wide diversity of political groups. Although they have strong opinions, many Israelis, as is true with citizens in other countries, often fail to express these opinions in the political arena.

This brief description of the Israeli political system illustrates the point made repeatedly in these pages: States are not monolithic entities. Instead, they are composed of individuals and groups with competing and often conflicting goals and visions for the future of the state. This was particularly evident in Israel during the fifteen months of the second National Unity government because of the profound differences among the coalition partners. In such a situation, foreign and domestic policies are the outcome of compromise, bargaining, and negotiation among these groups and individuals, rather than being based on a clearly defined national interest.

ISRAELI OCCUPATION OF
THE WEST BANK AND THE GAZA STRIP

As a result of the June 1967 War, Israel gained control of the remainder of the former Mandate of Palestine—East Jerusalem and the rest of the West Bank (which some Israelis refer to by the biblical names of Judea and Samaria) and the Gaza Strip—as well as the Syrian Golan Heights and the Egyptian Sinai Peninsula (see Map 2.1). The continuing Israeli military occupation of these lands is highly unusual. Although there are numerous other instances when territories gained during war have been incorporated against their will within the victorious country's boundaries—such

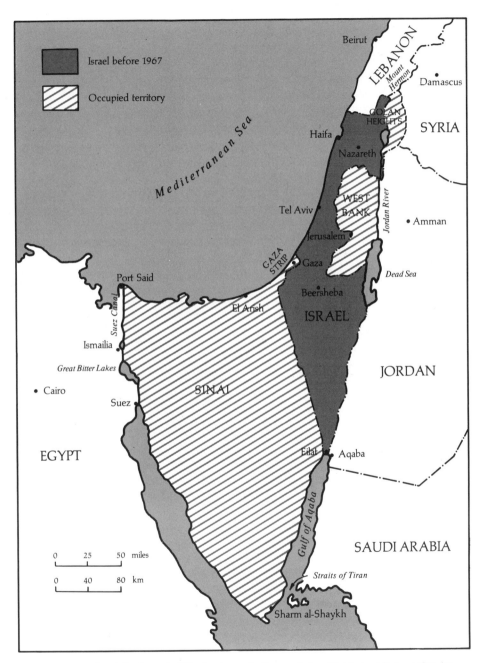

MAP 2.1 Israel and the Occupied Territories, 1967. *Source:* Arthur Goldschmidt, Jr., *A Concise History of the Middle East*, 3d ed., revised and updated (Boulder, CO: Westview Press, 1988), p. 196. Original cartography by Don Kunze.

as occurred with the lengthy Soviet occupation of the Baltic Republics of Estonia, Latvia, and Lithuania—the populations of such territories are generally made citizens of the conquering state and are granted some degree of equality with the rest of the citizenry of the country. In other instances, such as the U.S. occupation of Japan at the end of World War II, the occupation is short-term and the actions of the occupying power constrained by international law. Neither description fits the current Israeli occupation.

There have been changes in the official Israeli policies toward the territories occupied in the June 1967 War. The Sinai was returned to Egypt as part of the Egyptian-Israeli Peace Treaty. Israel extended its legal jurisdiction to East Jerusalem in 1967 and officially annexed it in 1980; the Golan Heights region was annexed in 1981. (Both these annexations were condemned by the international community.) The basic approach, however, has been to rule the Palestinian population through harsh military laws, while giving all rights and benefits of citizenship to those Jewish Israelis who chose to establish settlements in the area in anticipation of the territories' de jure incorporation into Israel. The principal justification given for this policy choice has always been that the security needs of Israel must be paramount and that in light of the continuing state of war between Israel and the Arab states that surround it (with the exception of Egypt since 1979), it is only prudent for Israel to protect itself through maintaining a significant presence in the Occupied Territories. In addition, some religious fundamentalists and some ultranationalists argue that the West Bank in particular was promised to the Jewish people by God and that therefore the Palestinians have no claim to that land and no rights if they choose to live there.

During the years of the occupation, the extent of integration of the West Bank and Gaza into Israel has been great. In 1987, former deputy mayor of Jerusalem Meron Benvenisti pessimistically described the situation this way:

> All Israeli objectives have been attained in the territories and Jewish interests have been assured. The process of economic integration has long since been accomplished; infrastructure grids have been linked (roads, electricity, water, communications), administrative systems have been unified; social stratification has become institutionalized and political relationships have settled into well established patterns.
>
> The Second Israeli Republic [post–June 1967 War] is a bi-national entity with a rigid, hierarchical social structure based on ethnicity. Three-and-a-half million Jewish Israelis hold total monopoly over governmental resources, control the economy, form the upper social stratum and determine the educational and national values and objectives of the republic.

The two million Palestinians divide into Israeli Palestinians and the Palestinians in the territories. Though the former are citizens of the republic, their citizenship does not assure them equality in law. ...

The remaining one-and-a-half million Palestinians ... are deprived of all political rights, ostensibly because they are under military occupation, though even their rights under international conventions governing military occupations are not assured, since the government of the republic does not recognize the application of these conventions to the territories. ...

Communal strife rages in the Second Israeli Republic. There is a perpetual conflict, not necessarily violent, between the Jewish majority group that seeks to maintain its superiority, and the Arab minority group that seeks to free itself from majority tyranny.[9]

Benvenisti makes several important points of relevance to analysts of international relations. First, he indicates that de facto state boundaries may have as much or more political and economic importance as de jure internationally recognized boundaries. This is seen in that until the beginning of the *intifada* in December 1987 it appeared that the Israeli incorporation of the West Bank and Gaza Strip was all but accomplished, although formal annexation had not occurred.

Second, Benvenisti points out the apparent irrelevance of international law if a state is willing to flaunt international norms, as Israel has done. Because international law operates through international pressure rather than through enforcement by an overarching global entity, a state that declares international law inapplicable to its situation suffers no specifically designated sanctions. (Despite the lack of formal sanctions, however, it can be argued that Israel suffered by being labeled a pariah state, particularly in the 1970s and 1980s.) Although Benvenisti does not mention it here, U.S. military, economic, and diplomatic support of Israel is of critical importance in this regard. In the absence of countervailing pressures, this support makes it possible for Israel to circumvent or ignore international law.

Finally, Benvenisti alerts scholars to the importance of internal strife even when it is not expressed violently. Until the *intifada* began, many people ignored the tensions between Israeli Jews and Palestinians because those tensions did not consistently reveal themselves in a physically violent form. The problems were present, nevertheless, and the eventual explosion should not have surprised those who were sensitive to the situation.

Among the many issues critical in understanding the implications of the Israeli occupation of the West Bank, including East Jerusalem, and the Gaza Strip, two stand out: Israeli settlement policies and human rights violations. Both exacerbate the conflict between Jewish Israelis and Palestinians; both have come under scrutiny by the international community; neither ceased with the onset of the *intifada*.

Settlement Policies

Customary international law developed in the nineteenth century placed certain restrictions on the actions of belligerent occupying powers against civilian populations under their control, such as forbidding the confiscation of private property. These restrictions, and others, were codified in the 1949 Geneva Convention Relative to the Protection of Civilian Persons in Time of War. Among the key elements are that a belligerent occupying power is not allowed to make changes in the laws, institutions, or government of the territory; place civilian settlements in the occupied regions; or annex part or all of the occupied territory. It is on this basis that most international legal scholars have condemned Israeli settlement activities.

Jewish settlement in the Occupied Territories began shortly after the June 1967 War (see Map 2.2). The settlements, which are located on lands purchased or confiscated from Palestinians (or in the case of the Golan Heights, from Syrians), are frequently established on the tops of hills overlooking Palestinian villages or in areas previously farmed by Palestinian peasants. Their existence is a constant thorn in the side of Palestinians, who see them as a continuation of the Israeli expansion and expulsion activities of the Palestine War and as evidence Israel will never withdraw fully from the West Bank or the Gaza Strip. The frequent land confiscations—about 60 percent of the land of the West Bank and 35 percent of the Gaza Strip is now controlled by the government of Israel— mean that increasing numbers of Palestinians are forced into ever-smaller amounts of territory and in many cases are denied their means of livelihood. Israel has also claimed a significant portion of the water resources of these areas. This problem is particularly acute in the tiny Gaza Strip, but it is also an issue in the West Bank.[10]

In addition, the areas around the settlements are frequently the sites of violent exchanges between Israeli Jewish settlers and Palestinian villagers. Often settler violence is ignored by official Israeli occupation forces. According to the *Karp Report,* submitted to the Israeli government by the Israeli attorney general's office in 1982 and made public in edited form in 1984, the security and police forces have been reluctant to investigate or prosecute instances of settler violence against Palestinians and instead have engaged in a "conspiracy of silence." Even when cases of settler violence are prosecuted and individuals convicted, their sentences are light compared with the sentences of Palestinians convicted of similar actions.

Settlement activities in the West Bank have gone through several distinct phases. Within six months of the June 1967 War, Israel began constructing large residential Jewish settlements in newly occupied and expanded East Jerusalem in order to create a united and predominantly

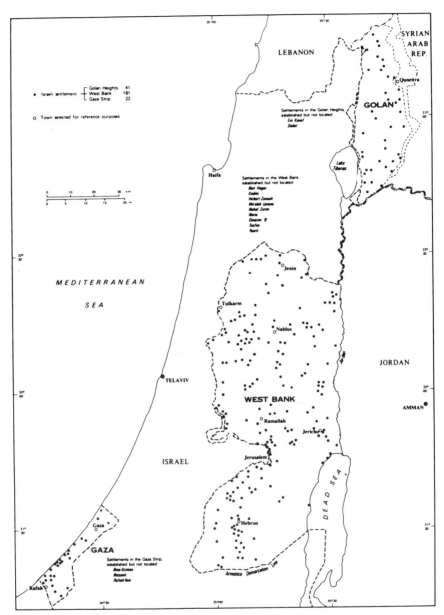

MAP 2.2 Pattern of Israeli settlements established in the territories occupied in June 1967. Information concerning the settlements has been furnished by the Special Committee to Investigate Israeli Practices Affecting the Human Rights of the Population of the Occupied Territories. *Source:* Based on United Nations map no. 3070, rev. 14, October 1993 (used by permission).

Jewish city. The first settlements in the West Bank outside of East Jerusalem were justified on the basis of a plan designed by Yigal Allon, which was intended to achieve maximum territorial increase for Israel with minimal increase in Palestinian population. In other words, Allon wanted to build settlements on, and eventually annex, as much of the West Bank as possible to provide "defensible borders," without having to add to the Palestinian population of Israel. In order to achieve this, a small Palestinian enclave would remain attached to Jordan, but the effective strategic eastern border of Israel was to remain the Jordan River. During the first ten years of the occupation, twelve settlements were constructed in the East Jerusalem area, with an additional thirty-six settlements in the rest of the West Bank. Important strategic locations also were identified as sites for future settlements. Most settlements were located in the Jordan Valley and around Jerusalem. Outside of Jerusalem, however, the number of settlers was relatively small—about 5,000 in 1977.

The second stage in Israeli settlement policy in the West Bank began with the 1977 election that resulted in the first Likud-dominated government in Israel's history. The new prime minister, Menachem Begin, shared many of the views of the increasingly influential Israeli settlers' movement Gush Emunim. Supporters of Gush Emunim consider the settlement and eventual annexation of the entire land of "Judea and Samaria" to be a religious and national responsibility and were in large part responsible for the dramatic increase in Jewish settlement in the West Bank during the years of Likud leadership. Although the U.S.-sponsored Camp David Accords of 1978 included a restriction on new Israeli settlements, this was completely ignored by the Likud government, which wanted to create a situation of de facto control. To facilitate this goal, newly appointed Army Chief of Staff Raphael Eitan (now head of the right-wing Tzomet party) began to provide settlers over the age of sixteen with army-issued weapons and ammunition and assigned men to do their reserve service in their home settlements. The settlers were also organized into virtually autonomous paramilitary Extended Defense Units that undertook independent actions against local Palestinians without any legal justification.

The third stage of West Bank settlement activities has been labeled by Meron Benvenisti as the "yuppiezation" of the West Bank. By this, Benvenisti means that the most recent settlers are often young, professional couples who have moved to a settlement for financial reasons rather than being motivated primarily by religious or nationalistic sentiments. Although this last group could conceivably be convinced through economic compensation to abandon the settlements as part of a "land-for-peace" exchange, those who are part of the Gush Emunim and similar movements are likely to resist any deals that would compel them to leave the West Bank.

In the early 1990s, the Israeli government established or enlarged dozens of settlements and developed plans for an expanded road system linking these settlements to each other and to the main population centers in Israel. New communities were also established just inside the Green Line (that is, within the pre-1967 borders of Israel) as part of Housing Minister Ariel Sharon's "Seven Stars Program," which was designed to connect towns in Israel with settlements in the Occupied Territories.

The settlement plan for the Gaza Strip was somewhat different from that seen in the West Bank, although the basic pattern of extensive land confiscation and settler penetration is the same. In the first five years of the Israeli occupation of the Gaza Strip, only one settlement was established. The high level of Palestinian resistance to the occupation made the area unattractive even for the highly committed. Once the resistance had been crushed in 1971, Israel was able to establish five additional settlements by 1978, but as in the West Bank the Jewish population remained small during the years of the Labor-controlled government. The year 1978 represented a turning point. The Camp David Accords resulted in the evacuation and destruction of thirteen Israeli settlements constructed in the Northern Sinai region as a buffer zone. Once the Sinai settlements were removed in 1982, a new strategy was developed to emphasize intensive settlement within the Gaza Strip area, and by 1985 twelve new Israeli settlements had been established.

At the beginning of 1992, there were approximately 247,500 Jewish Israelis living in 128 settlements in the West Bank, including 150,000 people in thirteen urban settlements around annexed Jerusalem. An additional 3,500 Jewish Israelis were living in sixteen settlements in the Gaza Strip.[11] Residents in many of these settlements can easily commute to their jobs in Jerusalem or Tel Aviv and still benefit from the generous housing subsidies provided to the settlers. The settlements, which are often completely self-contained, are tremendously expensive for Israel to establish and maintain. Many of the rural settlements are small but nonetheless require the full component of services—roads, water, electricity, schools, health clinics, and so forth—which increases the per capita cost. Thus, their existence strains an Israeli economy already stretched to the limit and heavily reliant on foreign aid from the United States and nongovernmental contributions from abroad.

The location of the West Bank settlements is also significant:

Officially, Israel claims to have placed its settlements along potential future borders in order to ensure strategic security. What has evolved, in fact, is a system of settlements set up along three different axes. The first is a line of settlements running along the Jordan river to separate the West Bank from Jordan. The second is a series of settlements which follow the 1948 cease-fire line designed to isolate West Bank Palestinians from Palestinians inside Israel. The final group consists of settlements that surround or penetrate major Palestinian population centers (i.e., Jerusalem, Nablus, Ramallah, and Khalil). The effect is not so much to provide strategic security as to isolate Palestinians from Jordan, Israel, and each other.[12]

Thus, the settlements are an integral part of a plan to incorporate the West Bank and Gaza Strip into Israel while cutting off easy contact among Palestinians and between Palestinians and other Arabs. Palestinian resistance to these settlements is based not on a reluctance to live near Jews, as it is often portrayed by Israel, but on the grounds that the settlements violate international law and are another way in which Israel is attempting to deny Palestinian nationalist identity and self-determination.

Human Rights in the West Bank and Gaza

The problem of human rights violations in the West Bank and Gaza Strip has been well documented. The International Red Cross, Middle East Watch, the Israeli human rights group B'Tselem, the Palestine Human Rights Information Center, and Amnesty International have repeatedly expressed concern regarding the treatment of Palestinians by Israel, pointing to the imprisonment of prisoners of conscience, arbitrary arrest and detention without charge or trial, demolition of houses, and the torture of detainees as violations of fundamental rights provided under international law. The U.S. Department of State's annual report on the human rights practices of recipients of U.S. foreign assistance has also criticized Israel for its failure to uphold internationally recognized standards of human rights. Among the violations of civil and human rights mentioned by these organizations and others are:

☐ shooting and beating of unarmed individuals, including targeted assassinations of "wanted" individuals
☐ confiscation of required identification cards without cause
☐ expulsion from the region without specific charges
☐ restrictions on residency rights for Palestinians who were not physically present in the West Bank or Gaza Strip in June 1967
☐ suppression of Palestinian culture
☐ the closure of Palestinian national institutions
☐ collective punishment such as curfews against entire neighborhoods, villages, or districts
☐ intimidation of families of individuals in whom the authorities are interested
☐ military censorship of all publications
☐ confiscation of land and water resources

□ differential taxation policies
□ restrictions on economic activities

In addition, since 1967 the Israeli military commander has imposed over a thousand regulations that affect every aspect of Palestinian life.

When Defense Minister Yitzhak Rabin announced the imposition of what he called the Iron Fist policy in August 1985, he was aptly naming a policy toward increased repression that had begun in 1982 under Prime Minister Begin. The explicit goals of the policy were to eliminate pro-PLO activities in the West Bank and Gaza Strip and to quash the continuing expression of Palestinian nationalist sentiments by significant portions of the population representing a wide range of socioeconomic groups. By definition, virtually any political or cultural activity by a Palestinian has been considered a security threat to Israel. Thus, trade unionists, journalists, academics, religious figures, and community leaders have all been defined as political activists who represent a sufficient danger to the security of Israel to justify detention or even expulsion.

PALESTINIAN NATIONAL MOVEMENT

The British expulsion of Palestinian leaders from Palestine in the late 1930s and the dispersion of the Palestinian people in 1947–1949 meant that Palestinian national organizations were frequently created among those living outside the borders of pre-1947 Palestine. The most important such organization was the PLO, which Israel declared an illegal organization and banned in all areas under Israeli control. It was not until September 1993 that Israel recognized the PLO as a legitimate political entity. Thus, the structures of Palestinian political expression, in particular the Palestine National Council, have evolved in an entirely different setting from that experienced by political actors within Israel. Nonetheless, there are similarities in the dynamics within the Knesset and the PNC. First, both attempt to be representative of the populations from which they are drawn. In Israel, this occurs through elections. Elections for the PNC were not feasible for nearly three decades, but efforts were made to assure broad representation. The two approaches are not equivalent, but the underlying intent is the same. Second, in both the Knesset and the PNC a wide range of opinions is expressed. In neither legislative body is there complete consensus on any topic; as a result, political decisions are inevitably compromises among alternative perspectives.

Creation of the Palestine Liberation Organization

By the mid-1960s there was a growing belief among Palestinians that they would have to take control of their own political future, as neither the international community as a whole nor the Arab states appeared willing or able to assist Palestinian self-determination efforts. It had been nearly two decades since the 1947 UN partition of Palestine, yet little progress had been made toward the objective of regaining the Palestinian homeland or even toward the goals specified by numerous UN resolutions: compensation for Palestinian property abandoned during the Palestine War, repatriation of Palestinian refugees to their original homes, rehabilitation and resettlement for Palestinians who did not wish to return to their homes in land now controlled by Israel, and the establishment of permanent Israeli borders that included adjustments to allow Palestinian villages to be rejoined with their agricultural lands. In the view of Palestinians, the United Nations clearly could not be counted on.

Nor were the Arab states much help. The collapse of the Egyptian-Syrian union in 1961 after less than three years and the failure of the 1963 unity talks among Egypt, Iraq, and Syria convinced many Palestinians that the Arab states lacked the necessary sense of cohesion to aid the Palestinian movement effectively. The Arab states had their own problems, and although they were rhetorically supportive of the Palestinian cause, few were willing to take political risks on behalf of the Palestinians. Some, it seemed, actually preferred the status quo. Certainly Jordan had benefited economically by its 1950 annexation of the West Bank, an action considered illegal by most of the international community and formally recognized only by Britain and Pakistan. At the same time, the ultimate success in 1962 of the lengthy Algerian revolution provided an example that suggested that armed resistance could aid in the achievement of self-determination. Thus, Palestinians began to organize guerrilla groups to engage in military actions against Israel. At this point, the Arab states were galvanized into action.

The idea for the Palestine Liberation Organization was proposed in January 1964 at the First Arab Summit, organized by President Gamal Abdel Nasser of Egypt. The official purpose of the organization, which was established at a meeting of over 400 Palestinians in May 1964, was to serve as an autonomous institutional expression of Palestinian national identity and to provide a means to achieve Palestinian self-determination. To facilitate the second purpose, the Palestine Liberation Army (PLA) was created at the same time as the PLO. In fact, however, the PLO was created not only to support Palestinian nationalism but primarily as a way for the Arab states to control the nationalist guerrilla groups. Egypt wanted to assure that Palestinian military actions did not involve Egypt in a war involuntarily; Jordan did not want to be forced to give up the West Bank.

In the beginning, the new body was controversial within the Palestinian community. One issue was whether it was appropriate to separate the cause of Palestinian self-determination from the more general pan-Arab national movement. Second was the charge that the PLO was an elite organization whose goals did not reflect the political views of the general Palestinian population. Some people viewed its first leader, Ahmed Shuqairi (who had previously served as a spokesperson for Palestinian affairs at the United Nations), as too much a part of the old establishment of traditional notables to lead a liberation movement. By December 1967 dissatisfaction with Shuqairi forced his resignation, and the PLO was led for a brief period by Acting Chairperson Yehia Hammouda. A third concern was the relationship between the PLO, which at this point was controlled by Egypt, and more autonomous Palestinian groups such as the Arab Higher Committee for Palestine, established in the mid-1930s, and the Palestine National Liberation Movement (Fateh), which began in the late 1950s and was headed by Yasir Arafat.

Despite these initial reservations, the need for an organization such as the PLO was obvious, and it rapidly gained a strong position in inter-Arab and international dialogues. It did not stop the creation and growth of other Palestinian groups, however. Fateh and the Popular Front for the Liberation of Palestine (PFLP) in particular began to gain strength and recognition. The PFLP was created after the devastating Israeli occupation of the West Bank and Gaza during the June 1967 War and was led by George Habash. Ultimately these groups challenged the initial internal structure of the Palestine Liberation Organization, which favored landowners and other notables, and gained a major role in its governance.

At the fourth Palestine National Council meeting in July 1968, the leadership of the PNC was effectively taken over by Fateh and other guerrilla groups, and seven months later, at the fifth PNC meeting, Yasir Arafat was elected chairperson of the PLO, a position he has continued to hold for twenty-five years.

In setting up the PLO as a nonstate national actor, Arab states were in some sense following the example of the Zionist movement fifty years earlier, with its plethora of prestate political, social, economic, humanitarian, and military institutions. Since the late 1960s, the PLO has developed an elaborate bureaucratic structure with virtually all the elements of a functioning government. This has allowed it to meet at least some of the economic and social service needs of the scattered Palestinian people. With its observer status at the United Nations and its membership in the Arab League, the PLO has served as the official voice of the Palestinian people in the international arena, providing the coherent, unified policy statements lacking since the 1930s.

Structure of the PLO

Most people associate the Palestine Liberation Organization with its military branches: the Palestine Liberation Army and the militia forces. In fact, the military dimension is only one part of a large organization that functions in many ways as a government-in-exile. The legislative body of the Palestinians is the Palestine National Council, composed of representatives from resistance organizations, unions, and popular organizations, as well as "independents" who are not affiliated with a particular group. The PNC is the supreme authority for the PLO and is responsible for creating general policy guidelines. Two-thirds of its members must be present for a quorum to exist, and decisions are made on the basis of simple majority rule. The PNC has met twenty times in the past thirty years, most recently 23–28 September 1991.

The legislative functions of the PNC are complemented by the Central Council, established in 1973, and the fifteen-member Executive Committee (Cabinet), which is elected by secret ballot during the PNC meetings. These bodies are responsible for implementing the policy directives of the PNC and, in the case of the Executive Committee, also handle the day-to-day running of the government. Each member of the Executive Committee has a specific portfolio that corresponds to a department of government, such as health, education, political affairs, planning, and the Palestine National Fund. Through these departments, the Palestine Liberation Organization provides social, economic, medical, cultural, and other services to the Palestinians living under Israeli occupation or in exile.

There are five main political and resistance movements within the PLO: Fateh, the Popular Front for the Liberation of Palestine, the Democratic Front for the Liberation of Palestine (DFLP), the Palestinian Democratic Union (Fida), and the Palestine People's party (PPP), formerly the Palestine Communist party (see Table 2.2). Fateh was created in the late 1950s by young Palestinian activists, including Yasir Arafat, Khalil Wazir (Abu Jihad, who was assassinated by Israeli operatives in April 1988), and Salah Khalaf (Abu Iyad, who was assassinated in January 1991). Since gaining a position of dominance within the PLO, Fateh has developed a significant political component in addition to its military dimension. From its inception, Fateh has remained independent of control by any Arab government and has emphasized Palestinian independence ahead of other goals such as pan-Arabism or class struggle. It is first and foremost a national liberation movement. Beyond this, it does not have a distinctive ideology. The majority of Fateh supporters are moderates and conservatives rather than progressives, and the group tends to align itself with the more traditional Arab states. Historically, Fateh has had a policy of restricting the armed struggle to Israel, the West Bank, and the Gaza Strip. Palestinians who identify with Fateh tend to support the 1993 Oslo Accords.

The Popular Front for the Liberation of Palestine emerged out of the Arab National Movement (ANM), which was established in Beirut in the early 1950s and was closely identified with Nasserism after 1954. The PFLP was created in December 1967 by Palestinians, including Christian

TABLE 2.2   Palestinian Resistance Organizations and Their Key Leaders

Group	Leader(s)
Democratic Front for the Liberation of Palestine (DFLP)	Nayef Hawatmeh, Tayseer Khaled
Palestine National Liberation Movement (Fateh)	Yasir Arafat, Farouq Kaddoumi, Mahmoud Abbas, Khaled Hassan
Palestinian Democratic Union (Fida)	Yasir Abed Rabbo
Palestine People's Party (PPP)	Sulayman Najjab, Bashir Barghouthi
Popular Front for the Liberation of Palestine (PFLP)	George Habash, Ahmad Yamani, Abu Ali Mustafa, Muhammed Abdel Rahim Mallouh
Arab Liberation Front (ALF)	Abdul Rahim Ahmad, Mahmud Ismail
Palestine Liberation Front (PLF)	Mahmud Zaidan (Abu al-Abbas), Ali Ishaq
Popular Front for the Liberation of Palestine–General Command (PFLP-GC)	Ahmed Jabril, Talal Naji, Fadal Shrour
Popular Palestinian Struggle Front (PPSF)	Samir Ghosheh
Saiqa	Muhammad Khalife, Issam Qadi, Majed Muhsen
Islamic Resistance Movement (Hamas)	Sheikh Ahmad Yassin, Abd al-Aziz Rantisi
Islamic Jihad	Fathi al-Shiqaqi, Abd al-Aziz Odeh

The first five organizations are consistently represented in the Unified National Leadership within the West Bank and Gaza and have significant leadership roles within the PLO Executive Committee. The second five organizations are those with a more minor role; of these, the Arab Liberation Front, Palestine Liberation Front, and Popular Palestinian Struggle Front were represented in the Executive Committee elected at the twentieth PNC meeting. As of mid-1994, the Islamic groups were not included in the PNC.

physician George Habash, who had been involved in the ANM since its inception and shared its pan-Arab, leftist orientation and its opposition to conservative or reactionary Arab regimes. In the past, the PFLP argued that the Palestinian liberation would be achieved only in the context of widespread structural change in the Arab world, although more recently it has deemphasized this somewhat. The PFLP has consistently supported the formation of a democratic secular state in Palestine. Its members reject the Oslo Accords and the "Gaza-Jericho" plan as delegitimizing the basic principles of the Palestinian struggle.

The Democratic Front for the Liberation of Palestine was created in February 1969 when a Jordanian, Nayef Hawatmeh, a Christian like Habash, broke away from the PFLP. The reasons for the split were complex, but one factor was Hawatmeh's objections to the PFLP's dramatic military operations outside of mandatory Palestine, which the DFLP believes are "limited in objective and negative in results."[13] Like the PFLP, the DFLP is left-wing, with an emphasis on grassroots mobilization. From

Yasir Arafat has been the PLO chairperson since 1969. The PNC elected him president of the newly declared State of Palestine in 1988.

its beginning, the DFLP advocated establishing a democratic Palestinian state in which the rights of Arabs and Jews to express their national cultures would be respected. This differed slightly from Fateh's early idea of a democratic secular state as it reflected an acceptance of a distinctly Jewish national identity and led in 1974 to the PNC's advocacy of a Palestinian entity in the West Bank and Gaza alongside the State of Israel. The DFLP split in 1990 over disagreements in political strategy. A slim majority of DFLP supporters continues to follow Hawatmeh, who has become increasingly critical of Arafat. Yasir Abed Rabbo, the former number-two person in the DFLP who is closely identified with Arafat, is the leader of the breakaway group, which took the name Palestinian Democratic Union (Fida). The DFLP is opposed to the Oslo Accords; Fida supports the agreement.

In addition to these four resistance organizations—which with the "independent" members formed the core of both the PNC and the PLO Executive Committee in the 1970s and 1980s—there are several additional groups of varying strength. The most important of these, the Palestine People's party, has had an autonomous, well-organized leadership inside the West Bank and Gaza Strip for many years. The Communists were a key underground opposition force against the Jordanians in the West Bank and against the Egyptians in Gaza prior to 1967, and they played a significant role in opposing the Israeli occupation of these areas after 1967. Particularly skilled at organizational activities, the PCP/PPP has been involved in trade unions and other institutions for a number of years. Its strength was acknowledged when it was brought into the PLO Executive Committee at the eighteenth PNC meeting in 1987. The PPP leadership initially supported the Oslo Accords but split with Arafat over subsequent Israeli-PLO agreements on their implementation.

Smaller Palestinian groups include the Syrian-controlled Vanguards of the Popular Liberation War (Saiqa), the pan-Arab and Iraqi-affiliated Arab Liberation Front (ALF), and the tiny Libyan-supported Popular Palestinian Struggle Front (PPSF), founded by Palestinian Bahjat Abu Gharbiyya (who died in 1989). A fourth organization, the Popular Front for the Liberation of Palestine–General Command (PFLP-GC), was originally part of the PFLP but broke off in October 1968. It is led by Palestinian (and former Syrian military officer) Ahmed Jabril. Although the PFLP-GC is small, its involvement in numerous terrorist actions and consistent rejectionist policies have damaged the Palestinian national movement in the eyes of many in the West. Jabril, who is extremely hostile toward Arafat, was expelled from the PLO at the seventeenth PNC meeting. The Palestine Liberation Front (PLF) is a small, violently anti-Israeli group that split from the PFLP-GC.

Evolution of Palestinian Politics

For most of its history, the PLO has been a relatively unified body. There have been differences in ideology or strategy, but until recently these did not prove internally destructive. Over the course of the late 1960s and 1970s, the PLO was able to deal with severe difficulties in its relationships with the governments of Lebanon, Jordan, and Syria and to evolve in its political sophistication.

The military and political agenda of the PLO in the late 1960s rejected the Balfour Declaration and the 1947 partition resolution; its goal was the establishment of a progressive, democratic, secular state in all of historic

Palestine. In a shift from its earlier position, the PLO indicated Jews living in Palestine would be allowed to remain as citizens as long as they were willing to live in a pluralist, nonsectarian society. This idea was formally accepted by the 1971 PNC meeting. But the focus on guerrilla activities as "the nucleus of the Palestinian popular war" remained in place. By the early 1970s there were two competing tendencies among Palestinian groups. Possibly inspired by the decision of the Islamic Conference to admit a PLO representative in September 1969 and the UN General Assembly's December 1969 resolution affirming "the inalienable rights of the people of Palestine," the mainstream groups, including Fateh, began to place a greater stress on political activities than they had immediately after the June 1967 War. This new focus was rewarded as the international community responded with recognition of and support for Palestinian self-determination. The states of the Non-Aligned Movement were particularly vocal in their acknowledgment of the inalienable rights of the Palestinians and in their willingness to recognize the PLO as the representative of the Palestinian people.

The PFLP and other members of what was called the Rejection Front disagreed with this diplomatic strategy and instead tried to gain attention for the Palestinian cause through a series of dramatic hijackings and bomb attacks, including the plane hijackings in September 1970 that triggered the Jordanian-Palestinian War and eventually led to the expulsion of the Palestinian fighters from Lebanon. One result of the war was the creation of the short-lived Black September Organization, which, like the PFLP, undertook military actions outside the boundaries of the Mandate of Palestine. Best known of these was the kidnapping of a group of Israeli athletes at the 1972 Munich Olympics. The operation, which was widely condemned internationally, ended in the deaths of eleven Israelis and five Palestinians and brought Israeli reprisal raids against Syria and Lebanon that killed several hundred people, mostly civilians.

The year 1974 was particularly significant for the Palestinian national movement. Virtually all African states had broken diplomatic relations with Israel after the October 1973 War in solidarity with Egypt, whose territory remained occupied by Israel. Although their support did not provide many tangible benefits for the PLO, it was an important morale boost. In February, Fateh, Saiqa, and the DFLP approved a working document that called for the establishment of a Palestinian "national authority" in any part of the British Mandate of Palestine evacuated by Israel. This "ministate" idea, which was accepted as the provisional political program by the PNC at the Cairo meeting in June, represented the beginning of a new approach to the achievement of Palestinian national autonomy that eventually developed into the current two-state model. A few months later, at the Arab League's Rabat summit conference in October, the Arab states acknowledged the PLO to be the "sole legitimate representative of the Palestinian people," giving it additional credibility in the international arena. The UN General Assembly also invited the PLO to participate in the Question of Palestine debate held in November, the first such discussions by the UN since 1952. As part of the deliberations, Arafat spoke to the UN delegates for nearly two hours, ending his speech with the now famous words: "Today I have come bearing an olive branch and a freedom fighter's gun. Do not let the olive branch fall from my hand." Two weeks later, the United Nations granted the PLO observer status.

While these developments were occurring in the Palestinian diaspora community, significant political changes were taking place within the West Bank and Gaza Strip, spurred on by Israeli actions. In the years immediately following the Israeli occupation of the West Bank, there was an effort by Israel to discredit and silence the traditional, generally pro-Jordanian, political elites. These notables made several moves to develop a consultative relationship with Israel during 1967 and 1968 but were repeatedly ignored or rebuffed. Israel's strategy backfired, however. It meant that the majority of West Bank Palestinians, who were already dissatisfied with Jordanian-Palestinian relations and who felt that the traditional leaders were more interested in protecting their own economic and political position than in enhancing the welfare of the Palestinian community, increasingly turned to indigenous, nationalist leaders to represent their interests. These new leaders generally identified with and were supported by the PLO. Although the PLO was illegal according to Israeli law, it worked through local institutions and came to serve as the principal expression of Palestinian nationalism. In particular, the PLO-affiliated Palestinian National Front (PNF), which was established in 1973, was able to provide and allocate material and political resources in the West Bank (and Gaza), just as the traditional leaders had done in the past. It was also responsible for the coordination of local political activities.

The only exceptions to Israel's elimination of a formal political role for the traditional elites were the city and village mayors, who were left in place and who maintained routine administrative responsibility for the West Bank. By 1975 there was widespread sentiment within the Israeli government that continued control of the West Bank required the tacit cooperation of the local population. As part of this new approach, municipal elections were held in the West Bank on 12 April 1976, resulting in widespread victories for PNF-backed nationalist and leftist candidates. After Likud came to power in 1977, Israel moved against these elected mayors and municipal councils. Two of the mayors were deported in April 1980, assassination attempts were made against three other mayors in May and June, and still other elected officials were jailed or dismissed. Soon, virtually none of the elected municipal officials remained in office. Israel also forced the PNF to dissolve in October 1978. Its functions were quickly taken over by the newly created National Guidance Committee (NGC), composed of West Bank mayors, professional and union leaders, and other political and community figures.

In the Gaza Strip, Palestinian political evolution was somewhat different. Immediately after the Israeli occupation in 1967, a strong guerrilla movement developed that prevented Israel from establishing a significant presence in the region. In January 1971 the commander-in-chief of the (Israeli) Southern Command, Ariel Sharon, instituted a systematic "pacification" campaign against the Gazan population through widespread curfews, massive repression, expulsions, and arrests. When these measures failed to crush the resistance, Sharon bulldozed parts of the Gazan refugee camps, leaving residents homeless and making it easier for Israeli troops to maneuver. By the end of 1971, Sharon had succeeded in temporarily destroying the guerrilla movement, and for the next ten years political control in Gaza reverted to the traditional elites such as Gaza City mayor Rashad Shawa.

In the fall of 1981, the Likud government created the Civil Administration for the Occupied Territories, headed by Menachem Milson. This freed the military from the need to provide municipal services and served as a first step toward the economic and later political integration of the West Bank and Gaza Strip into Israel. During the next year, Israel dissolved additional elected municipal councils and in their places set up Village Leagues whose Arab membership was appointed by Israel. March, April, and May 1982 were months of major unrest in the Occupied Territories; there were also demonstrations of solidarity by Palestinians living within pre-1967 Israel. Israel responded to these disturbances by forcing the National Guidance Committee to disband.

At this point, popular committees—agricultural, health, women's—began to emerge in the towns and refugee camps to address the service needs of the Palestinian communities. These local institutions, identified with various factions of the PLO, were an important aspect of the continuing development of Palestinian nationalism and political expertise in the Occupied Territories and paved the way for the establishment of the Unified National Leadership of the Uprising (UNL) after the beginning of the *intifada*.

Meanwhile, despite the diplomatic successes of the first half of the 1970s, the Palestinian national movement outside the Occupied Territories hit a plateau, and momentum toward international support for self-determination slowed. The Palestinian policy shifts in 1974 had gained little attention in the United States or in Israel, leading some Palestinians to question the wisdom of the compromises made. Nonetheless, the March 1977 PNC meeting repeated the call for the establishment of an "independent national state" in any part of Palestine. Significantly, the proposal did not specify the extent of the state, an omission widely interpreted as a further step toward a two-state strategy. At the time, there were hopes that the new U.S. president, Jimmy Carter, would be more sympathetic to Palestinian interests than Presidents Richard Nixon and Gerald Ford had been.

The end of the 1970s and beginning of the 1980s were difficult years for the PLO. The PLO used every opportunity available to reiterate its willingness to negotiate with Israel and its desire to establish an independent state in whatever part of Palestine from which Israel would withdraw. There were some diplomatic successes, particularly with the European Community (EC), Japan, and India. However, the signing of the Camp David Accords by Egypt, Israel, and the United States in 1978 put the PLO on the defensive internationally. Sadat's unilateral actions, and in particular his attempt to speak on behalf of the Palestinians, made it far more difficult for the PLO to pursue its goal of peace negotiations with Israel. Instead, the PLO was asked to explain its rejection of the limited autonomy formula worked out by the three parties, even though the majority of the international community by this point accepted the idea that the PLO was the only group with the right to speak officially for the Palestinian people.

In 1983 the PLO experienced a major, although temporary, split as a result of the 1982 War in Lebanon and Arafat's decision to pursue a strategy of international diplomacy on behalf of Palestinian self-determination. The constituent groups within the PLO divided into three distinct factions. The first was composed of Fateh members as well as independents who supported the thrust of Arafat's political and diplomatic agenda. In opposition to Arafat were members of the pro-Syrian National Salvation Alliance, a small group composed of Saiqa, the PFLP-GC, and the PPSF. In the middle was the Democratic Alliance, which included the PFLP, the DFLP, the PCP, and the PLF. The Democratic Alliance was in general supportive of Arafat but had reservations about the political line he had been following. In particular, they objected to Arafat's appearing to give Jordan's King Hussein the implicit right to negotiate on behalf of the PLO, felt Arafat had been acting too much on his own without consultation with members of the PNC, and disagreed with Arafat's decision to form closer ties with Hussein and with Hosni Mubarek of Egypt.

As a result of this split, the seventeenth PNC meeting, which was held in Amman, Jordan, in November 1984, was boycotted by members of the National Salvation and Democratic alliances and had difficulty obtaining the necessary quorum to conduct business. Consistent with the more accommodationist approach of the sixteenth PNC meeting, held in February 1983, this session passed a number of moderate resolutions and agreed to work with Israeli-Jewish groups—even if Zionist—that supported the Palestinian cause. In February 1985, Arafat signed an accord with King Hussein that established the basis for a Jordanian-Palestinian confederation. In direct response to this action, the PFLP joined the National Salvation Alliance the following month to form the Palestine National Salvation Front, which opposed the Jordanian-Palestinian accord. By February 1986 Hussein had abrogated the agreement, which paved the way for the reestablishment of unity at the next PNC meeting, in Algiers in April 1987. Only the PFLP-GC, Saiqa, and some fringe factions remained outside the PLO umbrella, and the Palestine National Salvation Front collapsed. During this session, the PNC reasserted the commitment of the PLO to an independent Palestinian state (implicitly in the West Bank and Gaza Strip rather than in all of historic Palestine), declared the Jordanian-Palestinian accords null and void, called for an international peace conference, and focused on a strategy of operations in the Occupied Territories.

The nineteenth PNC meeting was held in Algiers in November 1988, nearly one year after the beginning of the *intifada*. At this meeting, the PNC unanimously declared the independence of the State of Palestine on the basis of UN Resolution 181, the 1947 resolution that called for the partition of Palestine into Jewish and Arab states. At the same time, the PNC adopted a political platform that made significant concessions to Israel. Among the specific points of the political program were the following:

☐ The PLO is committed to pursuing a peaceful solution to the conflict with Israel on the basis of United Nations Resolutions 242 and 338 and in accordance with other relevant UN resolutions on the Question of Palestine.

☐ The PLO is willing to negotiate directly with Israel in the context of an "international peace conference ... under the auspices of the United Nations and with the participation of the permanent members of the Security Council and all parties to the conflict in the region." Any negotiations must be held on the basis of Israel's acceptance that Palestinians have political and national rights, including the right to self-determination, and are not to be treated as refugees only.

☐ The PLO retains the right to resist Israeli occupation inside occupied territories, but it rejects all forms of terrorism "in accordance with United Nations resolutions." These resolutions on terrorism have upheld the right of liberation movements to resist occupiers.

☐ The PLO believes that "the future relationship between the two states of Palestine and Jordan should be on a confederal basis as a result of the free and voluntary choice of the two fraternal peoples."[14]

These statements effectively superseded the controversial 1965 National Charter, which called for the abolition of the Zionist state of Israel. Although the vast majority of representatives to the PNC supported the Algiers Declaration (the vote was 253 in favor, 46 against, with 10 abstentions), the PFLP expressed skepticism that the PLO would be rewarded in the international community for its gestures of peace.

The same range of political perspectives reflected in the membership of the PNC is present in the West Bank and Gaza Strip as well. The Unified National Leadership, established in the early days of the *intifada,* included representatives of each of the major political groups and had substantial, if not universal, support among the Palestinian people. The UNL expressed itself through "communiqués" that activists secretly printed and distributed throughout the Occupied Territories. The first communiqué appeared in January 1988; throughout the *intifada* they were issued on average every two weeks. Each provided a schedule of resistance activities for the coming days and often reflected on recent events, gave encouragement and praise to groups or villages experiencing particular difficulties, warned collaborators not to work against the *intifada,* and presented the evolving political program of the UNL.

In recent years, the secular, pro-PLO groups have had to compete for the support of the Palestinian population with the Islamic Resistance Movement (Hamas) and, to a lesser extent, the Islamic Jihad. Unlike the PLO, whose power base is outside the Occupied Territories, both Hamas and Islamic Jihad were created by Palestinians living under occupation; thus, these organizations derive their legitimacy from inside the West Bank and Gaza Strip. Until the late 1980s

> the most important Islamic movement in the occupied territories, the Muslim Brotherhood, had shied away from active resistance against the Israeli occupation, a decision that stood in the way of its full development as a popular force. This situation was suddenly to change with the [*intifada*], which led the Muslim Brotherhood to play an active role in the resistance for the first time. ... It was thus that the Islamic movement, after many years in existence, was able to emerge as the first true challenge ever posed in the occupied territories to the dominant nationalist trend.[15]

The small Islamic Jihad movement stresses the religious importance of Palestine for all Muslims and calls for the overthrow of most of the Arab governments because they have turned away from Islam. Islamic Jihad is not averse to using violence against Israelis and has been actively working against the Oslo Accords. The broader-based Hamas, which Israel declared illegal in September 1989, was established by Sheikh Ahmad Yassin, the leader of the Muslim Brotherhood in Gaza, and others immediately after the outbreak of the *intifada.* Hamas is highly influential in

Gaza and has challenged the PLO's dominance in the conservative city of Hebron and other parts of the West Bank. Like Islamic Jihad, Hamas opposed the PNC's 1988 Algiers Declaration that recognized Israel within its pre-1967 borders and disagrees strongly with the terms of the 1993 Oslo Accords.

When the *intifada* first began, there was a great deal of discussion in the United States about how the local Palestinian leadership had replaced the PLO as the representative of the Palestinian people. The reality is more complex. It is unquestionably true that the *intifada* continued the transformation of old social, economic, and political structures of Palestinian society by contributing to the erosion of the authority of the traditional leadership—the old landowners, notables, and other elites—that began in the mid-1970s and accelerated with the creation of popular committees after 1982. The popular committees, which were responsible for underground education, garbage collection, policing the streets, the coordination of food distribution during curfews and sieges, and everything in between, required a high level of popular mobilization. Entire sectors of society that had not been politically involved in the past, most notably women, were brought into the process. These popular committees took on additional importance after King Hussein's announcement on 31 July 1988 that Jordan was disengaging legally and administratively from the West Bank.

These indigenous organizations did not replace the PLO, however; instead, except for Hamas and Islamic Jihad, they served as the internal manifestation of the PLO during the years that the PLO was a banned, illegal organization. They were expressions of Palestinian nationalism on the ground, whereas the PLO was the external, public symbol and the internationally recognized voice of the Palestinian people. Particularly in the early years of the *intifada*, there was constant interaction between these two dimensions of the Palestinian national movement, with each deferring to the other in certain situations.

After the Gulf War, this pattern of mutual support began to break down. During the nearly three years between the Gulf War and the Oslo Accords, there was growing dissatisfaction with PLO chairperson Yasir Arafat among some Palestinians in the Occupied Territories and the diaspora. At the same time, there was no consensus on an alternative to Arafat, and Palestinians emphatically rejected efforts by U.S. officials and others to promote a substitute for the PLO. Many Palestinians called for increased democratization within the PLO, greater equality between Palestinians inside and outside the Occupied Territories, increased PLO acknowledgment of the indigenous political leadership, and possibly even formal elections to pick the delegates to the PNC. Others argued that elections, whether for local offices or for the PNC, would be artificial as long as there was no independent Palestinian state because diaspora Palestinians would be unable to participate.

Not always articulated but on everyone's mind was the question of the relative political strength of the nationalist perspectives versus the Islamic fundamentalists. These concerns gained a new urgency in April 1992 when a sandstorm forced Arafat's plane to land in the Libyan desert. For eighteen hours it appeared likely that the PLO leader had died in the crash, which led to widespread speculation about a possible transition of power. Arafat survived, but the leadership issue became pressing again later that spring with reports that he had undergone serious brain surgery. By 1993, disagreements over the direction of the peace talks and internal political issues threatened the cohesion of the Palestinian national movement. These issues remain unresolved in the post-Oslo period.

From this discussion, it should be clear that the Palestinians, like the Israelis, are not a monolithic bloc. A range of constantly evolving political positions are represented in the PLO and in the organizations of the Occupied Territories. For convenience, scholars may ignore this diversity, referring to *the* position of the PLO or *the* position of Israel. What is generally meant in such cases is the official position of the government, that is, the view of the elites who are politically dominant at that time. But it is important to keep in mind that the seemingly unified position implied by such language may not reflect the actual views of all, or even a majority, of the people represented by the government.

THE "INTIFADA"

The Palestinian uprising began in December 1987. The trigger incident occurred on 8 December, when an Israeli army tank transporter collided with a line of cars filled with Palestinian workers waiting at the military checkpoint at the north end of the Gaza Strip. Four workers were killed and seven others seriously injured. Rumors spread that the accident was a deliberate act in retaliation for the killing in Gaza of an Israeli salesperson two days earlier. That night, the funerals for three of the workers turned into a massive demonstration; protests and demonstrations continued the following day and a young Gazan man was shot. The Palestinian *intifada* had begun. The deaths of the four workers was the precipitant cause, but the conditions under which Palestinians had lived for more than forty years formed the underlying or long-term cause. This, along with a feeling among Palestinians that external actors—the United Nations, the United States, and the Arab League (which had met in November 1987 and had virtually ignored the Palestinian issue)—could not be counted on to create a political solution, led to the explosion.

The *intifada* caught the Israelis unaware, and it took some time for the government to formulate a response to it. The massive size of the demonstrations in the early days of the *intifada*, its rapid spread from Gaza to East Jerusalem and the rest of the West Bank, the discipline shown by the demonstrators, the use of nonviolent actions such as tax resistance and commercial strikes, the rapid formation of an indigenous Unified National leadership to coordinate the *intifada* activities, and the breadth of involvement by Palestinians were all unexpected. Initially, the Israelis described the *intifada* as just a peak in the normal cycle of violence and considered it sufficiently minor that Israeli Defense Minister Rabin traveled to the United States three days after it began.

During the first several weeks of the *intifada*, the IDF had no specific instructions other than to "put down the disturbances," and there seemed to be complete confidence that Israel would be able to control the situation. This the military attempted to do through the use of massive quantities of tear gas and by shooting into crowds of unarmed demonstrators. The protesters were described as "hooligans and criminals" and Yitzhak Shamir claimed in an Israeli Cabinet meeting on 13 December that "most of the Arab population ... is anxious to see public order preserved, but they are intimidated and terrorized by a tiny minority."[16] Although a few scholars and commentators argued the disturbances appeared to be "the first signs of an uprising by the population," this idea was quickly dismissed.

After two weeks, there was a temporary lull in the protests, giving the Israelis reason to think the uprising had been successfully suppressed. It quickly became clear this was not the case. Soon Israel took more draconian measures to attempt to control the situation, such as cutting off water, electricity, and phone lines to some of the refugee camps in Gaza; banning all international phone calls not cleared through the military; establishing curfews and other collective punishment against entire villages; and expelling perceived Palestinian leaders. In an effort to reduce the large number of shooting deaths, the IDF implemented a policy of beating demonstrators with the intention of breaking bones. This new approach was loudly condemned by the international community, and soon soldiers reverted to the more frequent use of live ammunition, supplemented by deadly plastic and rubber bullets.

After the 1988 meeting of the Palestine National Council and the declaration of the State of Palestine, the *intifada* moved into a new phase, characterized by increased efforts at suppression by Israeli military forces and a steady, moderate level of resistance activity by Palestinians. The massive street demonstrations and other public displays of protest that typified the early months declined in frequency; however, moves toward political and economic disengagement from Israel, such as the boycott of Israeli

This demonstration in November 1989 against the Israeli occupation was held in the predominantly Christian West Bank village of Beit Sahour. Beit Sahour gained international attention for its nonviolent tax resistance activities during the *intifada*.

products, the refusal to pay Israeli taxes (most notably by the entire West Bank village of Beit Sahour), and the development of local industries continued, as did the construction of national Palestinian institutions to replace the ties to Israel.

When Moshe Arens took over as Israeli Defense Minister in June 1990, he modified significantly the Israeli approach to the uprising so that it was less confrontational on a day-to-day basis. In contrast to the first years of the *intifada*, primary and secondary schools were allowed to remain open, and by the middle of 1992, Israel had lifted the closure orders for all the Palestinian colleges and universities, permitting them to function legally for the first time since early in 1988. Other charitable, educational, and labor organizations also resumed operation when their closure orders expired. There was a decrease in the visible Israeli military presence among the general Palestinian population and in random killings by Israeli security forces, such as those that had been occurring when troops used gunfire to break up a demonstration.

The clash on al-Haram al-Sharif, or Temple Mount, that resulted in the deaths of seventeen Palestinians on 8 October 1990 was a major exception to the overall decline in violence.[17] The European Parliament and the United Nations condemned the actions of the Israeli forces, but there was no change in the rules regarding the soldiers' use of deadly force. To the contrary, since the beginning of the *intifada*, there has been a steady expansion in the circumstances under which regulations permit Israeli troops to use live ammunition against Palestinians. Soldiers may fire on unarmed Palestinians if they are masked, manning barricades, fleeing arrest, throwing stones, wanted by the authorities, fail to obey an order to stop, or appear to pose a threat to soldiers. Regulations permit soldiers to shoot on sight any armed Palestinian whether or not the person poses an immediate threat to life. In addition, Israeli settlers may open fire to protect their property.

At the same time, under Arens the security forces initiated new undercover operations against Palestinians and increased targeted ambushes and summary executions of identified Palestinian activists.[18] Prison sentences for Palestinian activists became longer and the treatment of Palestinian stone-throwers became harsher. In September 1992, Israel began using antitank missile fire to demolish Palestinian neighborhoods where the military suspected wanted persons of hiding. The deportation of Palestinians, which Israel had halted in 1989 because of international pressure, began again, most dramatically with the expulsion of over 400 alleged Hamas supporters into Lebanon in December 1992. In response to demands from increasingly militant and vocal Jewish settlers, there was also an increase in the frequency of roadblocks and random security checks of Palestinians throughout the Occupied Territories.

Analysts debate the economic impact of the *intifada* on Palestinians and Israelis, but two points seem clear. First, an initial drop in tourism, the decline in productivity in sectors relying on Palestinian labor, the Palestinian boycott of Israeli products, a decrease in Israeli revenues from taxes and fees collected from Palestinians, and the cost of controlling the *intifada* all damaged the Israeli economy, particularly in the first years of the uprising. Eventually, however, the economy reached a new equilibrium and began to recover. The harm to the Palestinian economy appears to be deeper. The decline in tourism affected Palestinians as well, frequent strikes and curfews meant lost income, and many wage earners spent significant time in jail. Furthermore, it became more difficult to bring funds into the West Bank and Gaza Strip from other Arab states or Europe than it was prior to the *intifada*. In 1991, changes in the tax structure imposed on the Occupied Territories reduced the financial burden on Palestinians somewhat but did not have a significant impact on the majority of people whose income was too low to be affected. There was also a loosening of restrictions on economic activities in the Occupied Territories to allow more business opportunities and to encourage investment and industrial development.

The human costs of the uprising have been severe. After six and a half years, more than 1,380 Palestinians had died as a result of direct actions by Israeli occupation forces: gunfire, beatings, stoning, tear gas inhalation, and other causes. Of these, nearly 25 percent were children sixteen years or younger; many were not yet in their teens. Although the majority of Palestinian deaths occurred at the hands of Israeli security forces, Israeli settlers, civilians, or collaborators were responsible for more than 120 deaths. Palestinians killed nearly 200 Israeli soldiers, civilians, and foreign tourists during this period as well as an estimated 500 Palestinians accused of collaborating with the Israeli occupation authorities.[19]

In an effort to undercut the leadership of the uprising, by the end of 1993 Israel had placed over 18,100 Palestinians under administrative detention for varying lengths of time from six months to several years, held more than 100,000 others on a variety of security charges such as distributing pro-PLO literature or belonging to an illegal organization, and expelled 70 people for secret "security" reasons (in addition to the one-year expulsion of the 400 alleged Hamas supporters). The military demolished over 500 homes and partially or totally sealed at least 395 others for "security" reasons; military forces destroyed an additional 1,442 buildings, mostly homes, for failure to be licensed.[20]

As the *intifada* stretched on, many Palestinians expressed frustration that an end to the Israeli occupation remained seemingly remote. Some sectors of the population argued for an escalation and broadening of the use of violence against Israelis living inside the Green Line and Israeli settlers in the Occupied Territories. The UNL opposed this strategy in its leaflets and, until the beginning of the fifth year of the uprising, was able to keep the *intifada* primarily nonviolent. Nevertheless, unsanctioned force by Palestinians—against other Palestinians as well as Israelis—escalated in the 1990s, and by the middle of 1992 there was a noticeable increase in the use of guns and explosives that continued in 1993 and 1994. Analysts frequently explained these acts of violence as a result of the deportations and repeated mass arrests that placed virtually all top and mid-level Palestinian leaders under detention and left strategy decisions to a younger, less well educated, less experienced, and less restrained group of political activists. Many Palestinians expressed apprehension that the stress of the continuing Israeli occupation had led the *intifada* to turn inward against itself, engaging in internal fighting and failing to maintain cohesiveness and discipline.

The endurance of the *intifada* caused Israelis from all political perspectives to question the policies of their government, although their conclusions on how Israel should change its approach differed radically. Some Israelis and Palestinians believe the *intifada* has collapsed in the post–Gulf War period. Others maintain the uprising is in a transition phase, the next stage of which will be determined by the outcome of negotiations following the Oslo Accords and the Cairo Agreement.

CONCLUSION

In a review of the interaction of Israel and the Palestinian people after 1948, several themes stand out. First is the continuing importance of nationalist identity and the search for self-determination on the part of Palestinians and Jewish Israelis. The creation of the State of Israel provided for this nationalist expression by one group of people. Palestinians were denied this basic form of political expression, although the same UN resolution that called for the establishment of a Jewish state also provided for a Palestinian state. This problem was further exacerbated with the 1967 Israeli occupation of the West Bank and Gaza Strip, among other territories, which has led to the continuing denial of the right of self-determination for the Palestinian people. The occupation also raised crucial issues for Israel, which had to decide how it would relate toward the Palestinians in those occupied lands. Thus, the problems raised in the first half of the twentieth century by competing nationalist claims over the Mandate of Palestine were not resolved in the second half of the century; they merely took different forms.

Finally, this chapter has described the viewpoints of various Israeli and Palestinian factions to stress that neither Israel nor the Palestinian nation is a unitary entity with a single, clear-cut, and agreed-upon national interest. Instead, there is a wide range of opinion about how best to deal with the ongoing conflict and the extent to which accommodation or aggression is appropriate. The interests of competing groups within these nations will have to be taken into account in formulating a proposal for conflict resolution that will be accepted internally. At the same time, it is important to recognize the tremendous impact the Israeli-Palestinian conflict has had on the political dynamics of the region and the international system. Chapter Three examines four Arab-Israeli wars, considers involvement of other state and nonstate actors—the superpowers, the United Nations, and the European countries—in this issue and explores briefly some related concerns of the international community.

THREE

□ □ □

The Crowded Stage: International Dimensions

The Israeli-Palestinian conflict does not exist in a vacuum. Both the regional and the global communities influence and have been influenced by the debate over the control of Palestine. This chapter discusses the numerous conflicts between Israel and the Arab states in the region, beginning with a brief consideration of the different types of crises that frequently precede international wars. The 1956 Suez War, the June 1967 War that led to the Israeli occupation of additional Arab lands, the effort of Egypt and Syria to regain control of those territories through the October 1973 War, and the 1982 Israeli invasion of Lebanon all illustrate the internationalization of the Israeli-Palestinian conflict.

Additional examples of Arab involvement include the initial creation of the Palestine Liberation Organization by Egypt and other members of the League of Arab States, the League's support for the PLO as the sole legitimate representative of the Palestinian people (both discussed in the previous chapter), and the 1973 oil price increase and embargo against the United States that resulted from the decision by the Organization of Petroleum Exporting Countries (OPEC) and the Organization of Arab Petroleum Exporting Countries (OAPEC) to link economic and political issues. Finally, although Iraq's 1990 invasion of Kuwait and the subsequent international war against Iraq was not directly related to the conflict over Palestine, the episode had wide-ranging implications for Israeli-Palestinian relations and is therefore considered here.

Chapter Three then turns to a discussion of the variety of global interests that may encourage, constrain, or otherwise affect the resolution of the Israeli-Palestinian conflict in the future. In this chapter the United States, the former Soviet Union, the United Nations, and other actors are generally discussed as though they are unitary actors. It is important to keep in mind, however, that this is a form of intellectual shorthand; as is true of the Israeli state and the Palestinian national movement, each of these international actors actually includes a wide variety of political perspectives.

In the post–World War II period, the United States has defined its national interests in the Middle East as maintaining secure, internationally recognized boundaries; protecting Western access to petroleum resources; and minimizing Soviet influence. Furthermore, in the past twenty-five years, U.S. support for Israel, as expressed through economic and military assistance and in the diplomatic arena, has become increasingly unqualified (with the exception of President George Bush's last two years in office). On several occasions, the United States has intervened in the region in an effort to direct affairs more to its liking, rather as the British tried to do while Palestine was under British mandatory control.

For four decades, the interests of the Soviet Union in many ways paralleled those of the United States. The Soviet Union wanted to decrease U.S. and Western European involvement in the region and desired a role in decisionmaking regarding the Middle East. Soviet interests also included support for nationalist or revolutionary movements, particularly but not exclusively those influenced by socialist ideas. Since the breakup of the Soviet Union, Russia and the Soviet successor states have been preoccupied with their own internal difficulties; Russia did, however, cosponsor with the United States the 1991 Madrid peace conference and subsequent Arab-Israeli negotiations.

Like the United States and the Soviet Union, the United Nations has been consistently concerned about maintaining stability in the region. In addition, it has been a strong advocate for Palestinian self-determination and has frequently—too often, according to some—criticized Israeli violations of Palestinian human rights. The European Community's role in the Israeli-Palestinian conflict was minor during most of the post–World War II period. Europe took center stage in 1993, however, when it was revealed that months of secret Israeli-Palestinian negotiations in Oslo, Norway, had led to the 13 September Israeli-PLO agreement. Related issues facing the international community in the 1990s include concerns about political terrorism and increasing militarization throughout the Middle East.

REGIONAL CONFLICTS

Israel has been involved in six major international wars since its declaration of independence. Whether as the initiator or as a defender, Israel has never lost a war, although the 1973 and 1982 conflicts should probably be judged as draws. Israel gained substantial territory as a result of two of these wars, but this has exacerbated rather than improved its security problem and increased regional hostility toward the state. Most signifi-

Reprinted by permission of Stuart Goldman.

cantly, none of the wars settled the basic conflict between Zionists and Palestinians.

War—the sustained, organized conduct of armed hostilities between states or nonstate national actors—involves enormous human, political, and economic costs for both victors and losers. Nonetheless, prior to this century war was generally considered an acceptable, possibly even desirable, and at any rate inevitable method of settling disputes. The view that war is an optimal approach to problem solving no longer has much support. In addition, a number of factors, such as the increased destructive capability of war, might be expected to decrease its appeal and utility. Still, in the twentieth century the frequency of war, whether civil or international, has not decreased as these changes in attitude and objective utility might suggest. But one shift *has* occurred: In the second half of the century wars tend to be fought in the Third World rather than between or within Western industrialized states. Furthermore, modern wars frequently begin without a formal declaration of hostility and end with an armistice agreement that falls short of being a peace treaty between the adversarial parties.

International relations scholars spend a tremendous amount of effort trying to identify the causes of war and violent conflict short of war. Theories include individual-level psychological arguments (instinctual aggression, relative deprivation, the role of misperception), state-level analyses (nationalism, separatism and irredentism, form of government, economic imperialism), and systemic approaches focusing on the structure of the international system or the possibility of long-term cycles of war and peace.[1] At present, there is no consensus that all wars can be explained by any single cause, or even by a consistent and predictable combination of factors. What *is* clear is that in spite of the costs and risks involved, the leaders of states and nonstate national entities continue to believe that under certain circumstances war is worthwhile or unavoidable.

Crisis as a Precursor of War

One of the most challenging issues facing scholars of international conflict is to understand the conditions under which a crisis situation leads to war or, alternatively, allows a crisis to be resolved short of war. In his 1981 book, *Between Peace and War*, Richard Ned Lebow analyzes three types of acute international crises that frequently, although not inevitably, result in war. The first type of crisis occurs when the initiator is engaged in **brinkmanship** behavior. Brinkmanship is similar to the game of "chicken," in which the drivers of two cars head straight toward one another at a high speed, each trying to force the other to swerve first. A brinkmanship crisis occurs when there is an effort to challenge an important but potentially vulnerable commitment of an adversary, hoping the adversary will back down. If the adversary does retreat from the commitment, the initiator of the crisis will have gained a significant economic, strategic, psychological, or territorial reward. If the adversary does not back down, war is likely to occur. In a variation of brinkmanship, the real objective of the initiator may be to force the adversary to make concessions unrelated to the original challenge, or to humiliate the adversary by making it appear weak.

The outcome of this type of crisis will depend on whether the adversary is prepared to go to war in order to defend its commitments. Historically, initiators have not been particularly skilled at identifying situations in which they can successfully challenge an adversary. Wishful thinking or domestic policy needs often create situations in which initiators perceive that a vulnerable commitment exists, even when the adversary has made it clear that the commitment will be defended if necessary. Once an actor has initiated a brinkmanship crisis, however, it is difficult for that actor to retreat from the challenge it has presented to the adversary. As a result, the initiator of the crisis may find itself in an unplanned, unintended, and undesired war.

Spinoff crises are secondary confrontations that result from an actor's involvement in or preparation for a primary conflict but are not desired by either the initiator or the third party. For example, a spinoff crisis might result from geographic proximity of the third party to the primary conflict, after a shift in the domestic power structure of the initiator in favor of the military, or as a result of public attitudes within the initiating actor. Although both the initiator and the third party in a spinoff crisis prefer that the crisis be resolved by diplomacy if possible, the leaders are prepared to escalate the crisis or even to go to war if necessary to protect perceived political or security interests. Despite mutual efforts to find a peaceful solution to such secondary crises, in each of the cases Lebow examined the ultimate outcome was war.

Finally, some crises arise as the result of a deliberate choice to go to war on the part of leaders of the initiating actor. In this case, "the leaders of the initiating nation make a decision for war *before* the crisis commences. The purpose of the crisis is not to force an accommodation but to provide a *casus belli*. ... Initiators of such crises invariably attempt to make their adversary appear responsible for the war. By doing so they attempt to mobilize support for themselves, both at home and abroad and to undercut support for their adversary."[2] This type of crisis, which Lebow calls a **justification of hostility,** is different from brinkmanship and spinoff crises in that there is no interest on the part of the initiator in avoiding war. Thus, accommodation efforts by the other party will not be successful in preventing a war from occurring.

Not all wars result from one of these three types of crisis. For example, prior to the 1956 Suez War there was no effort by Israel to create a single international incident that would provide an internationally acceptable excuse for the Israeli attack on Egypt, nor was Israel engaged in brinkmanship. The period prior to the October 1973 War also does not fit neatly into any of Lebow's categories of acute crisis, although a high level of tension was certainly present. On the other hand, the June 1967 War illustrates elements of two of Lebow's crisis types on the part of the protagonists. The prewar maneuvers of Egypt are an example of brinkmanship behavior, whereas a justification of hostility approach was taken by the Israelis. The onset of the 1982 War in Lebanon also illustrates a justification of hostility strategy by Israel.

The 1956 Suez War

The events that led to the 1956 Suez War (also referred to as the Sinai War or the Suez Crisis) are complicated and will only be summarized briefly here. Since the 1800s Egypt had been under the colonial control of Great Britain. Consistent with the 1936 Anglo-Egyptian Treaty, Britain relaxed its control to some extent but reserved the right to intervene in Egyptian affairs in several critical areas, including the maintenance of troops in the Suez Canal region and in Cairo during World War II. (Britain's position was similar to the status of the United States in Panama since the 1978 Panama Canal Treaty.) In 1952, the British-supported monarchy was overthrown by a group of military personnel known as the Free Officers. Shortly thereafter, negotiations were initiated that eventually resulted in a British agreement to withdraw their troops from the canal region by July 1956.

The Egyptian president, Gamal Abdul Nasser, was a strong advocate of foreign policy neutralism and was critical of the newly formed Baghdad Pact involving Great Britain, Iran, Iraq, Pakistan, and Turkey. Nasser also felt threatened by Israel, particularly after the Israeli raid on Gaza on 28 February 1955, and concluded Egypt needed improved weapons to deal with these challenges. Nasser first turned to Britain, France, and the United States. Each country declined his request for advanced military equipment, pointing to the 1950 Tripartite Declaration that specified none of them would supply any Middle Eastern country with weapons of a higher level of sophistication than were already present in the region. In April 1955, Nasser attended the Bandung Conference of nonaligned countries and established contacts that eventually facilitated an arms agreement with the Soviet Union (with the weapons channeled through Czechoslovakia).

Nasser's action stunned the Western powers, which apparently had not seriously believed Nasser might go elsewhere for Egypt's weapons supply. Some analysts in the United States and Britain argued the West should be more supportive of Egypt to prevent an Egyptian-Soviet alliance. This proposed shift in policy never occurred. To the contrary, U.S. rhetoric against Nasser escalated, and in July 1956 U.S. Secretary of State John Foster Dulles withdrew an offer of U.S. assistance (made the previous December) to help build the Aswan High Dam along the Nile River. Britain, which had also committed funds to the dam project, followed suit. The Western powers expected this to be a major economic and political blow to the Egyptian president, but they miscalculated. Nasser promptly nationalized the Anglo-French Suez Canal Company on 26 July and expelled all British oil and embassy officials from Egypt. In doing so, he regained some of the prestige he had lost over the British and U.S. withdrawal from the development project and gained $25 million in annual profits that Egypt could use to build the dam.

Britain and France were furious with Nasser's actions, even though Nasser promised that there would be freedom of passage through the canal. France was also angered by Nasser's support of the Algerian independence movement against French colonial rule; Britain was similarly dismayed by Nasser's advocacy of the Mau Mau rebellion in Kenya. Thus, the decision was made to restore Western control of the canal by force if negotiations failed. Israel had its own disagreements with Egypt. As part of the continuing state of war that had existed between Israel and the Arab states since 1948, Egypt refused passage through the Suez Canal to ships flying the Israeli flag. This action was explicitly criticized in 1951 by the UN Security Council, which called on Egypt to "terminate the restrictions on passage"; Egypt, however, ignored the condemnation. This was a continuing source of frustration for Israel, more because of its political significance than its economic ramifications, which were minor. In addition, there were muted pressures within Israel to increase the territory of the Jewish state to include the Sinai Peninsula.

Together, the three countries worked out a secret plan whereby Israel would attack Egypt along the Sinai Peninsula and in Gaza. France and Britain would then intervene, ostensibly to "protect the canal." Their ultimatum would demand that both belligerents, Israel and Egypt, withdraw from the vicinity of the canal, a demand Egypt would predictably refuse. Then Britain and France could occupy the area by force "to save world commerce."

Initially, at least, the plan worked perfectly. On 29 October 1956 Israel crossed the Egyptian border and attacked Egypt. Twenty-four hours later an Anglo-French ultimatum ordered Israel and Egypt to withdraw ten miles from the east and west banks of the Suez Canal and allow British and French troops to station themselves along the canal. As previously arranged, this was acceptable to Israel, especially because its troops had not yet reached the canal, but was rejected by Egypt. At this point, British and French aircraft began bombing Egyptian airfields in the Nile Delta and canal areas. On 31 October, Egypt responded by sinking forty-seven ships and blocking the canal. Three days later, the United Nations voted in favor of a U.S.-sponsored cease-fire. By 5 November, Israel and Egypt were no longer fighting. Only then did French and British troops appear at the canal, supposedly to separate the combatants, but by then the only fighting was between the French and British on one side and the Egyptians on the other. Two days later the UN cease-fire went into effect.

Nonetheless, it took another six weeks before all armies had left the canal zone, and the United Nations Emergency Force (UNEF) was able to restore the area to Egyptian control. Even then, Israel maintained a military presence at Sharm el-Sheik, overlooking the approach to the Gulf of Aqaba, and in the Gaza Strip. Between December and March, there were several UN resolutions calling on Israel to withdraw behind the 1949 armistice lines, and a continuous stream of communications between the United States and Israel indicated U.S. displeasure at Israel's continued military occupation. On 22 February 1957, Charles Malik, foreign minister of Lebanon, introduced a UN resolution calling for the imposition of severe economic sanctions against Israel: the end of all military, economic, and financial assistance. Once it became clear that the United States would support this resolution when it came to a vote, Israel capitulated and began to withdraw its troops from Sharm el-Sheik and the Gaza Strip.

The conditions leading up to the 1956 Suez War and the war itself illustrate several important points. First, they show that a series of seemingly unrelated factors—Britain's resistance in the 1950s to granting Egypt full independence, French and British anger at Nasser's support of African independence movements, Israel's desire to punish Egypt for its refusal to allow Israeli ships to use the Suez Canal and its interest in expanding the territory under its control—can create a situation conducive to international conflict. Israel alone might have been reluctant to attack Egypt. Britain and France would have been hard-pressed to come up with an excuse to do so themselves. But by acting in concert they were able to work toward the common goal of challenging Nasser's hold on power in Egypt.

In addition, this conflict is interesting in that it is one of the few occasions in which the United States sided with the Arab states rather than with Israel, and did so despite extensive domestic pressure to back down. U.S. President Dwight Eisenhower wanted to make it clear that the United States would not be manipulated by a foreign government into supporting actions it found reprehensible. This appeared to be the intent of the three allies in launching their attack on Egypt just prior to the U.S. election and while the United States was preoccupied with the Soviet repression in Hungary. The United States was also annoyed with its allies because their invasion of Egypt appeared to put the European states on a par morally with the Soviets in their invasion of Hungary. Additional motivations for U.S. support of Egypt included minimizing Soviet involvement in the region, protecting European access to petroleum, and maintaining legitimacy for the United Nations, which had called upon Israel to withdraw from the territories it occupied—all traditional U.S. foreign policy goals.

The June 1967 War

The ten years following the final Israeli withdrawal from Gaza in 1957 were relatively calm. Israel was preoccupied with internal political and economic development issues, Palestinian nationalism remained in a period of quietude, and the Arab states were disinclined to take on the seemingly invincible Israeli army. The presence of UNEF troops stationed in Egypt along the border with Israel was also an important factor in securing the peace.

The UNEF was established by the UN General Assembly under the Uniting for Peace Resolution, which was originally passed in response to the Korean War. This resolution allowed the General Assembly to hold an emergency session to adopt collective means to address "threats to the peace, breaches of the peace, and acts of aggression" in situations when the UN Security Council was unable to act because of a veto by one of the permanent members. In the days after the initiation of the 1956 Suez War, the Security Council was stymied by vetoes by Britain and France, so Canada called on the General Assembly to create a peacekeeping force. The responsibility of the UNEF, whose soldiers came from Colombia, Denmark, India, Norway, Sweden, and Yugoslavia, was to reestablish and maintain peaceful relations along the Israeli-Egyptian border and to make superpower intervention in the situation unnecessary. Israel refused to allow UN troops to be based on any Israeli-controlled territory; thus the UNEF was forced to operate only from the Egyptian side of the border, in the Sinai Desert, where it remained for nearly eleven years.

This interlude of relative quiet ended with the June 1967 War and the subsequent Israeli occupation of East Jerusalem and the rest of the West Bank, the Gaza Strip, the Golan Heights, and the Sinai. In the history of Israeli-Palestinian relations, the June 1967 War, also known as the Six-Day War, is second in importance only to the partition of Palestine and the establishment of the State of Israel. The war was preceded by a period of increasing tension in the region. For the first time there had been organized attacks against Israel by Palestinian guerrilla groups, beginning with the 1 January 1965 Fateh operation against the Israeli National Water Carrier. In the north, Israel had been engaged since the 1950s in a "creeping annexation" of the demilitarized zone separating Israel and Syria, building fortified settlements and basing military personnel there. In April 1967 the Israeli government announced it would begin cultivation of the entire demilitarized zone, including land owned by Syrian Arabs. This led to a clash on 7 April, which began when Syrian forces shot at an Israeli working on the land. In reprisal, Israel launched a massive bombing attack against Syrian border villages that ended only after the United Nations Truce Supervision Organization intervened. Although the shooting stopped, Syrian and Israeli threats continued to escalate.

To the west, Nasser was in a difficult position. He had been arguing for several years that the Arab states were not militarily strong enough to attack Israel. At the same time, his position in the Arab world was being challenged by other leaders, such as Saudi Arabia's King Feisal. When Syrian and Soviet intelligence reports were sent to Egypt indicating—whether accurately or not remains controversial—that Israel was planning a massive attack against Syria at the end of May, Nasser felt he had to respond.

On 15 May, Nasser put the Egyptian military forces on alert and began moving them into the Sinai. He also formally requested that the UNEF troops based in the Sinai pull out from Sharm el-Sheik. UN Secretary General U Thant said the UNEF could not withdraw selectively, so Nasser had to request its complete withdrawal. The UNEF left the Sinai on 19 May, leaving the Egyptian and Israeli troops face to face and the Sinai open to attack. After the UNEF withdrawal, Egypt again closed the Strait of Tiran to Israeli ships, an action Israel had said it would consider an act of war. The tensions along the Israeli-Syrian border, Nasser's actions in the Sinai, plus the sudden 30 May trip to Cairo by Jordan's King Hussein to sign a defense pact with Egypt provided the necessary external justification for Israel to launch what it labeled a preemptive, defensive attack on Egypt.

At the same time, one has to ask whether in fact Nasser had any intention of attacking Israel. It seems unlikely, given that Egypt had been involved since 1962 in a war in the Yemen Arab Republic between Egyptian-supported republican forces and Saudi-supported royalists. Egypt's role in Yemen meant that much of the Egyptian army was unavailable to use against Israel. Yitzhak Rabin, then chief of staff of Israel, shared this assessment, telling Le Monde in 1968, "I do not believe that Nasser wanted war. The two divisions he sent into Sinai on May 14 would not have been enough to unleash an offensive against Israel. He knew it, and we knew it."[3] U.S. President Lyndon Johnson agreed and on 26 May informed Israeli Ambassador to the United States Abba Eban that three separate U.S. agencies—the Central Intelligence Agency, the National Security Council, and the State Department—had investigated the issue and had concluded that no Egyptian attack was imminent.[4] Even Menachem Begin, who maintains the Israeli actions were justified, admitted: "In June 1967 we again had a choice. The Egyptian Army concentrations in the Sinai approaches do not prove that Nasser was really about to attack us. We must be honest with ourselves. We decided to attack him."[5]

Nonetheless, it could be argued that in the weeks preceding the initiation by Israel of the June 1967 War, Egypt was engaged in a series of actions that fit Lebow's brinkmanship model: using bellicose language, moving troops, reimposing the restrictions on Israeli ship movements through the Gulf of Aqaba. The goals for Nasser in pursuing this brinkmanship approach appear to have been to preserve or improve Egypt's position in the Arab world and to humiliate Israel by forcing it to accept what it said it would not accept—the renewed closure of the Strait of Tiran. In a serious miscalculation characteristic of failed brinkmanship efforts, Nasser did not actually expect that Israel would go to war over Egypt's actions.

Nasser's miscalculation occurred in part because Israeli leaders were themselves engaged in another of Lebow's crisis models: a justification of hostility strategy. The goal of a "Greater Israel," including all of the British Mandate of Palestine and beyond, had been the policy of the Jabotinsky faction of Zionism since its inception in 1925. For these advocates of expansion, virtually any action by an Arab state could be used to support an aggressive response by Israel. Further, Israel's attack on Egypt in 1956 had made it clear that Israel desired the overthrow of Egypt's President Nasser. These two goals—an increase in Israeli territory and elimination of a difficult adversary—were of great importance to some factions within Israel. In fact, the possibility of another war had been in the minds of military strategists almost before the withdrawal from the territories captured in 1956 was complete.[6] Thus, it seems clear Israel was quite willing to allow Egypt and the other Arab states to create a situation in which Israel could claim justification for attack, although Israel knew its actions were not necessary to prevent an invasion by Egypt.

On 5 June Israel moved against Egypt. The war was short, lasting only until 10 June. In those six days, the Israeli army defeated Egypt in the Sinai and the Gaza region and established itself on the East Bank of the Suez Canal. Fighting also broke out between Jordan and Israel around Jerusalem. As a result, Jordanian forces were driven back across the Jordan River, putting Israel in control of the West Bank as well as the eastern side of Jerusalem. In the north, Israel attacked Syria and demolished much of the Syrian army, gaining control of the Golan Heights, an area that had been demilitarized since 1949.

This war represented a watershed for Palestinian-Israeli and Israeli-Arab relations. For the Arab states, the material damage and loss of life—some 25,000 to 30,000 troops—was severe. The entire air force capability of Egypt was destroyed, and the extensive property damage set back economic development activities in Egypt, Jordan, and Syria. Even Lebanon, which had not been part of the war, experienced economic harm because of a drop in tourism. The psychological impact was equally significant. Yet again, the small state of Israel had thoroughly defeated the combined forces of three large Arab countries, leading to a collapse of Arab morale and self-confidence. Nasser even resigned as president of Egypt, although the resignation was rejected by the population and he remained in office until his death three years later. For the Palestinians, it meant the creation of another group of refugees, many of whom swelled the existing camps in Jordan, Lebanon, and Syria. It also meant that all of the old British Mandate of Palestine was under the control of Israel.

In Israel, the implications were equally profound. Initially, there was great excitement about the unexpected victories of the June 1967 War. Jerusalem, which had been split in the Palestine War, was reunited under Israeli control. Jews were delighted that the religious sites of the Old City of Jerusalem, as well as throughout the West Bank, were now accessible to them. Shortly after the end of the war, three laws were passed to expand the municipal boundaries of Jerusalem and extend Israeli laws to the entire area, thus effectively, although unofficially, annexing East Jerusalem and the surrounding area. The occupation also meant that, in theory, the security situation for Israel was improved. Now, the military strategists explained, Israel had "defense in depth." The Sinai could serve as a buffer between Israel and Egypt, and the West Bank and the Golan Heights would do the same vis-à-vis Jordan and Syria. For those Zionists who believed Israel should control all of the territory held by the ancient Hebrew people, "from the Nile to the Euphrates," the accomplishments of the June 1967 War were a crucial step in that direction.

The negative ramifications became obvious only later. Instead of being more secure militarily, Israel's occupation of the West Bank, the Gaza Strip, the Sinai, and the Golan Heights meant that Israel now controlled territories claimed by three Arab states—Egypt, Syria, and Jordan—rather than only occupying lands allotted by the United Nations to Palestinians. Israel now ruled over 1.5 million Palestinians within the "expanded" Israel, as well as Syrians in the Golan Heights and Egyptians in the Sinai Peninsula. This made Israel even less the homogeneous Jewish state than it had been previously.

There was little consensus regarding the appropriate international response to the June 1967 War once the cease-fire was in place. Thus, it was five months before the Security Council passed **UN Resolution 242** on 22 November 1967. This resolution was to serve as the basis for all future UN mediation activities:

Expressing its continuing concern with the grave situation in the Middle East,

Emphasizing the inadmissibility of the acquisition of territory by war and the need to work for a just and lasting peace in which every State in the area can live in security, [the Security Council]

1. *Affirms* that the fulfillment of Charter principles requires the establishment of a just and lasting peace in the Middle East which should include the application of both the following principles:

   (i) Withdrawal of Israeli armed forces from territories occupied in the recent conflict;

   (ii) Termination of all claims or states of belligerency and respect for and acknowledgement of the sovereignty, territorial integrity and political independence of every State in the area and their right to live in peace within secure and recognized boundaries free from threats or acts of force;

2. *Affirms further* the necessity

   (*a*) For guaranteeing freedom of navigation through international waterways in the area;

   (*b*) For achieving a just settlement of the refugee problem;

   (*c*) For guaranteeing the territorial inviolability and political independence of every State in the area, through measures including the establishment of demilitarized zones; ...

In order to mediate the fundamental differences that remained between the protagonists, the United Nations sent Swedish diplomat Gunnar V. Jarring to the region. Although Jarring made two lengthy attempts to work with Israel, Egypt, and Jordan, he was unable to make significant progress on a compromise solution. (Jarring did not meet with Syria, which at this point had not accepted UN Resolution 242.) Egypt was prepared to negotiate on the basis of the repatriation of Palestinians and Israeli withdrawal from the captured areas, but Israel was firm in its position that the Palestinian refugees should be resettled in Arab states and that direct negotiations must occur prior to the withdrawal of any of its military forces. The result was a stalemate.

The cease-fire that officially terminated the June 1967 War did not indicate an end to violent conflict among the principal adversaries. With the failure of the Jarring mission in 1968, sporadic fighting broke out along the Suez Canal and in the Golan Heights. The fighting, which escalated early in 1969, was labeled the War of Attrition. For the next eighteen months, artillery battles and air encounters were a daily occurrence along both fronts. Not until July 1970 was a cease-fire finally arranged between Egypt and Israel; it went into effect 7 August. Two months later, on 28 September, Nasser died of a heart attack.

The October 1973 War

Throughout the early 1970s Egypt, Jordan, and Syria unsuccessfully attempted to negotiate for the return of the territories occupied by Israel. Israel made it clear that it had no intention of returning to the 1949 armistice lines, citing security concerns and the unwillingness of neighboring states to recognize the legitimacy of Israel. Israel also began to establish Jewish settlements throughout the territories captured in 1967. By the late summer of 1973, the tension between Israel and its Arab neighbors had again reached a high level, with military sparring, such as the 13 September air battle between Israel and Syria, occurring on a regular basis. Public statements by Nasser's successor, Anwar Sadat, that Egypt would be compelled to retake the Occupied Territories by force if negotiations failed were ignored. Israeli leaders seem to have created an illusion of their own invulnerability to attack, and through rationalization and stereotyping of Egypt apparently concluded that Sadat would not order a move against Israel regardless of his rhetoric. They also did not believe Egyptian troops were capable of successfully crossing the Suez Canal, which they would need to do in order to attack Israel.[7]

The war began on 6 October with an attack by Syrian and Egyptian forces against Israeli troops in the Occupied Territories. It was Yom Kippur, the Day of Atonement, the most important Jewish religious holiday; for this reason some people refer to the October 1973 War as the Yom Kippur War. Jordan was not heavily involved in the fighting, although King

Hussein sent a token force toward the end of the war to assist the Syrians. Nor was the newly formed Palestine Liberation Army a significant factor in the conflict.

Although the war had been initiated by Egypt and Syria, Israel assumed it would follow the pattern established in previous military confrontations: a quick and overwhelming victory for the Israelis. In fact, it was nearly three weeks before the Israelis were able to drive the Syrians back over the 1967 cease-fire lines, and the death toll was massive. The introduction of newer and more sophisticated weapons, particularly antitank and antiaircraft missiles, into the region meant the level of destruction on both sides was substantially greater than anyone had anticipated. The Egyptian strategy was one of limited engagement, focused on regaining the lands lost in 1967. Initially this approach was quite successful; by the third week in October, however, Israel had received a fresh supply of weapons from the United States and the war turned in its favor.

On 22 October, the Security Council passed **UN Resolution 338**, which called for a cease-fire-in-place and the implementation of UN Resolution 242. Now on the offensive and making successful gains in territory, Israel resisted the idea of a cease-fire. After two additional UN Security Council resolutions, fighting along both the Egyptian and Syrian fronts finally ended on 25 October. Egypt and Israel signed a disengagement agreement in January 1974 (the Sinai I Accord), but intermittent fighting continued along the Syrian-Israeli border until the May 1974 disengagement agreement between those two states. As part of the disengagement agreements, Israel had to withdraw to several miles east of the Suez Canal and also evacuate from territory conquered in Syria during the October 1973 War.

Israel had no significant loss of territory under its control on either front. Still, this was not nearly the victory for the Israelis that the previous wars had been. Only six years after the stunning successes of the June 1967 War, Israel had faced initial failures and the possibility of defeat. If the United States had not been willing to resupply Israel with military equipment, the outcome might have been very different. The reactions in Israel reflected this sense of uncertainty, as well as the awareness that the country was isolated internationally and only the United States could be considered a fully reliable friend. The war also represented a challenge to the idea that the post-1967 status quo of military occupation of the West Bank, Gaza Strip, and other territories could be maintained indefinitely. Internally, there was a crisis of leadership. In the Israeli elections of 31 December 1973, the dominant Labor party fell dramatically in popularity, whereas the right-wing Likud coalition, which had never been in the majority, gained an impressive eight seats. Shortly thereafter, in April 1974, Prime Minister Golda Meir, who had led Labor and the country since early 1969, resigned and was replaced by Yitzhak Rabin.

If the aftermath of the October 1973 War was depressing for the Israelis, the opposite was true for the Arab states. Although their military successes were negligible, politically and psychologically the war was a tremendous victory. They had challenged Israel and for the first time had not been humiliated. Furthermore, by publicly stating that the intent of the war was limited to regaining territories lost in the previous war, the Arab states achieved a positive status in much of the world. In the post-war period Egyptian and Syrian diplomatic relations with the United States, broken in 1967, were reestablished. Egypt was also able to obtain the involvement in peace negotiations of U.S. National Security Adviser Henry Kissinger, whose diplomatic efforts led to the Sinai I Accord and subsequent disengagement agreements. Finally, U.S. actions during the October 1973 War led directly to a petroleum embargo and price increases by the Organization of Petroleum Exporting Countries and the Organization of Arab Petroleum Exporting Countries.

Petroleum as a Tool of Foreign Policy

The economic consequences of the October 1973 War extended far beyond the immediate participants in the conflict. Thus, it serves as an excellent example of the complex interactions among military, economic, and diplomatic relations, and the ways in which a seemingly peripheral player—in this case, Saudi Arabia—can have a significant impact on a specific issue and on the international system as a whole. It also illustrates that power can take a variety of forms and should not be conceptualized solely in terms of military capability.

In the midst of the October 1973 War, OPEC unilaterally implemented an increase in the price of petroleum. At the same time, in response to the decision by the United States to provide Israel with extensive military equipment resupply, Arab members of OPEC imposed an oil embargo on the United States and several U.S. allies. Saudi Arabia's decision to support both actions should not have come as a shock to the leadership of the United States, although it did. For some time Saudi Arabia had been sending signals that if the United States expected to continue favorable relations with Saudi Arabia and to have its petroleum needs met by that country, the United States would need to indicate greater appreciation for Arab concerns regarding the return of the territories captured by Israel in the June 1967 War.

By early 1973 Saudi Arabia had begun to reconsider its past willingness to separate its policy on petroleum from its concerns regarding the Palestinian issue. Beginning in April, King Feisal, Minister of Petroleum Ahmed Zaki Yamani, and others began to drop hints to the United States about the way the Saudis were thinking. First, Yamani went to Washington, where he met with a number of top U.S. leaders: Secretary of State William Rogers, Assistant Secretary of State Joseph Sisco, Henry Kissinger, Secretary of the Treasury George Shultz, and Deputy Secretary of the Treasury William Simon. To each, he conveyed the same message: Saudi Arabia would not continue to increase production of petroleum (which was already providing Saudi Arabia with greater revenues than it could easily absorb) to meet U.S. needs unless the United States made some movement on justice for the Palestinians and Israeli withdrawal from the territories occupied in 1967, including from the Islamic religious sites in East Jerusalem. Yamani also gave an interview to the *Washington Post* on 19 April in which he said, "We'll go out of our way to help you. We expect you to reciprocate. America should be more evenhanded in its dealings with Israel and the Arabs." It was important that the United States create "the right political atmosphere" to allow U.S.-Saudi relations to flourish.

The next month King Feisal held several meetings with U.S. oil executives in Saudi Arabia to convey similar points. Despite these efforts, Feisal recognized his message was not being heard—or at least was not believed. In July he invited reporters from the *Christian Science Monitor* and the *Washington Post* to Taif, Saudi Arabia, so he could stress to them that the warnings given by Yamani and by Minister of State for Foreign Affairs Omar Saqqaf were coming from him, personally. He also gave his first-ever interview to a U.S. television company. In a program shown on 31 August, the king told the National Broadcasting Corporation, "We do not wish to place any restrictions on our oil exports to the United States, but America's complete support of Zionism against the Arabs makes it extremely difficult for us to continue to supply U.S. petroleum needs and even to maintain our friendly relations with America."[8] None of this seems to have sunk in for U.S. policymakers. The assumption was that Feisal was bluffing. And why not? Although OPEC had been in existence since 1960, it had not yet had a significant impact on either the price or the extent of production of petroleum. An Arab oil embargo attempt in 1967 had been a complete political and economic failure. No one believed the Arab states would risk humiliation a second time.

On 6 October, the Egyptians and Syrians attacked Israel. At the time, Yamani was on his way to Vienna for a conference with other oil ministers and the petroleum companies. At this meeting, the oil ministers indicated that the price of oil paid by the oil companies should be increased from $3.01 to $5.12 per barrel; the oil company representatives said they were not prepared to budge on their original offer of less than $4.00 per barrel. Although negotiations had been scheduled to last a week, the oil company representatives left Vienna on 9 October, saying they had to return home for further consultation. The oil ministers agreed to meet in a week in Kuwait.

Meanwhile, the October 1973 War was continuing, and both the United States and the Soviet Union were under pressure from their respective allies to provide weapons resupply. On 10 October the United States began a limited and secret resupply operation to Israel; the Soviet Union began a similar airlift to the Arab states. (Kissinger initially held back large, public shipments of weapons to Israel in an effort to control the course of the war and to compel Israel to accept a cease-fire-in-place. Finally, on 13 October, after Israel agreed in principle to such a cease-fire, Kissinger approved a major airlift of weapons.)

On 17 October a group of four Arab foreign ministers, headed by Saudi Arabia's Saqqaf, met with both Kissinger and President Nixon. King Feisal of Saudi Arabia and Egypt's President Sadat had been notified of the U.S. airlift to Israel before it was made public; one of the purposes of the meeting was to provide the United States with the response of the Arab states. Kissinger appeared sympathetic to the concerns raised by the foreign ministers: the need for an immediate settlement based on complete Israeli withdrawal from lands occupied in the 1967 war, plus the restoration of Palestinian rights as specified in UN Resolution 242. When the president met later with the Arab ministers, he reiterated that he understood the concerns they raised.

For both Kissinger and Nixon, it should be noted, their main concern was not the Israeli-Palestinian issue per se, but the same U.S. foreign policy goals that had dominated U.S. thinking throughout the post–World War II years. Nixon's comments at the time make this quite clear: "No one is more keenly aware of the stakes: oil and our strategic position. ... Some of the [Arab countries] are desperately afraid of being left at the mercy of the Soviet Union. ... This is bigger than the Middle East. We can't allow a Soviet-supported operation to succeed against an American-supported operation. If it does, our credibility everywhere is severely shaken."[9]

Meanwhile, the oil ministers had reconvened in Kuwait without the oil companies and had decided unilaterally to implement a significant oil price increase. It was the first time the price of oil had been announced by the oil-producing countries, not negotiated with, or determined by, the oil companies. The next day, while the Arab foreign ministers were meeting with Kissinger and Nixon, the Arab oil ministers announced they were cutting production by 5 percent a month until Israel withdrew from the Arab territories they had occupied in 1967. At this point, events began to move quickly. On 19 October Nixon formally submitted to Congress a request for $2.2 billion in economic and military assistance to Israel. When King Feisal learned of this, it was a slap in the face and seemed to contradict everything Kissinger and Nixon had told the Saudi foreign minister.

Saudi Arabia immediately announced a complete oil embargo against the United States as well as additional production cuts. The other Arab oil-producing countries quickly followed Saudi Arabia's lead, and the list of embargoed countries grew to include the Netherlands, Portugal, and South Africa.

The United States did not depend heavily on oil from OAPEC. Still, the price increase and embargo were sufficient to disrupt the sensitive balance of U.S. energy supplies for several months, resulting in long lines at gas stations, the imposition of a 55 mile-per-hour speed limit, serious consideration of rationing systems, and a temporary shift to smaller, more fuel-efficient automobiles (where the U.S. auto manufacturers were at a distinct disadvantage compared to the Europeans and Japanese). For perhaps the first time, events in the Middle East had a direct and obvious impact on the day-to-day lives of ordinary U.S. citizens. Although the embargo was eventually lifted, petroleum prices did not return to their earlier levels and in fact rose dramatically in the 1970s, in part because of the turmoil surrounding the Iranian Revolution of 1979 and the short-term Iranian decision to drastically curtail oil production.

For the next ten years international oil prices were controlled primarily by the decisions of OPEC acting as a producer cartel. Analysts differ on whether the events of 1973 resulted in a fundamental restructuring of the relationship between the Arab oil-producing countries and the Western industrialized countries. There is also debate on whether any changes in U.S. policy toward the Israeli-Palestinian conflict could be clearly attributed to the actions of OPEC and OAPEC. What does seem clear is that the high level of U.S. support for Israel was now recognized to have a potential economic "cost," something that had not been true previously. This gave Saudi Arabia and the other Arab oil-producing states, none of which was particularly powerful in traditional military terms, a new tool they could use to redress partially the power imbalance between the Arab states and the West, including Israel.

Jordan, the Palestinians, and the Lebanese Civil War

At the end of the June 1967 War, Jordan became a home for thousands of new Palestinian refugees fleeing the Israeli occupation of the West Bank. Palestinian national identity was repressed, and relations between Jordanians and Palestinians were frequently tense. Many Palestinians looked down upon the Jordanian fighters for having lost the West Bank to Israel and pointed out that it was the Palestinian community, not the Jordanians, who suffered as a result of Jordanian failures. Members of some Palestinian groups, such as the PFLP, called for the overthrow of the Arab monarchies, including the Hashemite regime in Jordan, arguing that this was an essential first step toward the liberation of Palestine. Not surprisingly, these views did not endear the Palestinians to the Jordanian government or to the military. Jordanians also resented the economic stress placed upon their society by the increased Palestinian presence, and saw the well-educated and politically astute Palestinians as a threat to the positions of power held by Jordanians. Finally, there was widespread concern that the military activities of the Palestinian fighters against Israel would result in Israeli retaliatory military attacks against Jordan.

Jordanian fears became more pronounced after the 1968 Battle of Karameh. On 21 March Israel launched a massive attack on the Karameh refugee camp and Fateh guerrilla base located there. Although Palestinian troops, assisted by Jordanian forces, were outnumbered and took heavy casualties, they also inflicted severe losses on the Israeli forces, which had not expected such intense resistance. The Battle of Karameh provided a needed boost to the self-confidence of the Palestinians, and the number of volunteers joining the guerrilla movement multiplied dramatically. At the same time, the events at Karameh signaled the Arab world that the Palestinian resistance movement had become an autonomous factor in the conflict with Israel that could not easily be ignored.

With the increased number of guerrilla fighters, Palestinians gained greater power and influence within Jordan and began to develop a state-within-a-state over which the Jordanian monarchy had virtually no control. Thus, Palestinians were free to attack Israeli troops in the West Bank without restraint, and cross-border attacks by both Israelis and Palestinians became more frequent. By the summer of 1970, there was a high level of anxiety in Jordan, with Palestinians and Jordanians ready for confrontation. Nasser's decision in July to accept a U.S.-mediated cease-fire agreement with Israel exacerbated Palestinian unease. Palestinians interpreted this as an indication that the Arab states would forsake Palestinians if doing so would enhance their own interests.

The final impetus for the Jordanian-Palestinian War was the hijacking of four commercial airplanes by the PFLP in early September. Three of the planes were set down in the eastern desert of Jordan, where the PFLP held the passengers hostage in defiance of Jordanian efforts to negotiate their freedom. Although the passengers were eventually released, the challenge to King Hussein's authority was too much for him to tolerate, and on 17 September he gave the order for his military forces to attack the Palestinian guerrillas. The Palestinians expected military support from Iraq and Syria, but neither country provided reinforcements. Iraq actually had troops stationed on Jordanian soil, but they did not intervene. In the case of Syria, the army sent troops across the border into Jordan, but they were forced to retreat when Hafez Assad, who was in charge of the Syrian air force, refused to provide the necessary air cover. In ten days of intense fighting, thousands of Palestinians were killed, and the guerrilla movement in Jordan was broken.

Within a year of "Black September," as the events were labeled by Palestinians, virtually all of the Palestinian fighters had been expelled from Jordan. For Palestinians, the Jordanian action and the lack of Syrian and Iraqi support represented a betrayal of what was supposed to be the most sacred Arab cause. It reinforced the belief that the Palestinians could not rely on the Arab states for assistance but must find their own way to achieve self-determination. Although relations between King Hussein and the PLO improved somewhat after the October 1973 War, the lessons drawn from Black September stayed with the Palestinian national movement. Black September had another result as well: Palestinian fighters regrouped in Lebanon, where their presence was to provide the pretext for Israeli invasions in 1978 and 1982.

Between 1975 and 1990, Lebanon was embroiled in an off-and-on war with both civil and international dimensions. The roots of the conflict can be traced to the governmental structure of the state, another legacy of the League of Nations' mandate system. As part of the mandate arrangement, France took over responsibility for Syria and Lebanon after the collapse and defeat of the Ottoman Empire. Originally, Lebanon referred to a small area surrounding Mount Lebanon. France added to this territory the port cities of Tripoli, Beirut, Tyre, and Sidon, as well as the adjacent rural areas and the Bekaa Valley, all of which had originally been part of Greater Syria. France held these areas until 1941, when Britain invaded and occupied the region. Lebanon was granted independence in 1944. Its constitution provided for a "confessional" system of government whereby each main religious group was allocated specific positions in the government based on its population as of the last official census in 1932. As the largest religious group, Christian Maronites were given the greatest number of seats in a chamber of deputies, as well as the position of president. The **Sunni** Muslims had control of the position of prime minister; the speaker of the chamber was to be a **Shiite** Muslim. According to this system, the defense minister would be a Druze, and the head of the foreign ministry would be a Greek Orthodox.

This rigid structure did not include a place for Palestinians. After the Palestine War, 100,000 Palestinian refugees had fled to Lebanon. In the 1970s the Palestinian population had grown to 300,000 through high birthrates and a second influx of refugees after the June 1967 War. Most Palestinians remained in refugee camps, and even well-off Palestinians who owned homes and had professional jobs were never fully integrated into Lebanese society. Virtually none was granted citizenship rights by the

Christian-dominated government as this would upset the delicate balance of forces in favor of the Muslims.

After the 1967 Arab defeat, the Palestinians in Lebanon became more highly politicized and began to put pressure on Lebanon to make the recovery of at least a portion of Palestine a more central concern than it had been previously. Lebanese accommodation was reflected in the November 1969 Cairo Agreement, mediated by Nasser, which legitimized armed PLO presence in Lebanon although restricting somewhat its actions and its locale of operations. A series of additional agreements supported the basic outline of the Cairo Agreement, which became particularly important once Palestinian fighters originally based in Jordan arrived in Lebanon in 1970 and 1971.

Meanwhile, however, the political structure that had held Lebanon together in the 1950s and 1960s by preserving the status quo was unable to deal with the changes occurring in the country, separate from the issue of the increased Palestinian refugee community. Population growth in Lebanon had been uneven, and the structure of government no longer reflected the actual balance among Christians, Sunnis, Shiites, and Druze. Nor were the benefits of government—schools, health services, improved roads, and so forth—evenly shared; the Shiites consistently ended up with the short end of the stick, despite their growing numbers.

These problems were reflected in tensions between two factions: the Lebanese Front (LF) and the Lebanese National Movement (LNM). The LF, which was made up primarily of Maronite Christians, was dominated by the Phalangist party that had been founded in 1936 by Pierre Gemayel. It was opposed to the presence in Lebanon of the PLO and Palestinians in general and argued against any changes in Lebanon's political system. In contrast, the LNM was a coalition of progressive parties, including the Nasserites and various socialist and communist groups. It was supportive of the PLO and called for fundamental changes in the Lebanese confessional system. The conflict between the Lebanese Front and the Lebanese National Movement came to a head with the beginning of the Lebanese Civil War on 13 April 1975. The war lasted through the summer of 1976, when the Syrian military intervened, and officially ended with the Riyadh Summit in October 1976. The formal end of fighting, however, failed to resolve the basic problems of resource allocation and the distribution of political power in Lebanon. Instead, it left the country badly weakened and effectively divided up into separate areas of military authority.

For much of the war, Palestinians remained relatively uninvolved, reasoning that it was an internal Lebanese fight. But when their participation was solicited on the side of the LNM, which had been supportive of the PLO presence in Lebanon, they could not easily refuse. Palestinians were to pay dearly for their involvement in Lebanon's Civil War, most dramatically at the East Beirut refugee camp of Tal Zaatar. Between 22 June and 12 August 1976, the camp was held under siege by Phalangist forces. An estimated 2,500 Palestinians died during the siege or were killed in the massacre that occurred once Tal Zaatar fell. This massacre provided further evidence for Palestinians that they, as with the Jews prior to 1948, would be secure only in their own state.

This situation illustrates a dilemma that has haunted Palestinians since 1947 and particularly since 1967. On the one hand, the guerrilla groups needed the territorial sanctuary only the Arab states that bordered on Israel could provide. At the same time, Palestinians did not trust the Arab leaders and recognized that the position of the Palestinians in the host states was never secure. This is one reason the PLO leadership has insisted that Palestinians not get involved in the internal conflicts of host countries: Palestinian security would not be enhanced by making enemies with factions within the government. This policy broke down in Lebanon, with continuing disastrous consequences for both Palestinians and Lebanese.

The Palestinians remained in Lebanon after the end of the 1975–1976 Civil War and continued low-level operations against Israel. Syria also maintained its military presence in the Bekaa Valley and elsewhere. On 14 March 1978 Israel invaded southern Lebanon up to the Litani River in order to end these attacks and to extend Israel's de facto border further north. The invasion had been planned for some time in advance, although the trigger event providing the external justification was a Fateh hijacking of a passenger bus along the Tel Aviv–Haifa road that resulted in the deaths of thirty-six Israelis and eight Palestinians when Israeli troops stormed the bus. After establishing control of what they labeled a buffer zone, the Israeli military forces gave in to strong U.S. pressure and withdrew on 13 June, turning the area over to their allies, the Maronite Christians. But Israel continued to attack southern Lebanon and to supply the Maronite forces with military equipment during the next four years. The Israeli invasion, which resulted in heavy casualties for Lebanese and Palestinians, was criticized by a number of countries, including the United States, which objected to the use of U.S.-supplied cluster bombs provided to Israel on the condition that they be used for defensive purposes only.

The 1982 War in Lebanon

Operation Litani, the 1978 invasion of Lebanon, had not accomplished the Israeli goals of ridding Lebanon of the Palestine Liberation Organization and isolating Lebanon from the Arab world through a peace treaty with the politically dominant, although no longer numerically superior, Lebanese Christian Maronites. During the spring and summer of 1981, there were a series of attacks back and forth across the Israeli-Lebanese border and heightened tension between Israel and the Arab states. On 28 April, Israeli planes attacked two Syrian helicopters in Lebanon; in response Syrian troops moved antiaircraft missiles into Lebanon's Bekaa Valley. The United States quickly sent special Middle East envoy Philip Habib to the region to negotiate an agreement between Israel and Syria, but he was unable to gain the necessary concessions to have the missiles removed.

In this highly charged atmosphere, the Israeli bombing raid on 7 June against an Iraqi nuclear reactor resulted in strong condemnation by both the United States and the Soviet Union, and the United States temporarily suspended the delivery to Israel of four previously ordered F-16 fighter planes. Meanwhile, Israeli and PLO raids and counterraids across the Israeli-Lebanese border became more frequent. In July, Israel bombed southern Lebanon steadily for a week, culminating this thrust with an attack on Beirut on 17 July that killed an estimated 300 people, mostly civilians. At this point, Habib was again sent to the region and, working with Saudi Arabia, was successful in arranging a cease-fire agreement between Israel and the PLO that went into effect on 24 July 1981.

The cease-fire merely delayed for ten and a half months a second Israeli invasion of southern Lebanon, one which was to result in the most controversial war in Israel's history. On 9 July 1982 Israeli Defense Minister Ariel Sharon told the *Jerusalem Post* he had been "planning this operation since [he] took office" the previous summer, and as early as October 1981 Prime Minister Begin told U.S. Secretary of State Alexander Haig that Israel intended to move militarily into Lebanon but hoped to avoid Syrian involvement. All that was required was an appropriate excuse. This proved difficult. According to the United Nations Interim Force in Lebanon (UNIFIL), which was set up in the aftermath of the 1978 Israeli invasion, there were no hostile acts against Israel from Lebanon during the first eight months of the cease-fire.[10]

Thus, Israel, which by this point had become a major global military power, had to create a reason to invade. First, some 25,000 Israeli troops were moved north to the border area, where they conducted a variety of provocative training maneuvers during the first months of 1982. When these brought no Palestinian response, Israel sent a convoy of military vehicles into Lebanon, passing near to PLO bases. The PLO ignored the soldiers. April and May brought Israeli air strikes into Lebanon, but the only response by the PLO was to shoot off some rockets, carefully avoiding any populated areas. No one was killed. The restraint shown by the PLO fighters can be attributed to Arafat, who wanted to prove he was a strong leader and could maintain the cease-fire, even under difficult conditions. He also recognized that Israel was trying to provoke the PLO into retaliation that would then provide Israel with its necessary justification to attack. But Arafat's decision in favor of restraint was controversial among Palestinians, and when Israel engaged in a massive shelling of Beirut on 4 June under the pretext of retaliating for the attempted assassination of the Israeli ambassador to London the previous day by an anti-PLO splinter group, the PLO responded with air attacks against the northern Galilee. Israel had its "justification of hostility," to use Lebow's phrase, and on 6 June Israel launched its invasion, labeled Operation Peace for Galilee.

Officially, the goals of the invasion were to remove Palestinian fighters out of range of the northern Galilee and to eliminate the political and military infrastructure of the PLO. Critics of the invasion pointed out that because the PLO had consistently maintained the cease-fire for the previous year, even when provoked, the military-strategic argument was flawed. The real agenda, these critics suggested, was to distract attention away from Israel's economic problems, to repair the psychological damage done to Israel in the October 1973 War, and to create an atmosphere in Israel that might improve the immigration/emigration ratio.

At the beginning of the war, Defense Minister Sharon announced that Israeli troops would advance into Lebanon only 25 miles—to the Litani River—but when this goal had been accomplished the troops continued northward. It was later revealed this had been Sharon's plan from the beginning of the operation. By 14 June Israeli forces had completely encircled Beirut, where they remained for over two months. Israeli forces cut off electricity and water in the western (Muslim) side of Beirut, and waves of bombardment hit the city in an effort to force Arafat and the Palestinian fighters to evacuate. In Tel Aviv on 3 July 100,000 Israelis demonstrated against the continued Israeli presence in Lebanon, and soldiers began publicly to state their refusal to serve in Lebanon.

Philip Habib was sent back to the region to negotiate between the PLO and the Israelis. A deal was finally made whereby Israeli attacks on Beirut would end, the Palestinian fighters would leave Lebanon and redeploy in several Arab countries willing to accept them, and a multinational peacekeeping force, including U.S., French, and Italian troops, would assure the security of the Palestinian civilians remaining in Lebanon. The PLO evacuation began on 21 August, and the last of the PLO fighters left Beirut on 1 September. Ten days later, the United States withdrew its forces.

The cease-fire was a false calm. In response to the assassination of the newly elected Lebanese president and head of the Lebanese Front, Beshir Gemayel, Israeli troops defied the August Habib agreement and returned to Beirut on 15 September. By the end of the following day, Israeli forces had occupied the entire city, something they had been unable to do during the summer when the city was protected by Palestinian fighters, and sealed off the Sabra and Shatilla refugee camps, which were home to Palestinians and poorer Lebanese. The massacre in the Sabra and Shatilla camps by Lebanese Maronite Christian forces allied with Israel began late in the afternoon of 16 September and continued for forty hours. When the camps were finally unsealed, as many as 1,000 people had been murdered, the majority of whom were Palestinian women, children, and old men. The international community was united in its condemnation of both the invasion of Beirut on 15–16 September and of the subsequent Sabra-Shatilla massacre, and the UN Security Council passed two strongly worded resolutions criticizing Israel. Palestinians and other Arabs also blamed the United States, which had guaranteed the safety of Palestinian civilians left unprotected when the PLO evacuated Beirut.

A three-person commission headed by Israeli Supreme Court President Yitzhak Kahan was set up by the Israeli government to investigate the massacre. It found Ariel Sharon guilty of "indirect responsibility" for the deaths because he had given the signal for the Phalangist soldiers to enter the camps for what were called "mopping up" operations. Other Israeli officers were also condemned for having deliberately turned a blind eye to the events occurring in the camps. The commission said if Sharon did not resign he should be fired. Instead, Sharon gave up his position as defense minister but remained in the Cabinet as a minister without portfolio. The report of the International Commission of Inquiry, headed by Nobel Peace Prize recipient Seán MacBride, went still further in its censure of Israeli government officials: "The Commission concludes that the Israeli authorities bear a heavy legal responsibility, as the occupying power, for the massacres at Sabra and Chatilla. From the evidence disclosed, Israel was involved in the planning and the preparation of the massacres and played a facilitative role in the actual killings."[11] These findings shocked many Israelis, who joined in the worldwide condemnation of their government and the actions of the Israeli military. For Israel, it was a bad ending to an unsuccessful military action.

An estimated 15,000 to 20,000 Palestinians, Lebanese, and Syrians, the majority civilians, were killed during the three months of the war, as were nearly 500 Israeli military personnel. Even though the military, political, and administrative structures of the PLO were destroyed and had to be reconstructed in Tunis, where Yasir Arafat eventually was granted permission to establish new headquarters, the 1982 War in Lebanon, as with those that had preceded it, failed to resolve the Israeli-Palestinian conflict in any of its fundamental elements. Arguably, Israel's position in Lebanon was worse after the war than it had been before 1982, because the factionalization in Lebanon that resulted from the invasion led to increased instability in the region.

By June 1985 Israel had withdrawn from most of Lebanon, although it maintained troops in a "security zone" along Lebanon's southern border. At this point, a Syrian-backed Lebanese Shiite militia group known as Amal attacked Palestinian refugee camps and former guerrilla bases in an effort to prevent the PLO from reestablishing a military presence in Lebanon. The War of the Camps, as this fighting came to be called, lasted intermittently for nearly three years. Despite opposition from Amal and from Israel, the PLO was able to return about 10,000 troops to Lebanon, to be based primarily around the port city of Sidon, south of Beirut.

The **Taif Accord** marked the beginning of a new period in Lebanese history. The agreement, negotiated in Taif, Saudi Arabia, in September 1989, became part of the Lebanese constitution a year later. It implemented a cease-fire, required Syrian troops to redeploy to areas near the Syrian border, and called for all the militias—the Syrian-backed Amal; Amal's Shiite rival, Hizballah, an Islamic movement backed by Iran; the Christian Maronite Lebanese Forces, and others—to disband. In addition, the accord set up a new structure for the Lebanese Parliament with an equal number of seats allotted to Muslims and Christians. In the fall of 1992, Lebanon held its first general elections in twenty years; Rafiq Hariri, a Lebanese-Saudi national, became prime minister.

The Taif Accord stabilized Lebanon domestically but did not fully resolve its international problems. Hizballah refused to disband as long as Israel occupied part of southern Lebanon; Syria did not fully redeploy its forces for the same reason. Further violence occurred. After Hizballah killed seven Israeli soldiers in Israel's self-declared "security zone" in southern Lebanon, Israeli troops launched "Operation Accountability" on 25 July 1993. The stated purpose of this week-long bombardment of Lebanese towns and villages was to drive Lebanese civilians from their homes so they would force the Lebanese government to end Hizballah's attacks against Israeli soldiers. The Israeli offensive, which 93 percent of Israelis polled supported, left some 130 people, mostly Lebanese civilians, dead and 450 wounded. More than fifty towns and villages were heavily damaged, and 400,000 Lebanese had to flee their homes.[12]

A number of countries called for an emergency session of the UN Security Council to discuss the Israeli attack, which was the most severe since the 1982 invasion; the United States blocked these efforts, however. Eventually, Syria, under pressure from the United States, apparently urged Iran to force Hizballah to agree to a cease-fire. The 31 July agreement specified that Israel would end its attacks on civilian areas of southern Lebanon and Hizballah would halt its rocket attacks against northern Israel. Hizballah did not agree to suspend attacks against Israeli troops in the "security zone," however, nor did it agree to disarm.

Iraq's Invasion of Kuwait and the War Against Iraq

On 2 August 1990, Iraq invaded its southern neighbor Kuwait. Whether Iraq's grievances and historical claims against Kuwait were valid or invalid is less relevant here than are the implications of the crisis for Israeli-Palestinian relations.[13] In a close vote that pitted an unusual coalition composed of the Arab Gulf states, Egypt, Morocco, and Syria against most of the other Arab countries, the League of Arab States condemned Iraq's invasion, a denunciation that led to a serious split in the Arab world. Within days, the United States and its European and Arab allies began a massive troop mobilization that continued throughout the autumn and early winter. On 16 January 1991, one day after Iraq failed to respond to a UN Security Council deadline calling for its withdrawal from Kuwait, the U.S.-led forces began an air bombardment campaign. Iraq responded with largely ineffective but frightening Scud missile attacks against Saudi Arabia and Israel. The ground war began on 24 February and ended just one hundred hours later with the military defeat of Iraq.

In the initial days of the air campaign, thousands of Israelis fled from the urban areas to the countryside, hoping to avoid being hit by one of the Iraqi missiles; those who remained in the cities huddled in air-tight rooms wearing gas masks whenever the air-raid alerts sounded. For some older Israeli Jews, the feeling of helplessness was frighteningly reminiscent of their experiences during the Shoah. Many Israelis called on their government to retaliate against Iraq, but at the request of the United States (which feared such an attack would cause a breakdown of the coalition against Iraq and a widening of the war), Israel refrained from doing so.[14] Although the Scud attacks killed only two Jewish Israelis directly, reports that the warheads might carry deadly chemical or biological weapons led to widespread anxiety, and several dozen more people died because of stress-induced heart attacks or difficulties in using their gas masks.

Iraq's invasion of Kuwait further damaged relations between Palestinians and Israeli Jews already strained by nearly three years of the *intifada*. International attention focused on widespread support for Saddam Hussein among Palestinians, including Arafat, who viewed him as a strong Arab leader prepared to stand up against the West and the oil-rich countries. Although some Palestinian leaders condemned the invasion and called for Kuwaiti self-determination and an end to the Scud attacks against Israel, their voices received less attention. Israeli Jews were strongly critical of Palestinian enthusiasm for Iraq's actions. Many leftist Israelis felt betrayed by Palestinian support of an Arab leader who was directing an attack against Israel. On the other side, Palestinians, regardless of their view of Iraq's invasion and occupation of Kuwait, criticized the explicit international double standard that demanded Iraq's immediate and unequivocal withdrawal from Kuwait but counseled Palestinians to be patient and use negotiation to achieve Israeli withdrawal from Palestinian territories occupied not for months but for decades.

Israel used the crisis as a justification for new restraints against the Occupied Territories. When the air war began, Israel declared a state of emergency and imposed a full curfew on the entire Gaza Strip, extending it to the West Bank the following day. Restrictions on movement remained in effect for virtually the entire Palestinian population of the Occupied Territories through January and February 1991. At its most severe, the curfew allowed people to leave their homes for only two or three hours a week to do essential errands. This confinement was gradually eased in some West Bank villages, but the restrictions on refugee camps remained severe. Once the ground war against Iraq began, a total curfew was reinstituted for two days, and many areas remained under at least partial curfew well into March. (The nighttime curfew of Gaza, imposed at the beginning of the *intifada,* remained in effect even after the curfew was lifted elsewhere in the Occupied Territories.)

These curfews caused grave economic hardship to the Palestinian population. The restricted Palestinian industrial sector was unable to function because employees could not reach the factories; farmers were unable to work their fields or to harvest, transport, or market crops, which resulted not only in immediate financial difficulties but also a lack of capital for future growing seasons. Once the military had lifted the curfews, some Palestinians who had worked before the war for Israelis inside the Green Line found their employers had replaced them with recent Jewish immigrants. Other Palestinians were unable to obtain the permits necessary for employment. An expanded and formalized pass system required every holder of a West Bank or Gaza identity card to obtain a special permit from the military authorities to enter Israel or East Jerusalem as well as a separate pass from an Israeli employment bureau or employer.

Palestinians in the Occupied Territories were also affected by the fate of relatives who had been living and working in the Gulf. Most Palestinians in these countries, including about 400,000 living in Kuwait, suddenly found themselves unemployed and, in many cases, deported. Because many of these people were supporting family members in the Occupied Territories, this led to additional financial difficulties throughout the West Bank and Gaza Strip. Finally, external contributions from Saudi Arabia and other Arab Gulf states for Palestinian institutions, such as hospitals, schools, universities, and social welfare organizations, dried up almost instantly. The Gulf states also withheld the special taxes collected from Palestinians working in their countries that the governments had previously forwarded to the PLO. The impact of all these changes was devastating to the Palestinian economy, which was already battered by the *intifada* and restrictions on development dating back to the beginning of the occupation.

U.S. POLICY TOWARD THE CONFLICT

As the major Western power at the end of World War II, the United States was expected by the international community to take a leading role in dealing with the Palestinian-Israeli conflict. The U.S. government first became intimately involved in the controversy over Palestine in the 1940s and was instrumental in the passage of UN Resolution 181 on the partition of Palestine and the creation of Israel. At this point, however, the overall goals of the United States in the Middle East were still being formulated, and it did not have a clear policy toward Israel or the Palestinians.

The Eisenhower administration fully developed the U.S. foreign policy orientation toward the Middle East and the Israeli-Palestinian issue. Since the early 1950s, the principal goals have been to protect the supply of petroleum for the United States and its European allies and to prevent or minimize Soviet involvement in the region. The concern about Middle Eastern petroleum has been part of U.S. calculations since the 1930s. President Franklin Roosevelt's decision to declare Saudi Arabia "vital to the defense of the United States" and therefore eligible for lend-lease assistance in February 1943 reflected this desire to assure U.S. and European access to petroleum resources, as did U.S. actions in support of the shah of Iran against a coup attempt in 1953 and President Carter's creation of a Middle East Rapid Deployment Force in 1980. Similarly, the need to keep the Soviet Union out of the Middle East was a theme raised repeatedly by U.S. decisionmakers.

An additional factor in understanding U.S. actions in the Middle East, particularly in the 1950s and early 1960s, is the U.S. relationship with former European colonial powers. Presidents Eisenhower and Kennedy wanted the United States to take a public anticolonial position as a way of improving ties with the newly independent states in Africa, the Middle East, and Asia. At the same time, France and Britain, which remained influential in the Middle East, were important U.S. allies in the cold war against the Soviet Union, and the United States did not want to alienate them unnecessarily. Only when Britain and France forced the issue, as they did during the Suez crisis, was the United States compelled explicitly to take a position in opposition to its European friends. Otherwise, the United States frequently appeared willing to minimize its own involvement in the Levant, particularly regarding Palestine, in deference to Europe's prior claims.

The U.S. policy regarding the Palestinian-Israeli conflict came directly out of these more general concerns. Successfully managing the dispute was important to the extent that the failure to do so could damage U.S. and Western relations with the Arab world and Iran, make states in the region susceptible to Soviet influence, and risk the security of Middle Eastern oil sources. In this context, the most important element in U.S. policy was that the issue of Palestine was formulated in terms of the *states* in the region. According to U.S. preferences, Jordan should maintain control of most of the portion of Palestine intended by the United Nations for an independent Arab state (that is, the West Bank) and when necessary could speak for the Palestinians. Egypt would continue its military presence in the Gaza Strip. The United States would not challenge Israel's annexation of the remaining areas originally intended for the Palestinian state, that is, the territories it captured during the Palestine War.

It is obvious that this policy did not recognize the Palestinians as a distinct national group with political rights. In dramatic contrast to the positive, inspiring portrayal of the Jewish Israelis, the Palestinians were viewed exclusively as a refugee population that needed to be resettled, repatriated, rehabilitated, compensated, and otherwise taken care of so that the Arab-Israeli dispute could be resolved and the United States could continue to forge political links with conservative Arab states such as Jordan and Saudi Arabia, with Iran, and also with Israel. In recent years, this attitude toward Palestinians has shifted somewhat in the United States, and there is greater recognition of the *national* identity of the Palestinian people, but the preferred U.S. solution to the conflict still excludes an independent Palestinian state.

This rejection of the political and national rights of Palestinians has had a number of important implications. First, it meant that from the beginning of U.S. involvement in the conflict U.S. decisionmakers made few if any efforts to identify Palestinian groups or individuals who had the authority to speak on behalf of the Palestinian community. It is striking to note that although officials in Washington meet regularly with representatives of the Israeli government, until recently conversations with Palestinian leaders have been all but nonexistent. Second, the U.S. decision to focus only on the states in the region ignored that any proposed solution that satisfied the leaders of Syria, Jordan, and other Arab states was useless unless it was also acceptable to the Palestinians themselves. The political aspirations of the people of Palestine and their sense of betrayal by the United States and the UN had to be considered. Third, because of the way the issue was framed, the United States initially directed its attention to improving conditions for the Palestinian refugees through economic development activities such as the United Plan for Jordan Valley Development, rather than pushing strongly for repatriation, which was the preferred international solution for most other refugee populations. These factors partially explain why initial U.S. efforts at settling the Palestinian-Israeli dispute in the 1950s were unsuccessful: They were based on a series of false premises, including the assumption that if economic issues related to the Palestinian refugees could be addressed to the satisfaction of the Arab states, the political dimensions of the problem would be more easily resolved.

Most significant was the U.S. belief that the vast majority of Palestinian refugees from the Palestine War should be settled as residents and citizens of the surrounding Arab states rather than being allowed to return to their homes within the new State of Israel. This was true despite public and private statements in which the United States indicated it would like to see Israel permit significant Palestinian repatriation, and despite repeated U.S. cosponsorship of UN resolutions supporting such repatriation. About 8,000 Palestinians were allowed to reenter Israel as part of a family reunion plan that ended in March 1953, but this barely touched the massive numbers of Palestinians wishing to return to their homes. Israel has consistently refused to consider the possibility of significant repatriation of the 1948 refugees, citing security concerns and economic constraints. There is no evidence to suggest that U.S. decisionmakers have pressured Israel on this issue. The June 1967 War created a second group of refugees who also desire repatriation and who have had equally limited success in gaining U.S. support for this goal. The Oslo agreement does provide for limited repatriation of some 1967 refugees, but final details have not yet been determined.

On the question of compensation for property left in Israel by the Palestinian refugees, the U.S. position in the 1950s was that this was an essential element in any final peace agreement between Israel and the Arab states. At the same time, it was clear that Israel's economy could not support such compensation while maintaining the standard of living expected by its European immigrants. Therefore, in August 1955 U.S. Secretary of State John Foster Dulles indicated the United States would be willing to underwrite substantially an international loan to Israel to help cover the costs of compensation; Israel, however, did not pursue this possibility, and no compensation occurred. Officially, there has been no change in the U.S. policy regarding compensation, but the issue has been relegated to a far back burner.

In terms of the official borders of the countries in the region, the United States has repeatedly said that it considers the 1949 armistice borders to be binding on all parties until permanent boundaries are negotiated. Furthermore, at least through the first half of the 1950s, the United States stressed that the permanent borders might require some minor adjustments from the armistice borders in order to reunite Palestinian villages with their agricultural lands. After the June 1967 War, the United States reiterated its commitment to the 1949 armistice lines and has continued to do so through subsequent presidential administrations. At the same time, even though the United States verbally criticizes the gradual incorporation into Israel of the territories captured in the June 1967 War, it has appeared implicitly to condone such actions through continued and increased financial assistance to Israel. U.S. policy regarding Jerusalem has been particularly ambiguous. Although the United States frequently reiterates that it supports "a united Jerusalem whose final status should be determined by negotiations," regular U.S. abstentions on UN Security Council resolutions condemning Israel's effort to extend its rule over all of Jerusalem have sent a different message. For this reason, within Israel the assumption developed that the United States did not really mean it when it said that *all* territories captured in the June 1967 War were considered occupied until a peace treaty determined their final status. When President George Bush explicitly stated in March 1990 that the United States viewed East Jerusalem as part of the Israeli-occupied territories, there was a tremendous outcry in Israel. Although Bush later backed off slightly, saying that in his opinion "Jews and others can live where they want, East or West, and the city must remain undivided," he did not retract his previous statement on East Jerusalem.[15]

The status of Jerusalem was again at issue the following month when a group of Jewish settlers moved into a complex of buildings near the Church of the Holy Sepulcher in the Christian Quarter of the Old City. It was later revealed that nearly half the money to purchase the lease on the buildings had come directly from the Israeli government. The settlers' action and the covert role of the Israeli government, which originally denied any connection with the settlers, were condemned both within Israel and by the international community; however, some in Israel felt it was legitimate for Jews to settle in any area under Israeli control.

Particularly during the first decade after the establishment of the State of Israel, there were serious problems with border violations by all parties. Most incursions from Egypt (at least until after the February 1955 Israeli raid against Egyptian military outposts in Gaza) or Jordan were by unorganized groups or individual Palestinians crossing to retrieve property in Israel, pick crops, and so forth. Israeli border crossings, in contrast, frequently took the form of formal military actions that resulted in a significant number of Palestinian civilian deaths. The United States openly censured such preplanned actions and on several occasions cosponsored UN General Assembly or Security Council resolutions critical of Israel.

Israel consistently ignored these resolutions, causing increased tension between the United States and Israel. In a public statement following the 11 December 1955 Israeli attack against Syrian outposts overlooking Lake

Tiberias (which led to a UN Security Council "condemnation" of Israel's "flagrant violation" of the cease-fire and armistice agreements), U.S. Representative to the United Nations Henry Cabot Lodge reflected:

> It is always deplorable for any government deliberately and willfully to plan and carry out an attack against its neighbor in violation of its solemn international commitment. What makes these particular deliberations more serious is the fact that a member of the United Nations—indeed, a member created by the United Nations—should now be before this Council for the fourth offense of this kind in 2 years. … Each of the incidents from Qibya in [October] 1953, through Nahalin [in 1954], Gaza [in 1955], and now in the Tiberias area, has resulted in a deterioration in the situation in Palestine. This is something that the Security Council cannot ignore.[16]

The United States felt that the apparent inability of the UN to compel Israeli compliance with its declarations damaged the UN's credibility in the eyes of the Arab countries; the United States also judged Israel's actions to be counterproductive to regional stability and the prospects for peace.

The second Eisenhower administration began with the unresolved issue of the Israeli withdrawal from territories captured in the 1956 Suez War. Once this had been settled, U.S. attention was pulled in other directions. Hungary, the arms race with the Soviet Union, the 1958 crisis in Lebanon, concerns about the possible spread of communism, the Bay of Pigs, the Cuban missile crisis, and growing U.S. involvement in Southeast Asia preoccupied Presidents Eisenhower, Kennedy, and Johnson. As a result, the Israeli-Palestinian and Arab-Israeli conflicts dropped to a relatively low priority for the United States. One critical shift in U.S. policy did occur during this period. Under President Kennedy, the United States began to develop the "special relationship" with Israel that characterizes current U.S. policy in the Middle East. Under Presidents Truman and Eisenhower, Israel had received some $700 million in financial assistance. Kennedy continued this aid and also began to sell Israel sophisticated U.S. weapons, something Eisenhower had refused to consider.

Strengthening of U.S.-Israeli Ties

The June 1967 War had widespread implications for U.S. policy in the Levant and marks both the initiation of significant mobilization of U.S. Jewry on behalf of Israel as well as the beginning of almost unqualified support of Israel by the U.S. government. Prior to 1967, Zionists in the United States had lobbied intensely on behalf of Israel on only a few occasions, such as prior to the UN vote on the partition of Palestine and during the resolution of the 1956 Suez War. After the June 1967 War, Zionists among the U.S. Jewish community became increasingly involved in promoting U.S. political, military, and economic support for the expanded state and far more outspoken against leaders elected and appointed by the U.S. government whose views differed from those of the supporters of Israel.

Zionists found a sympathetic audience for their views among the general U.S. population for some of the same reasons that led many to support Zionism before Israel was established as a state. The most significant factor remained continuing guilt feelings about the Shoah and a recognition that U.S. immigration restrictions prior to World War II contributed to the deaths of European and Soviet Jews at the hands of the Nazis. Furthermore, there was an immediate and positive identification with the formerly European Israelis, whose culture, values, and religion (unlike those of the predominantly Muslim Palestinians, who appeared alien and therefore frightening) were familiar to people in the United States.

Official U.S. governmental rhetoric and actions also became increasingly supportive of Israel. The foreign policy community continued to express concern for regional stability, protection of petroleum resources, and possible Soviet involvement in the Middle East; however, the implementation of this policy came to rest not only on Iran (prior to the revolution in 1978–1979) and Saudi Arabia, as it had done in the past, but also on Israel. In the eyes of the United States—mired in the Vietnam War and increasingly isolated internationally—Israel's dramatic victories in 1967 provided evidence that Israel could serve as a strategic asset for the United States in the Middle East. Economic and military assistance to Israel began to rise dramatically, and the public U.S. commitment to Israel was strengthened.

President Nixon, like his predecessors, viewed the Middle East primarily in the context of the continuing rivalry between the United States and the Soviet Union; this remained the case even after the moves toward détente that characterized the second term of the Nixon presidency. Israel was important to the United States because it could serve as a surrogate for U.S. interests in the Middle East. As U.S. scholar Cheryl Rubenberg writes: "According to proponents of the surrogate thesis, by providing Israel absolute military superiority the American interests of containing Soviet expansionism, promoting regional stability and preventing war, and assuring Western freedom of access to the area's raw materials, markets, and investment opportunities would be maximized. ... The strategic asset thesis came to be accepted during these years as absolute dogma in the conventional wisdom of American political culture."[17]

The War of Attrition that followed the June 1967 War provided an opportunity for the United States to attempt to mediate between Israel and its opponents in the context of this approach. In November 1969, U.S. Secretary of State William Rogers gave a major policy speech in which he reaffirmed the U.S. commitment to UN Resolution 242, proposed negotiations between Israelis and Palestinians, expressed concern for the Palestinian refugees of 1948 and 1967, and stated U.S. opposition to the unilateral de facto annexation of Jerusalem by Israel. Over the next few months, these points formed the basis of a U.S. initiative to end the War of Attrition. The plan was accepted in July 1970.

The real foreign policy architect under Nixon was not Rogers, however, but National Security Adviser (and later Secretary of State) Henry Kissinger. Kissinger, who remained secretary of state under President Ford, quickly concluded that the Palestinian issue was unsolvable in the short term, so he essentially ignored it in his step-by-step diplomatic approach in the region. Instead, particularly after the October 1973 War, Kissinger focused on negotiations to bring about a partial Israeli withdrawal from the Egyptian Sinai and the creation of a UN buffer zone in the region. These goals were achieved in September 1975 with the signing of the Sinai II Accord between Israel and Egypt.

Camp David Accords

In his first two and a half years in office, U.S. President Jimmy Carter approached international politics very differently from most of his predecessors. He was a hands-on president whose ideology was as close to the political idealism of the interwar period as any president since Woodrow Wilson. Shortly after Carter took office in 1977, he began to address the Israeli-Palestinian conflict, which he saw not only as a security concern but also as a human rights issue. In a speech on 6 March, Carter indicated there were three conditions for peace in the Middle East. Two of the conditions were standard U.S. policy: recognition of Israel's right to exist and the establishment of permanent boundaries, based on the pre-1967 situation. Carter's third condition, however, was new: "a homeland for the Palestinian refugees." In saying this, Carter acknowledged the crux of the problem that had been consistently ignored by previous U.S. presidents. The following day, Carter shook hands with a PLO observer at the United Nations. This symbolic action, in the context of Kissinger's 1975 pledge not to negotiate with the PLO until it had accepted UN Resolutions 242 and 338 and recognized Israel's right to exist, upset the Israelis but gained Carter little with the Arab states or the Palestinians, who understood its limited significance.

In the months that followed, Carter attempted to convene an international conference to address the Middle East situation. His efforts were complicated by the results of the Israeli election in May, which gave Likud control of the Knesset and made Menachem Begin the prime minister when the new government was formed in June. Although Israel officially accepted the idea of peace negotiations and an international conference, Begin had little interest in them. The Arab states were more enthusiastic, recognizing that in such an arena the United Nations and the superpowers could be called upon to enforce international opinion, which generally favored the Palestinians. Although the PLO argued it should be included in the international conference, the United States felt constrained by Kissinger's pledge. The Soviet Union also indicated its support for an international conference in a joint declaration with the United States made public on 1 October. Israel was intensely upset by the joint statement, which referred to the "legitimate rights" of the Palestinians, and said it would refuse to participate in an international conference based on the document. Carter immediately backed away from the statement, placating Israel at the expense of angering the Soviet Union.

Meanwhile, Jordan and Saudi Arabia were working to find a common ground between Egypt and Syria, which were unable to agree on the composition of the Arab delegations. The main problem was the high degree of mistrust between Egyptian President Sadat and Syrian leader Assad. Sadat feared that Assad would veto any Egyptian-Israeli accord reached at an international conference, whereas Assad was afraid he would lose the ability to regain the Golan Heights if Sadat cut a separate deal with Israel. Ultimately, Sadat decided to attempt an initiative on his own. Against the advice of the Egyptian foreign minister—who resigned over the issue—Sadat announced that he wished to go to Jerusalem to meet with Prime Minister Begin to discuss peace. An invitation was forthcoming, and on 20 November 1977 Sadat addressed the members of the Israeli Knesset and stated his desire for peace with Israel.

Sadat had several motives for this decision, in addition to his distrust of Assad. Although the October 1973 War had been a psychological success for Egypt, the subsequent disengagement agreements (Sinai I and II) had not fully restored the Sinai to Egyptian control. Sadat badly wanted to accomplish this. In addition, the economy in Egypt was experiencing severe difficulties, and Islamic fundamentalists were challenging the government's competence and legitimacy. A peace treaty with Israel would allow Egypt to reduce its military expenditures and might result in increased military and economic assistance from the United States. At minimum, a foreign policy success could distract attention from those domestic problems. Finally, the grand gesture, and its potential for equally sweeping changes in the Israeli-Egyptian relationship, had the power to take Sadat out of the shadow of Nasser and assure him a place in history. By acting unilaterally rather than with the support of Arab allies, however, Sadat placed himself in a weak and vulnerable bargaining position vis-à-vis Israel.

Sadat's visit was followed by months of fruitless discussions between Israel and Egypt, and the talks broke off in July. At this point, Carter stepped in and invited Sadat and Begin to meet with him for direct negotiations at the presidential retreat at Camp David, Maryland. For thirteen grueling days Carter attempted to discover common ground between the two leaders. The result was the Camp David Accords, signed on 17 September 1978 and composed of two main documents. "A Framework for Peace in the Middle East" dealt with the West Bank and Gaza Strip. It called for a Palestinian self-governing authority to be followed by a five-year transition period, with the final status of the West Bank and Gaza Strip to be negotiated. The "Framework for the Conclusion of a Peace Treaty between Egypt and Israel" outlined an understanding for an eventual peace treaty between the two states. Six months later, on 26 March 1979, Sadat and Begin met in Washington, D.C., to sign that treaty. Among the attachments to the treaty was an annex that set forth the details of Israeli withdrawal from Egyptian territory and another that specified the new relations that were to exist between the two states.

In the end, each of the three leaders seemed to get at least some of what he wanted, although in retrospect most analysts believe Israel came out ahead of Egypt. Sadat achieved a peace treaty with Israel, which allowed him to reduce military expenditures; he obtained increased economic and military assistance from the United States; and Egypt regained control of the Sinai Peninsula. The price, however, was that Egypt lost its influential position as a leader of the Arab world and was ostracized for the next decade. Begin gained the neutralization of Israel's most powerful regional adversary, a demilitarized zone between Israel and Egypt, an Israeli embassy in Cairo, and increased economic and military assistance from the United States. In exchange, Israel had to give up the oil-producing Sinai and the Israeli settlements located there. Finally, Carter had what he felt was a major foreign policy success to which he would point with pride.

Many crucial details pertaining to the Palestinian people and the land of the West Bank and Gaza Strip were left unspecified in order to achieve an agreement. For example, Jerusalem was not mentioned, although its political status is one of the most significant points of disagreement between Israelis and Palestinians. The phrase used in the accords, "legitimate rights of the Palestinian people," had no legal meaning. It was later defined by Begin to refer only to Palestinian inhabitants of the Occupied Territories, rather than all Palestinians, and to mean much less than the self-determination intended by Sadat and Carter. There was nothing in writing to confirm Carter's conviction that Begin had promised to suspend Israeli settlements in the Occupied Territories indefinitely; instead, Israel put a three-month moratorium on settlement development, then returned to their construction with renewed energy.

Finally, there was no way to compel Israel to move quickly on the proposed autonomy for the Palestinians. The Camp David framework had called for a "self-governing [Palestinian] authority ... freely elected by the inhabitants of [the West Bank and Gaza] to replace the existing [Israeli] military government." The exact modalities for the establishment of this authority were to be agreed upon by Egypt, Jordan, and Israel. After a year of negotiations over the format of Palestinian autonomy, however, nothing had been accomplished. By then Carter's attention was focused on the overthrow of the shah of Iran and the subsequent taking of U.S. hostages in Tehran, and he was unable to pressure Israel to negotiate in good faith.

If most people in Israel and the United States and some in Egypt cheered the Camp David Accords and the Egyptian-Israeli Peace Treaty, the majority of the Arab world was highly skeptical of what they perceived as a separate peace, that is, a peace with one party to the conflict without addressing the issues of importance to other involved actors. On 5 November 1978 an Arab summit meeting held in Baghdad strongly condemned Egypt and the Camp David Accords and warned Egypt against signing a peace treaty with Israel. At the same time, the Arab League stripped Egypt of membership and voted to transfer its headquarters from Cairo to Tunis, where it remained for the next twelve years. (In 1989, Egypt was readmitted to the Arab League, and on 1 January 1991 the League headquarters returned to Cairo.)

The Arab states raised a number of concerns. First, Arab analysts pointed to the areas of ambiguity in the Camp David Accords and argued that Israel would find loopholes to avoid abiding by the spirit of the agreements. (Israelis similarly feared that Egypt would find such loopholes; they pointed to the lack of full normalization between the two states as evidence that their concerns were legitimate.) Second, Arab states believed Egypt had sold out the Palestinians by not negotiating for complete Palestinian independence from Israeli control and settling instead for a vague autonomy plan. Third, Arabs feared the peace treaty was a way of co-opting Egypt—then the strongest Arab military power in the Levant—so that Israel would be free to attack elsewhere. The 1982 invasion of Lebanon was seen as proof that this had been Israel's intent from the beginning.

U.S. Involvement in Lebanon

U.S. President Ronald Reagan came to power in 1981. One of the first trips taken by the new secretary of state, Alexander M. Haig, Jr., was a tour of the Middle East in April, during which he met with Egyptian President Sadat, Israeli Prime Minister Begin, Jordan's King Hussein, and

Saudi Crown Prince (now King) Fahd. Haig's agenda included a proposed U.S. arms deal with Saudi Arabia and the continued fighting within Lebanon and between Israeli and PLO forces. Arab-Israeli tensions escalated throughout the spring and early summer until the United States negotiated a cease-fire between the PLO and Israel in July.

With the Israeli invasion of Lebanon the following year, the United States again found itself involved in the Israeli-Lebanese-Palestinian triangle. In the wake of the invasion, the United States supported repeated UN Security Council resolutions calling on Israel to withdraw. Throughout June and July, the United States attempted to mediate an end to Israel's attack on Lebanon. Finally, in August the PLO agreed to a U.S. plan that called for the PLO to withdraw from Beirut in exchange for an Israeli cease-fire and protection of Palestinians by a multinational force including U.S. troops. A week later Israel also acceded to the plan and the PLO troops left Lebanon.

On 1 September, President Reagan presented a peace initiative that called for "self-government by the Palestinians of the West Bank and Gaza Strip in association with Jordan" and a halt to the building of new Israeli settlements or the expansion of existing settlements. Reagan also said that the future of Jerusalem should be determined by negotiations. The plan was immediately rejected by the Israeli Cabinet; the PLO's response indicated they saw some positive elements to the plan, although they did not fully accept it. Israel also rejected the Fez Summit peace plan presented by the Arab League on 9 September, disappointing U.S. Secretary of State George Shultz, who had seen the proposal as an opportunity for a breakthrough in the long stalemate between Israel and the Arab world.

U.S. forces, joined by French and Italian troops as they had been in August, returned to Lebanon on 29 September after the Sabra and Shatilla massacres. Their mandate was to help the Lebanese government restore order and to train the Lebanese army. The multinational peacekeeping forces were not universally welcomed, and hostility toward their presence grew during subsequent months. On 18 April 1983 a suicidal car-bomb attack on the U.S. embassy in Beirut killed sixty-three persons, including a number of CIA employees; responsibility was claimed by the pro-Iranian Islamic Jihad. Six months later, on 23 October 1983, there was a second suicide mission against U.S. citizens: a truck-bomb attack against the U.S. military barracks that left 241 U.S. military personnel dead. A virtually simultaneous attack against French peacekeeping forces resulted in fifty-eight deaths. Although Reagan reaffirmed the U.S. commitment to remain in Lebanon as part of the peacekeeping mission, U.S. public opinion was outspoken against continuing the military presence. Finally, on 7 February 1984 Reagan announced U.S. troops would be redeployed to ships off the coast of Lebanon. On 30 March the U.S. ships left the area, ending a military action the goals of which were unclear from the beginning and the success of which was dubious at best by the end.

U.S.-PLO Relations

In the late summer of 1975, Secretary of State Kissinger made a pledge to Israeli Prime Minister Rabin that the United States would not recognize or negotiate with the PLO until the PLO recognized Israel's right to exist and accepted UN Security Council Resolutions 242 and 338. This remained the U.S. policy for thirteen years, during which time the United States did not speak to the PLO officially. When unofficial contacts occurred, such as when Andrew Young, the chief U.S. representative to the United Nations under Carter, met with the head of the PLO's UN mission in a private home one evening, these actions were quickly denounced. Young, for example, was fired.

The Reagan administration added the requirements that the PLO had to renounce the use of terrorism and revise the Palestinian National Charter that called for the abolition of the Zionist state. On 14 December 1988 the U.S. policy of nonrecognition of the PLO ended, although the United States has not yet established official diplomatic relations with the PLO or the State of Palestine. The events that led to this change reflect a modification in at least the outward appearance of both U.S. and PLO policies. They also illustrate that if much of foreign policy is conducted by massive bureaucracies that move ponderously, in some instances dramatic changes in international relations can occur.

After the PNC meeting and the Palestinian declaration of independence in November 1988, Yasir Arafat was riding a wave of international support. Within two weeks, over sixty countries recognized the State of Palestine, and others expressed support for the principle of creating such a state. The United States was not in either group. To the contrary, Arafat's request for a visa from the United States so that he could address the United Nations was rejected, despite the U.S. host country agreement with the UN to allow free access to anyone invited to the United Nations on official business. In an unprecedented action, the United Nations then voted to move the entire General Assembly to Geneva, Switzerland, so that Arafat could speak during a special session on the Question of Palestine. A total of 154 countries supported the resolution, with only the United States and Israel voting against it. Great Britain abstained.

Meanwhile, Arafat flew to Stockholm, Sweden, where he met with a delegation of five prominent U.S. Jews on 6–7 December. At the end of their two-day meeting, Arafat and the delegation issued a joint declaration that included reference to the PNC's call for an international conference to be held on the basis of UN Resolutions 242 and 338. It also said that the PNC had "accepted the existence of Israel as a state in the region" and had "declared its rejection and condemnation of terrorism in all its forms." Much of the international community praised the Stockholm Declaration. But the U.S. government gave it a cool response, making it clear that Arafat would have to be more explicit in order to gain U.S. recognition.

Arafat's speech to the United Nations on 13 December was carefully crafted. It had to balance the demands of the United States against Arafat's need not to alienate the more radical groups within the PNC (which were already skeptical of elements in the political document from the Algiers PNC meeting, and which were concerned that Arafat had gone beyond his mandate with the Stockholm Declaration). Arafat again stated that the PNC rejected "terrorism in all its forms, including state terrorism" and added, "The PLO will seek a comprehensive settlement among the parties concerned in the Arab-Israeli conflict, including the state of Palestine, Israel, and other neighbors within the framework of the international conference for peace in the Middle East on the basis of Resolutions 242 and 338 and so as to guarantee equality and the balance of interests, especially our people's rights in freedom, national independence, and respect the right to exist in peace and security for all."[18]

When the speech ended, many were convinced Arafat had satisfied the U.S. requirements, but Secretary of State Shultz, speaking for the United States, said this had not yet occurred. U.S. allies quietly told the United States that it would damage peace prospects and look foolish in the eyes of the international community if it continued to deny recognition of the PLO despite Arafat's recent statements. Behind-the-scenes messages were also sent to Arafat indicating he needed to be still more explicit in his language regarding Israel and the renunciation of terrorism. By this time Arafat had gone too far to turn back without gaining some political advantage for his concessions. He decided to hold a press conference on 14 December and make one further attempt:

> In my speech yesterday, it was clear that we mean our people's rights to freedom and national independence, according to Resolution 181, and the right of all parties concerned in the Middle East conflict to exist in peace and security, and, as I have mentioned, including the state of Palestine, Israel and other neighbors, according to the Resolutions 242 and 338. As for terrorism, I renounced it yesterday in no uncertain terms, and yet I repeat for the record that we totally and absolutely renounce all forms of terrorism, including individual, group and state terrorism.[19]

Late in the afternoon of 14 December 1988, Shultz announced that Arafat had met the long-standing U.S. conditions for negotiation and that the United States and the PLO would begin discussions immediately. On 16 December the first round of talks began in Tunis.

By making the decision to open a dialogue with the PLO at the very end of Reagan's term in office, Shultz handed the incoming Bush administration a fait accompli. It would have been difficult for the incoming secretary of state, James Baker, to make such a dramatic move early in the Bush presidency, whereas the political cost of maintaining an existing dialogue was much less. According to a Gallup poll conducted in October 1989, a majority of U.S. citizens supported the U.S.-PLO dialogue. When asked "Do you think the U.S. government should continue the talks [with PLO leaders] at the present level, expand the talks to include higher-level PLO leaders, or end talks with the PLO?" 26 percent thought the talks should remain at the present level, and a plurality of 37 percent believed the talks should be expanded. Only 17 percent believed the talks should be ended; 20 percent said they were not sure. These responses are particularly interesting given that a mere 12 percent of those polled said that in the Israeli-Palestinian conflict they sympathized more with the Palestinians than with Israel.[20]

In Congress, however, support for the dialogue was tenuous. Under pressure from U.S. legislators, the Bush administration suspended talks with the PLO on 20 June 1990, three weeks after an unsuccessful attack on an Israeli beach by members of the tiny Palestine Liberation Front. The talks remained on hold for more than three years. Israel praised the U.S. decision. For Palestinians, already embittered by the U.S. veto on 31 May of a UN Security Council resolution calling for a commission to investigate Israel's policies vis-à-vis the Palestinians and provide recommendations to ensure their safety, it was another sign that the U.S. held Palestinians and Israelis to different standards.

There were few concrete results from the initial year and a half of U.S.-PLO discussions, although many analysts believed that their occurrence was itself a significant development in U.S.-Palestinian relations. In its first year, the Bush administration did not view the Israeli-Palestinian conflict as a matter of great urgency; by the middle of 1990, however, the Middle East had moved into a prominent position on the U.S. agenda. The Iraqi invasion of Kuwait in August diverted the United States for the next seven months, but once Iraq had been defeated, Israeli-Palestinian relations became the focus of sustained U.S. attention. Throughout this period, the United States continued to reject the idea of an independent Palestinian state in favor of a Palestinian-Jordanian federation (although Hussein's disengagement from the West Bank in 1988 had put that option on hold and left the United States without a clear policy alternative).

Soviet Immigrants, Israeli Settlements, and U.S. Loan Guarantees

Since at least the mid-1970s, there has been friction between the United States and Israel over the establishment of Jewish communities in the Occupied Territories. This became more pronounced during the Bush administration as Israel embarked on a massive expansion of its settlement program. In January 1990 Israeli Prime Minister Shamir indicated that an anticipated influx of Jews from the Soviet Union provided a new justification for Israel to maintain permanent control of the West Bank and Gaza Strip. Shamir argued that a "big Israel" was necessary to accommodate the new immigrants, approximately 10 percent of whom have chosen to settle in East Jerusalem and the rest of the Occupied Territories. Shamir's comments caused alarm in the Arab world and internationally, particularly when he later added that the Israeli government was unwilling to restrict immigrants from settling in any area controlled by Israel.

The United States challenged this assessment, and on 1 March, Secretary of State Baker announced that Israel must cease the growth in new and existing Jewish settlements before the United States would consider an Israeli request for $400 million in loan guarantees that would allow Israel to borrow money at a favorable rate despite its poor credit rating. Without such a halt in settlement activity, Baker argued, there was no way to assure that the guaranteed funds did not end up indirectly subsidizing housing in the Occupied Territories. After extensive debate, the U.S. Congress passed the necessary legislation to guarantee the $400 million in housing loans on 25 May 1990, but the State Department initially refused to provide the loan guarantees until it received clear assurances that no Jewish immigrants would settle in any of the Occupied Territories. The United States finally granted the loan guarantees in February 1991, without Israel's promise.

Throughout the early 1990s, emigration to Israel from the former Soviet Union and its successor states continued, with an estimated 450,000 people arriving between December 1989 (when Soviet emigration policy changed) and the end of 1993.[21] From Israel's perspective, this latest *aliyah* is an important step toward ingathering the whole of the Jewish people. The educational level and professional qualifications of the new citizens are high, and their presence will eventually strengthen the Israeli economy; however, the rapid influx strained a system already burdened with heavy social welfare expenditures, inflation, rising poverty and unemployment, and the cost of maintaining the military occupation. Israeli leaders feared that the difficulties newcomers experienced in finding jobs and housing might result in a decline in immigration. Therefore, during the Gulf War, Israeli leaders indicated that they would soon request more substantial loan guarantees from the United States.

Israel's position was that because of past U.S. support for the immigration of Soviet Jews, the United States should view the loan guarantees as a form of humanitarian assistance and should not link them to Israeli foreign or domestic policies. The United States disagreed. Baker was particularly upset because he believed the continuing Israeli settlement boom interfered with his attempts to gain agreement for an Arab-Israeli peace conference. In testimony before the U.S. House Appropriations Foreign Operations Subcommittee, Baker commented: "Nothing has made my job of trying to find Arab and Palestinian partners for [peace negotiations with] Israel more difficult than being greeted by a new settlement every time I arrive. I don't think there is any bigger obstacle to peace than the settlement activity that continues not only unabated but at an enhanced pace."[22] Bush, too, was blunt. When some members of Congress criticized Baker's comments, Bush backed him up: "Secretary Baker was speaking for this Administration and I strongly support what he said and what he is trying to do. Our policy is well known, and it would make a big contribution to peace if these settlements would stop."[23]

Shamir discounted these remarks and insisted that development would continue in all the areas controlled by Israel. He also disagreed with the U.S. contention that the settlements were an obstacle to peace and appeared convinced that the United States would not withhold the requested assistance. Shamir's optimism proved misplaced. When Israel officially requested the $10 billion in loan guarantees at the beginning of September 1991, the Bush administration asked Congress to delay discussion of the issue for 120 days so it would not be dealt with until after the Madrid peace conference. Bush also indicated that before the United States would grant the loan guarantees, he wanted Israel's pledge that it would halt further settlements, a position supported by 86 percent of the U.S. public.[24] The result was a nasty series of exchanges between U.S. and Israeli leaders, including an accusation of anti-Semitism against Bush by one Israeli Cabinet member that other Israeli leaders promptly disavowed.

Some members of Congress expressed dismay over the linkage of U.S. assistance to a change in Israel's settlement policy but ultimately concluded they lacked the votes to overturn the promised presidential veto of any loan guarantee legislation passed in the fall. In the months that followed, the American-Israel Public Affairs Committee (AIPAC) and other U.S. supporters of Israel lobbied hard for the loan guarantees. They proposed a variety of plans that would reduce the loan guarantees by the amount Israel spent on settlements or would allow Israel to complete existing construction as long as no new settlements were started. Ultimately, however, none of the compromises offered was acceptable to Israel, and the United States did not grant the loan guarantees while Shamir remained in power. Bush's strong stand was the first time since the 1950s that a U.S. president had used economic pressure against Israel. It was also the first time a president explicitly stated that unless Israel halted settlements in the Occupied Territories, the United States would limit its economic assistance.

Since their confrontation, the political fortunes of both Bush and Shamir have shifted, leading to a new configuration of key leaders in the United States and Israel. Shamir was the first to lose power, when the Labor party scored a victory in the June 1992 Israeli elections. The United States was enthusiastic about this outcome and pleased that the new prime minister was Yitzhak Rabin. Rabin's attitude toward the settlers is pragmatic rather than ideological and reflects most of all his desire to improve the weak Israeli economy. He has said, for example, that he wants to reorder national priorities so that the government serves primarily "those 3,900,000 of Israel's 4,000,000 Jews who do not live in the territories."[25]

To obtain the U.S. loan guarantees, Rabin agreed to a partial freeze on new settlements. Of more than 15,000 housing units previously approved for construction in the West Bank, work was halted on approximately 7,000 (primarily units still in the planning stage). The freeze did not apply, however, to what the Israeli government labeled "security settlements," communities located in the 51 percent of the West Bank that Israel considers essential to its security, including East Jerusalem and the Jordan Valley. Indeed, Israel accelerated land confiscation and settlement in East Jerusalem and elsewhere at the same time the settlement freeze was in force. After Rabin and Bush met in August 1992, Bush signaled Congress he was ready to reconsider the contentious loan guarantees. Congress passed the necessary legislation in October (with the stipulation that Israel can use these funds only within its pre-1967 borders), and on 5 January 1993 Bush signed a bill providing the first $2 billion.

Bill Clinton's inauguration as the forty-second president of the United States further modified the U.S.-Israeli relationship. Arguably in contrast to Bush's foreign policy team, several of Clinton's initial key appointments were strongly supportive of Israel: Defense Secretary Les Aspin, former AIPAC employee Martin Indyk as National Security Council Middle East adviser, Dennis Ross as coordinator of the Middle East peace talks, former U.S. ambassador to Israel Samuel Lewis as State Department director of public planning, and presidential adviser Richard Schifter. All were experienced in lobbying on Israel's behalf.

The Clinton administration's attitude toward Israeli settlements is illustrated by the way officials have dealt with restrictions on the loan guarantees. Consistent with the legislation passed the previous fall, the White House announced in October 1993 that it was deducting $437 million from the $2 billion allocated for Israel for fiscal year 1994 (which began on 1 October 1993) to reflect money Israel spent on settlement activity in the Occupied Territories during FY 1993. Shortly thereafter, Clinton indicated he hoped to reinstate the $437 million but did not want to raise the issue until

Congress had passed the FY 1994 foreign aid bill with its $3 billion in direct military and economic assistance for Israel. Clinton's position was that the Oslo Accords modified the context in which Israeli settlements occurred and invalidated the need for the earlier restrictions.

The intensity of the initial disagreement in 1991 over the loan guarantees raised the question of future Israeli-U.S. relations in a post–cold war era, an issue not fully resolved by the Clinton administration's pro-Israel stance. This is perhaps ironic as it comes at a time when Israel has gained a new measure of acceptance in the international community. In December 1991, the United States spearheaded a successful drive to supersede the 1975 "Zionism is racism" resolution in the United Nations, and in 1993 the Israeli delegation to the UN was seated without the traditional protest from the Arab states. The negotiations that followed the 1991 Madrid conference and the 1993 Oslo Accords further legitimized Israel for many countries, and during the early 1990s more than forty countries, including China, Russia, and India, established or renewed diplomatic relations with that state.

Yet the same shifts in the international environment that led many countries to change their attitude toward Israel may also decrease Israel's importance to the United States. Strong U.S. support for Israel in recent decades has been due, at least in part, to Israel's role as a counter to Soviet influence in the Middle East. Now that the Soviet Union no longer exists and communism has collapsed in Eastern Europe, the strategic concerns of the United States have turned elsewhere. Furthermore, as the coalition against Iraq demonstrated, in the "new world order" the United States might find the political cooperation of conservative Arab states more useful than the purely military power of Israel. In response to such arguments, Israeli leaders point out that the Middle East remains unstable and suggest that Israel is still a critical strategic asset to the United States. It is quite likely Israel and the United States will remain allies in the coming years; whether their ties remain as close as in the past remains to be seen.

SOVIET/RUSSIAN FOREIGN POLICY

For most of the twentieth century, the Soviet Union was not a major player in the Palestinian-Israeli conflict—at least not when compared with the United States. This is in some ways surprising, given its geographic location, bordering on Turkey and Iran; its large Islamic population concentrated in its southern republics; and its status as a superpower in the international arena since the end of World War II. The Western European states, however, had already staked out a clear claim through their colonial ties, and the United States had identified the Middle East as a region in which it had—and was prepared to defend—significant economic, political, and strategic interests. Soviet leaders realized they would have to work around these relationships and do so in a way that did not directly challenge the militarily superior United States. They did so primarily by focusing on low-risk opportunities and by continually pressing for the inclusion of the Soviet Union in peace initiatives and decisionmaking activities regarding the region. The success of this strategy was mixed.

The Soviet Union recognized Israel immediately after its declaration of independence in 1948, and for the next nineteen years the Soviet Union maintained an active diplomatic mission in Tel Aviv. From the beginning, there were multiple linkages between the two states. Weapons from Soviet allies were used by the Zionists in the Palestine War; many of the first leaders of Israel were from the Soviet Union or Poland; and there were many elements of socialist ideology in the mainstream Zionist movement. In fact, a principal concern of the U.S. government in 1948 was that Israel would immediately form an alliance with the Soviet Union when it declared independence.

After the death of Stalin in 1953 and the creation of the U.S.-sponsored Baghdad Pact, the Soviet Union began to forge political, economic, and military links with a variety of Arab countries. These states included Egypt after the 1952 coup that toppled the monarchy and brought Nasser to power; Iraq after the 1958 coup that overthrew the Hashemite regime; Algeria after its independence in 1962; Syria in the 1960s; PDR Yemen after 1967; and Libya after Muammar Qaddafi came to power in 1969. In dealing with the Arab countries, Soviet leaders Nikita Khrushchev (1953–1964) and Leonid Brezhnev (1964–1982) emphasized the themes of peaceful coexistence, mutual respect, and noninterference in internal affairs. These were appealing concepts to countries that had recently been under the control of European states. The Soviet Union also pursued a vigorous trade-and-aid policy toward the Arab states, providing them with low-interest loans and technical assistance. At least initially, Soviet policy was to support any government that followed an anti-Western foreign policy. A country did not need to become pro-Soviet, but it could not be allied with the West. This allowed the Arab countries a greater degree of political autonomy than the United States permitted and was an important factor in the Soviet Union's initial successes in the Middle East.

The Soviet position in the Arab world was enhanced by the June 1967 War. On 10 June the Soviet Union cut diplomatic ties with Israel and promised to assist the Arab states of the Levant if Israel refused to withdraw from the territories it conquered during the war. At the same time, the lack of a strong U.S. condemnation of Israel led to a deterioration in U.S.-Arab relations. Arab states were also angered at the continuing U.S. refusal to provide them with the same sophisticated weapons made available to Israel, Turkey, and Iran. Together, these factors pushed the Arab states into a greater dependence on the Soviet Union than might otherwise have developed.

Egypt was the most important Soviet ally in the Middle East during this period. Although Nasser was not a Marxist, the revolutionary rhetoric of the Soviet Union, its anti-imperialist foreign policy, and its willingness to provide Egypt with economic assistance and weapons—in contrast to the Western states—strengthened the connection. The Czech arms deal of September 1955 and the subsequent refusal of the United States to lend Egypt money for the Aswan Dam project in 1956 represented a watershed. From that point on, Nasser increasingly relied on the Soviet Union, and the Soviet Union in turn made Egypt the linchpin in its Middle East strategy. The Soviet Union joined the United States in supporting Egypt diplomatically against Israel during the 1956 Suez War, and it soon became Egypt's main weapons supplier and military adviser.

After Nasser's death in September 1970, Vice President Anwar Sadat became Egypt's second president. The Soviet choice to follow Nasser was Ali Sabri, who attempted to overthrow Sadat in May 1971. In light of Soviet support of the attempted coup, Sadat grew to distrust the Soviet Union, and he made it clear that the Soviets could no longer assume Egypt would remain an unquestioning client state. By 1972 relations between the two states were badly strained. Finally, under pressure from his own military forces, and with the encouragement of King Feisal of Saudi Arabia, Sadat ordered the expulsion from Egypt of approximately 20,000 Soviet military advisers and their dependents on 15 July 1972 and sent Egyptian military units to take control of Soviet bases and equipment.

This move was popular with the Egyptian people, who were not overly fond of the Soviet military presence, but it failed to bring about a change in U.S. policy toward Egypt or toward Israel, as Sadat had hoped. In retrospect, this appears to be an instance when the right hand of the U.S. government did not know what the left was doing, and vice versa. Saudi Defense Minister Prince Sultan had been consulting regularly with Assistant Secretary of State Joseph Sisco on Saudi efforts to move Egypt away from the Soviet Union. Yet National Security Adviser Kissinger expressed surprise when Sadat expelled the Soviet advisers. As a result, Kissinger did not come through with an appropriate gesture of appreciation in response to Sadat's action, leaving Sadat (and the Saudis) disappointed and puzzled.

The Soviets had invested heavily in Egypt and were reluctant to give up this important ally, so they continued to court Sadat. In particular, intermittent arms transfer negotiations continued between Cairo and Moscow, and the Soviet Union provided Egypt with a major airlift of weapons during the October 1973 War. In April 1974, however, Egypt announced that it would no longer rely exclusively on Soviet weapons, and on 14

March 1976 Sadat announced the abrogation of a 1971 Soviet-Egyptian Treaty of Friendship and Cooperation.

In the decade and a half following the split with Egypt, the Soviet Union was less involved in the Middle East and played only a minor role in the Israeli-Palestinian issue. It continued its patron-client relationship with Syria, Iraq, and PDR Yemen, and was nominally supportive of the PLO. It began to discover, however, that the Arab states felt the Soviet Union had little to offer them except military assistance and that this was insufficient for them to follow Soviet policy preferences when these conflicted with their own perceived interests. Syria proved a particularly independent-minded client, as the Soviet Union found when it unsuccessfully attempted to keep Syria from intervening in Lebanon in the mid-1970s. As its own economic problems worsened, the Soviet Union was forced to reduce the economic assistance it provided to the Arab states, further limiting its influence.

The Soviets tried to compensate for this decline in power through support of a number of international resolutions on the Israeli-Palestinian conflict. But with the exception of the joint Soviet-U.S. communiqué of 1 October 1977 calling for an international peace conference to deal with the conflict, the Soviet Union was not included in U.S. mediation activities after the October 1973 War, nor was it invited to participate in the Camp David meetings in 1978. The Soviet Union was critical of the resulting accords, which could have provided it with an opening to improve its relationship with Arab states. Any such prospects were damaged with the Soviet invasion of Afghanistan in December 1979.

Soviet policy began to take a new direction when Mikhail S. Gorbachev came to power in 1985. Almost immediately Gorbachev began to initiate contacts with moderate Arab states and with Israel. In August 1986, Soviet and Israeli diplomats met in Helsinki, Finland, to discuss the possible reestablishment of diplomatic relations—the first formal diplomatic contact since 1967. A year later, a Soviet consular delegation traveled to Israel to continue the dialogue. Gorbachev also offered to participate in joint security arrangements for the Middle East, called for an international peace conference on the Israeli-Palestinian issue, worked to bring about a reconciliation between Arafat and Syrian leader Assad, and played an important role in the reunification of various factions within the PLO prior to the 1988 PNC meeting.

In the past, the Soviet Union had frequently expressed its desire to have a role in the Middle East, motivated, as was the United States, primarily by superpower competition. In contrast, by the late 1980s, the Soviet Union appeared to be searching for positive, collaborative contributions it could make to increase stability in the region. The comments of Soviet Foreign Minister Eduard A. Shevardnadze after a ten-day Middle

East tour in February 1989 clearly reflected this shift: "The policy of [the United States and the Soviet Union] pushing each other out of the region has to be abandoned in favor of constructive cooperation for the sake of peace and tranquillity in the Middle East."[26] During his trip, the first to the region by a Soviet foreign minister in fifteen years, Shevardnadze tried to persuade Israel to negotiate with the PLO under the auspices of the UN Security Council, offered to act as a guarantor of Israeli national security after the conclusion of a peace agreement with the Palestinians, indicated Soviet terms for renewing diplomatic ties with Israel, agreed to increase political and military consultations with Syria, even as it was reducing its economic commitment to that state, and called for a ban on all chemical and nuclear weapons in the region.

In the autumn of 1989, change began sweeping across Eastern Europe. The Berlin Wall that had dramatically symbolized the division between East and West was dismantled, and the two Germanys were reunited. Czechoslovakia, Romania, Poland, and Hungary held free elections; civil war broke out in Yugoslavia. The collapse of the Soviet Union in 1990–1991 dramatically signaled the end of the cold war and the beginning of a radical transformation of the international system. At present, Russia and the Soviet successor states are preoccupied with internal problems and are not in a position to influence directly the course of Arab-Israeli or Israeli-Palestinian relations. However, the possibility of future U.S.-Russian cooperation in the region may not be as far-fetched as it first appears. Since World War II the United States has wanted to limit Soviet influence, which was perceived as a destabilizing force that would jeopardize the U.S. political and military position and put the region's oil resources at risk. If the United States is convinced that Russia shares its interest in regional stability, this reduces the threat to other U.S. goals.

An improved East-West political climate and serious economic difficulties in Russia and the Soviet successor states have led to a radical reduction in financial support for Syria, Libya, Iraq, and other traditional Arab opponents of Israel. This may provide justification for a similar decrease in U.S. financial support of Israel, which has for a number of years been the largest recipient of U.S. military and economic assistance. Official U.S. aid to Israel through the Foreign Military Sales Financing Program, the Economic Support Fund, and other aid programs currently totals more than $3 billion a year. The United States wants to provide increased foreign aid to Eastern Europe and Central America to encourage and support the political and economic transformations occurring in those areas. It has also committed itself to assist Palestinian economic development. Those resources have to come from somewhere; one possibility is to decrease the funds given to other major U.S. aid recipients, including Israel. This idea, which received a mixed reception, was first proposed by Senate Minority

Leader Robert Dole in January 1990. Three years later, newly appointed U.S. ambassador to Israel William Harrop made a similar comment, indicating it might be difficult for the United States to continue to provide Israel with such a high level of foreign aid. (Harrop was promptly dismissed from his post.) Although President Clinton has promised to maintain Israel's share of the foreign aid budget, he may find this commitment difficult to keep.

THE INTERNATIONAL COMMUNITY

The full implications of this global restructuring remain to be seen. One arena in which the changes may be significant is in the United Nations, where for most of the post–World War II period the United States and the Soviet Union were at loggerheads over a variety of issues, including the Palestinian-Israeli conflict. Although the Soviet Union was quick to recognize Israel's declaration of independence, since the late 1950s the Soviet Union has been closely identified with the Arab opponents to Israel. At the same time, after the June 1967 War the United States became a much stronger and more vocal supporter of the Jewish state. Given these alliances, the conflict between Israel and the Arabs came to take on cold war garb and to be discussed in cold war rhetoric, although in its earliest form (Zionists versus Palestinians) it predated the East-West split and had a reality quite separate from the U.S.-Soviet confrontation. Thus, there is a possibility that the improvement in U.S.-Russian relations could result in some kind of cooperation for dealing with the conflict through the United Nations.

For this to occur, Russia will need to encourage the Third World states toward greater moderation and acceptance of Israel, even as the PNC has accepted Israel. This has begun to occur. At the same time, the United States will have to move closer to the international consensus regarding Palestinian self-determination and the future status of the West Bank and Gaza Strip if it is to take a leadership role in resolving the conflict. During much of the past three decades, the United States has been isolated internationally on this issue because of its seemingly automatic justification of virtually any action Israel takes. In the early years of the United Nations, the Soviet Union repeatedly used its veto to block Security Council resolutions on a variety of topics, whereas the United States refrained from doing so until 1970 (when it prevented passage of a resolution critical of southern Rhodesia). Between September 1972 and May 1990, however, the United States used its veto power twenty-nine times to protect Israel from criticism by the Security Council. The Reagan administration used the U.S. veto on behalf of Israel on eighteen occasions, five times in 1988 alone. Although President Bush broke this pattern in the second half of his administration, President Clinton appears likely to follow in Reagan's footsteps in this respect.

The United Nations and the Question of Palestine

Virtually from its establishment in 1945, the United Nations has been dealing with the conflict over Palestine. The UN

- □ voted in 1947 to partition Palestine and create a Jewish state in part of the territory
- □ created the United Nations Relief and Works Agency to take responsibility for the Palestinian refugees
- □ has maintained armed forces and military observer groups in the Levant since 1948
- □ sent mediators such as Count Folke Bernadotte, Ralph Bunche, and Gunnar V. Jarring to the region in the 1940s, 1950s, and 1960s
- □ affirmed the right of "the people of Palestine [to] self determination" in 1969
- □ in 1975 declared that Zionism is a form of racism, a resolution repealed in 1991
- □ has passed dozens of General Assembly and Security Council resolutions calling for cease-fires, condemning aggressive actions by each of the parties, and suggesting approaches for conflict resolution

More generally, Article 2 of the Charter of the United Nations states that "all members shall settle their international disputes by peaceful means in such a manner that international peace and security, and justice, are not endangered" and that they "shall refrain in their international relations from the threat or use of force against the territorial integrity or political independence of any state, or in any other manner inconsistent with the purposes of the United Nations." The ongoing conflict among Israel, the Palestinians, and the Arab states is clearly in contradiction with both the spirit and the letter of this part of the charter to which all members must agree when they join the international body. In addition, the Israeli occupation of lands captured in the June 1967 War is widely argued to violate elements of the 1948 United Nations Universal Declaration of Human Rights:

> *Article 2.* Everyone is entitled to all the rights and freedoms set forth in this Declaration, without distinction of any kind, such as race, colour, sex, language, religion, political or other opinion, national or social origin, property, birth or other status. ...
>
> *Article 9.* No one shall be subjected to arbitrary arrest, detention or exile.

Article 10. Everyone is entitled to full equality to a fair and public hearing by an independent and impartial tribunal, in the determination of his rights and obligations and of any criminal charge against him.

Article 11.-1. Everyone charged with a penal offense has the right to be presumed innocent until proved guilty according to law in a public trial at which he has had all the guarantees necessary for his defense. ...

Article 13.-1. Everyone has the right to freedom of movement and residence within the borders of each state.

2. Everyone has the right to leave any country, including his own, and to return to his country. ...

Article 19. Everyone has the right to freedom of opinion and expression; this right includes freedom to hold opinions without interference and to seek, receive and impart information and ideas through any media and regardless of frontiers.

Article 20. Everyone has the right to freedom of peaceful assembly and association.

Finally, UN peacekeeping forces have been employed in the conflict with greater frequency, and for longer duration, than anywhere else in the world. In light of all these factors, it is not surprising that the United Nations as an international organization believes it has a stake in the just and peaceful resolution of the Israeli-Palestinian issue.

The policies of the United Nations have not always been consistent. Over the years, the composition of the United Nations has changed, and its political sympathies have reflected this. In 1945 the UN had barely fifty members. Nearly all were either European countries, members of the British Commonwealth, or states from the Americas. The United States was the obvious leader in the UN, as it was elsewhere in the world. Fifty years after the founding of the United Nations, the dominance of the United States and its allies has declined, and the new African, Arab, and Asian states hold the majority of seats in the General Assembly. Their agenda is focused on issues relevant to their own needs and experiences, just as the objectives of the founding states had reflected an earlier and different set of concerns.

Many of the states that helped form the United Nations were strongly committed to the establishment of a Jewish state in Palestine, often to support their own political objectives, and Israel maintained close ties to these early allies. In contrast, more than half of the UN members in 1994 were not even independent when Israel was created. Their perception of the Jewish state is influenced by their own colonial past, and for many years they viewed Israel more as a manifestation of European imperialism than as an expression of nationalism similar to their own aspirations for autonomous identity. The image of Israel among African states in particular was damaged by the Israeli occupation of Egyptian territory as a result of that war. Israel's political, economic, and military links with South Africa have also adversely affected its status among newly independent states. This shift in the balance of power in the United Nations from the American and European countries to the Afro-Asian bloc in part explains why UN resolutions on the Arab-Israeli and Israeli-Palestinian conflicts became increasingly critical of Israel and supportive of the Palestinians in the 1970s and 1980s.

With the end of the cold war and the ascendance of the United States as the only superpower, the United Nations began to return to a less hostile position toward Israel. This is seen most clearly by the General Assembly revocation of its 1975 condemnation of Zionism as a form of racism. The vote, in December 1991, was lopsided—111 countries voted in favor of the motion, and only 25 voted against. Thirty states, including a number of Arab countries, abstained or were not present for the vote. The United States and Israel lobbied hard for this resolution, the importance of which was primarily symbolic.

The European Community

In recent years, the European countries, like the Third World, have been more critical of Israel and more supportive of the Palestinians than has the United States. After the October 1973 War, the European states (and Japan) were among those who called for Israel's withdrawal to its 1967 borders; in June 1977, leaders of the European Community issued a statement calling for a peace settlement based on UN Resolution 242 and the recognition of the "legitimate right of the Palestinian people to its national identity" in the form of a "homeland."

In June 1980 the European states announced the Venice Declaration, which represented a policy that had been evolving over a period of ten years. In this document, the (then) nine-member group proclaimed its support for the right of Israel to exist within secure, recognized, and guaranteed borders, as well as its support of the legitimate rights of the Palestinian people and its belief that the PLO "will have to be associated with the negotiations" on any peace agreement. It criticized the Israeli occupation of the Golan Heights, West Bank, and Gaza Strip, and said that the Israeli settlements in those areas were illegal under international law.

Since the Venice Declaration, the European states have grown increasingly outspoken in their criticisms of Israeli policy toward the Palestinians. They voted in favor of the UN resolution condemning Israel's annexation of the Golan Heights in December 1981, and were quite critical of the 1982 Israeli invasion of Lebanon. In October 1986 the foreign ministers of the EC decided to grant direct financial assistance to the West Bank and Gaza Strip and agreed to assure preferential access to Palestinian industrial and agricultural products. It took over a year to work out a compromise with Israel on the export of Palestinian agricultural products to Europe, by which point the *intifada* had begun; nonetheless, the statement of intent by the European states was clear.

The European response to the declaration of the State of Palestine in November 1988 and the subsequent policy statements by Arafat was also far more supportive and warm than was the U.S. reaction. Although the EC as a body stopped short of formally recognizing the new state, several individual countries expressed strong support for the principle of such a state, and a number of countries on the European periphery, such as Malta, Cyprus, and Yugoslavia, formally extended diplomatic recognition to Palestine. Subsequent statements reiterated the EC's position that a resolution to the Israeli-Palestinian conflict must be balanced between security requirements and the rights of self-determination for both parties. In addition, in the late 1980s and early 1990s, EC member states hosted official visits by Arafat, an action the United States did not take until September 1993 (and even then only in the context of the signing of the Oslo Accords). At the same time, EC policy has not been completely one-sided; for instance, it praised Israel for its restraint during the Gulf War and lifted economic restrictions imposed earlier in response to Israeli human rights violations.

The key point is that the European states are pursuing their own policy preferences vis-à-vis the Palestinian-Israeli conflict rather than following the lead of the United States as they once did. Indeed, the EC's political independence was an important factor in explaining Norway's role in the secret negotiations that led to the 1993 Oslo Accords. The increasing economic and political integration of the European states as a result of the Maastricht Treaty enhances the prospect that they will present a strong, coherent, and unified foreign policy alternative to the United States.

Militarization of the Middle East

One issue of great concern to the international community is the high level of militarization in the Middle East. Among Third World states, the Middle East is the primary arms-importing area. In the 1980s, between 27 and 41 percent of all conventional weapons transferred from one country to another in a given year went to Israel, Iran, or one of the Arab states. For the five-year period 1987–1991, just six Middle East countries—Egypt, Iran, Iraq, Saudi Arabia, Syria, and Israel—accounted for more than 30 percent of the world's weapons trade.[27] Historically, the United States and the Soviet Union (now Russia) have been the region's principal suppliers; however, France, Britain, and China also provide a significant percentage.

Although imports remain a major source of sophisticated weapons, most Middle Eastern countries now have a modest conventional arms enterprise. Several countries also have developed a chemical, biological, or nuclear weapons industry. Israel, for instance, is widely acknowledged to have become a nuclear power in the late 1960s and now has a stockpile of 100–200 nuclear weapons. Iraq is one of several states in the region to have produced chemical weapons; it was in the process of developing a nuclear weapons capability before its defeat in the 1990–1991 Gulf War and the subsequent UN-mandated destruction of all of its weapons of mass destruction.

There are a number of explanations for this general situation, including a desire for the international prestige associated with major weapons systems and high oil revenues in the 1970s and early 1980s that allowed countries such as Saudi Arabia to purchase more weapons than would normally be possible. But one of the most significant factors is the multitude of antagonistic relationships within the region, including the Israeli-Palestinian conflict: Each state believes that it needs the weapons it imports or produces domestically in order to be safe in an insecure environment.

Are these states correct? There is some evidence to suggest that their efforts may be counterproductive and that the continual arms acquisitions may at some point result in a decrease rather than an increase in security. The reason has to do with a concept developed by John Herz in 1950 called the **security dilemma.** The basic problem Herz identified is this: In an uncertain environment, particularly one where there is little trust among actors, how can a state provide for its own legitimate security needs without appearing to threaten the legitimate security needs of its opponents? As Actor A increases its military capabilities, purely for defensive purposes it argues, it may well seem to Actor B that Actor A is planning an aggressive move against Actor B. Thus, Actor B concludes it must obtain additional weapons to protect itself against Actor A. "Since none can ever feel entirely secure in such a world of competing units," Herz writes, "power competition ensues, and the vicious circle of security and power accumulation is on."[28] Before either actor realizes it, they are involved in an arms race unlikely to enhance the security of either party.

What are the problems with such an arms race? First, the economic costs are great. Middle East countries that spent an average of at least 15 percent of their gross domestic product on military expenditures between 1972 and 1988 include Iraq, Israel, Jordan, Oman, and the People's Democratic Republic of Yemen (now part of the Republic of Yemen), with Egypt and Syria close behind them.[29] These resources could otherwise have been spent providing for the basic needs of the population or increasing economic development. Furthermore, the high concentration of domestic revenues spent on the military may increase the likelihood that the military will play a more significant role in the political affairs of the country than would otherwise be the case. Third, as Kuwait discovered in August

1990, high military expenditures do not by themselves bring security and may in fact lead to an inappropriate sense of complacency.

Finally, there is widespread concern that this great concentration of weapons, when combined with the high level of tension that has characterized the Middle East region, could result in an escalating war of such magnitude that in the end little would be left of the Levant region. If weapons by themselves do not create a war, they certainly can affect the intensity with which it is fought. This was the rationale for the 1950 Tripartite Agreement among the United States, France, and Great Britain and was behind a U.S. initiative following the Gulf War to limit weapons proliferation and arms sales. As Yahya Sadowski explains:

> In May 1991, President Bush called for a regional freeze in the acquisition, production and testing of surface-to-surface missiles. He advocated a ban on the production of plutonium or any other material that could be used as fissile material for nuclear weapons. He reiterated an earlier call for an end to the production of chemical and biological weapons. Finally, he called for negotiations among the major arms suppliers.[30]

Unfortunately, although few countries rejected Bush's initiative outright, none of the major suppliers, including the United States, acted on it either.

Another issue is the role of Middle East states in exporting weapons abroad. In this regard, most attention has focused on Israel, which has developed one of the largest arms export industries outside of the NATO countries. After the October 1973 War, Israel made a deliberate decision to expand its arms industry. Since then, Israel has not only moved toward sufficiency in certain categories of armaments but has also become a major supplier of high-technology weaponry to numerous Third World states, including El Salvador, Paraguay, Chile, Argentina, Ecuador, Guatemala, and Nicaragua under the Somoza regime. These arms sales help Israel cover the costs of its domestic military industry, which otherwise would be prohibitively high despite U.S. financial assistance. In addition, both advocates and critics of Israel's arms transfer program point out that Israel frequently acts as the United States' gendarme and surrogate around the world by providing weapons to U.S. client states for which open U.S. support and arms sales would be politically awkward for the United States or the recipient country. Israel's central role in the Iran-Contra arms deal gained international attention in 1987; it was, however, simply the best publicized of numerous cases in which Israel and the United States collaborated to supply weapons to third parties.

More recently, South Africa acknowledged it had a long-term military arrangement with Israel. Israel received enriched uranium and access to a long-range missile test site in South Africa in exchange for which Israel provided South Africa with advanced missile and nuclear weapons technology that allowed South Africa to build six nuclear bombs. Even before this story broke, the close military ties between Israel and South Africa had been a source of embarrassment for the United States. Certain aspects of the relationship may also violate U.S. law, if Israel provided South Africa with any technology that was originally received from the United States or was developed with U.S. funds.

Political Terrorism

Leon Klinghoffer, a U.S. citizen and a Jew, was murdered when the Italian cruise liner *Achille Lauro* on which he was traveling was hijacked by four Palestinians in October 1985. In the aftermath of the hijacking, the U.S. media covered his death in great detail. Hundreds of lines of newsprint and many minutes on television and radio news programs were devoted to describing the hijacking, the precise events that occurred just before Klinghoffer was thrown overboard into the Mediterranean, the grief of his family, and the history of Klinghoffer's life. There were calls for massive retaliation against Palestinians in response to this terrorist attack.

The same week, Alex Odeh, a U.S. citizen of Palestinian descent who was the West Coast director of the American-Arab Anti-Discrimination Committee, was murdered by a bomb explosion when he opened the door to his office in southern California. The Federal Bureau of Investigation issued a statement saying, "We have attributed the bombing to the Jewish Defense League." Odeh apparently was killed as punishment for a television interview he had given the night before in which he condemned the *Achille Lauro* hijacking and terrorism in general but defended Yasir Arafat, saying that the PLO had not been involved in the action. Odeh's death was virtually ignored by the national media, even though Odeh was a gentle man known for his work for peace. Few talked of terrorism, and there were no calls for retaliation.

The words "terrorism" and "terrorist" provoke strong emotions in almost everyone. Yet when asked to explain what makes something a terrorist act, many people fall back on an argument akin to saying, "I can't define it but I know it when I see it." When pushed, such people often end up classifying as terrorism any violent act against "us" by "them"— hardly a rigorous or scholarly approach. In light of this, it is not surprising that the phrase "one person's terrorist is another person's freedom fighter" has gained popularity in some circles. But this characterization, which implies that labeling an act as terrorism is nothing more than a normative judgment, is also problematic.

The first step out of this definitional morass is to separate the definition of terrorism from an ethical judgment about whether, and if so under what circumstances, terrorism is justified. George Lopez and Michael

Stohl, who have written a number of works on political terrorism, have defined it as "the purposeful act or threat of violence to create fear and/or compliant behavior in a victim and/or audience of the act or threat."[31] This definition makes it clear that political terrorism is a form of intimidation or coercion used deliberately and consciously and must be understood by its motivations as well as its violent nature. Political terrorism is not random violence, although one of its attributes is that it can occur at any time and in any place; it is violence with a specific goal that transcends the harm or threat of harm done to the individual or group against which it is most immediately directed. Political terrorism is often a tool of the militarily very strong (such as Stalin's reign of terror in the Soviet Union) or the militarily very weak (such as the use of terror by the Algerians against the French civilian population during the Algerian war of independence). When used by a state, terrorism can occur through economic coercion, the legal system, or the police or military. When used by nonstate groups, terrorism may involve murder, physical or psychological harm short of murder, or destruction of property.

This way of defining terrorism avoids making moral judgments about the appropriateness of terrorist tactics as a political or military tool a part of the definition of the word. Some people believe that terrorism is unacceptable under any circumstances and that it puts the person who engages in such acts completely beyond what is considered civilized behavior. Others argue that terrorism is one of many forms of violence and that a group lacking access to what is often labeled legitimate power (that is, the power of the state) has the right to use other tools available to it in order to promote its cause. Regardless of which of these two views one holds, it should be clear that not all violence done by a state or group of which one disapproves is terrorism, nor does approval for the goals of a state or group mean that nothing they do deserves to be labeled terrorism. Opinions about the state or group need to be kept separate from judgments about the nature of their violent actions.

In the context of the Israeli-Palestinian issue, the word terrorism is used a great deal, often inappropriately or to describe the actions of one group only. Under the Stohl and Lopez definition given above, terrorist tactics were used by Zionists and Palestinians during the British mandate over Palestine and have been used on occasion since 1948 by Palestinians, by the Israeli government, and by Israeli civilians. When a combined force of Irgun and Stern Gang members massacred two-thirds of the residents of the small Palestinian village of Deir Yassin on 9 April 1948, despite the nonbelligerency agreement the village had signed with nearby Jewish villages, and then drove around other Palestinian villages warning residents that they too might be murdered if they did not leave, that was terrorism. When members of the PFLP hijacked four airplanes in September 1970 and blew up three of them after releasing the passengers in order to gain publicity for the Palestinian nationalist claims, that was terrorism. The hijackers had nothing against the people they took hostage—the act was directed to a wider audience. When Israel bombed PLO headquarters in Tunis on 1 October 1985, killing at least twelve Tunisians and sixty Palestinians, mostly civilians, that too was an act of terrorism, for its intent was not only to assassinate Yasir Arafat and retaliate for the killing of three Israelis in Cyprus but also to promote a sense of fear and intimidation among all Palestinians. The massacre by Israeli settler Baruch Goldstein of twenty-nine Palestinians praying at the Tomb of the Patriarchs in Hebron on 25 February 1994 fits the description of terrorism. So also do the April 1994 car bomb attacks in Afula and Hadera, claimed by Hamas, that killed more than a dozen Israeli civilians, including children. In short, none of the parties to the current conflict has a monopoly on the use of terror.

Second, not all terrorist actions done in the name of a group are authorized or endorsed by that group. Thus, without clear evidence or a claim of responsibility, it is not always possible to know whether a particular group can legitimately be held responsible for a specific terrorist act. Individuals may act completely on their own, hoping to gain attention for themselves or their cause, or possibly to receive anticipated praise from the group in whose name they performed their deed.

Finally, it is important to reiterate that not every action that results in death or other violence is terrorism, no matter how much we dislike the action. For example, when on 27 November 1987 a Palestinian on a hang glider landed in northern Israel and killed six Israeli soldiers before being killed himself, that was a military action directed against a military target. The goal of the operation was not intimidation against a broader group of people; the intent was to kill Israeli soldiers and that is what was accomplished. Similarly, when Israel attacked Egyptian airfields without warning in the opening hours of the June 1967 War it was not engaged in terrorism, but in a surprise attack comparable to Iraq's invasion of Iran in 1980. These acts can be judged either reprehensible or justifiable as a legitimate use of force, but they are not terrorism as it has been defined here. Admittedly, the line between terrorist actions and other forms of violence is often difficult to draw, particularly because any use of violence can serve as a tool of intimidation or as a warning to the opponent that they had best not cross the party using the violence. The key issue is the *primary* intent and audience.

CONCLUSION

The Israeli-Palestinian conflict is primarily an issue between these two ethno-nationalist communities; however, it is also situated within a larger set of regional and international concerns and cannot be viewed in isolation from them. Israeli-Palestinian hostility has directly or indirectly spawned half a dozen regional wars in the past five decades, threatened Western access to critical petroleum resources, provided a justification for increased militarization throughout the region, and led to the deaths of innocent civilians due to terrorism. It is not surprising, therefore, that the international community sees itself as having an important role in the process and outcome of any proposals to resolve the conflict, for it is affected by the current problems and will equally be affected by any solution. The final chapter will pull together these diverse strands in an examination of the future of the Israeli-Palestinian conflict, including a discussion of the Madrid conference and Oslo Accords. It will not indicate the specific form an eventual resolution of the conflict must take but will instead suggest the types of issues that negotiators will need to address to create a proposal acceptable to Palestinians, Israelis, the Arab states, the United States, Russia, the European countries, the United Nations, and other relevant actors.

FOUR

□ □ □

Conflict, Compromise, or Conciliation? Constructing the Future

The *intifada* stunned the world and shattered the illusion that the status quo in the West Bank and Gaza Strip could be maintained indefinitely. The question then became: What now? Under whose authority and under what conditions will the West Bank and the Gaza Strip be governed in the future? In examining the political dynamics in Israel, within the Palestinian national movement, and in the international community, it is clear that there have been and are today an assortment of opinions on this issue. Prior to 1948, the majority of Zionists desired a far larger territory than was allotted to them by the United Nations; for their part, the majority of Palestinians saw the Zionists as European colonialists and resisted any Zionist control of the region. The United Nations partition satisfied neither party. The Zionists, however, accepted the partition because they had nothing to lose and everything to gain by doing so. Control over some territory was more than they had prior to the partition, and they maintained the hope that the state could be further expanded in the future. The Palestinians and the Arab states rejected the partition, for they gained nothing and lost a great deal from the United Nations decision. These conflicting reactions have been portrayed as Zionist accommodation versus Arab intransigence, but in fact the difference in the benefits and losses to the two groups makes it clear why each would react in the way it did.

Over the years there have been dozens of proposals for how to resolve the continuing conflict over Palestine. They range from expelling the Palestinians and creating an exclusively Jewish state in all the land controlled by the ancient Hebrews to establishing a Palestinian state in the Mandate of Palestine and expelling all Zionists and their descendants who came to Palestine after the 1917 Balfour Declaration. Some Palestinians still advocate the "elimination of the Zionist presence" in Palestine; some Israelis

165

and U.S. Zionists continue to espouse the solution of exclusive Jewish control over an expanded State of Israel. Neither of these positions is realistic in the present political environment, however, no matter how desirable they may appear to their proponents. Israeli Jews and Palestinian Arabs alike will be in Israel/Palestine in the future, and any serious plans for conflict resolution need to take this into account.

Most proposals fall between these two models. Their nuances are significant and may ultimately determine the specific outcome of the conflict, but virtually all the proposals can be collapsed into several options. Israelis and Palestinians continue to debate all of the possibilities described here, although the 1993 Oslo Accords and 1994 Cairo Agreement make certain alternatives more likely than others. From the Israeli side, Israel can either withdraw from part or all of the West Bank and Gaza Strip, or it can attempt to maintain control over those territories. If Israel continues to occupy the territories it captured in 1967, it can either preserve the status quo of a military occupation over the Palestinian population, or it can annex the areas and formally incorporate them into Israel.

Increasingly, many Israeli Jews have come to believe there are significant obstacles to permanent Israeli control of the West Bank and Gaza Strip. Governing the Occupied Territories under military law and without annexation is no longer viable in the long term: It is expensive and it does not increase Israel's security. Furthermore, the continuing occupation puts great stress on Israeli society. In a few cases, Israeli military officers who fought honorably in past wars have refused to serve in the West Bank and Gaza Strip and have been willing to go to jail if necessary to support their position. More generally, debates over the future of the Occupied Territories are bitter and divisive, splitting families and damaging friendships.

If Israel formally annexes the West Bank and Gaza Strip, as it has already done with East Jerusalem and the Syrian Golan Heights (although the actions are not recognized by the international community), it has several further choices. First, it can grant citizenship rights to the Palestinians but continue to impose military law on the areas with a high concentration of Palestinian residents. This would be similar to the situation of Palestinians in Israel until 1966. It is unlikely that this action would gain international acceptance, however, nor can one imagine that the highly politicized *intifada* generation of Palestinians would set down their stones because they had the right to vote if little else had changed. Israel's policy toward its Palestinian minority population prior to 1966 succeeded in part because the number of Palestinians remaining in Israel after 1949 was small, the society was politically weak, and the eyes of the international community were not focused on their situation. None of these factors exists today.

Alternatively, Israel could lift military control of the West Bank and Gaza Strip and grant full civil and political rights to all Palestinians. Either of these two possibilities creates a dilemma for Zionists, however, euphemistically referred to as the demographic problem. As of the end of 1987, there were approximately 3.6 million Jews and nearly 2.2 million Christian and Muslim Palestinians in Israel, the West Bank, and the Gaza Strip. By the end of 1993, another half million Jews from the former Soviet Union had emigrated to Israel, increasing the numerical gap between Jews and Palestinians. Nonetheless, the differential birthrate of Jewish and Palestinian women means that by the first decades of the twenty-first century the Jewish and Palestinian populations within the boundaries of the Mandate of Palestine will be roughly equal.[1] The implications of this for the distinctly Jewish identity of Israel should be immediately clear.

Third, Israel could annex the West Bank and Gaza Strip but not grant citizenship to the Palestinian residents. This would be functionally equivalent to an apartheid system of government, in which one group rules over another and denies them basic civil and political rights on the basis of race, religion, or ethnicity. An apartheid system would do nothing to improve Israel's position in the world community. It would also be as expensive in military terms as the occupation so would offer little improvement when compared to the status quo. In addition, many Israelis consider it morally unacceptable.

Finally, Israel could attempt to expel the Palestinian population from the newly annexed areas, as it did during and immediately after the Palestine War and, to a lesser extent, since the June 1967 War. International opinion would likely make this a nonviable option as well. Even the United States, which is generally supportive of Israeli actions taken under the guise of security concerns, has been critical of the expulsion of Palestinian political activists during the *intifada* and would be unlikely to tolerate the massive population transfer necessary to eliminate a significant Palestinian presence in an expanded Israel.

Thus, each of the scenarios in which Israel maintains control over the West Bank and Gaza Strip is problematic for that country. Israel can continue to rule the territories under oppressive military law, in violation of many of the ethical principles of Judaism and in a state of constant insecurity. This option, which is increasingly unacceptable to many Israelis for both moral and practical reasons, would leave Israel isolated internationally. Or Israel can grant citizenship rights to all residents of an expanded State of Israel, and give up the distinctively Jewish and Zionist character of the state that is its raison d'être. Neither choice is a happy one. For this reason many Israelis from across the political spectrum have concluded, in some cases reluctantly, that a settlement to the Israeli-Palestinian conflict requires at least partial Israeli withdrawal from the West Bank and Gaza Strip.

On the Palestinian side, most of the options are constrained by Israeli decisions. If Israel withdraws from part or all of the West Bank and Gaza Strip, an independent Palestinian state could be established in those areas, or the Palestinians could form a federation of some type with Jordan. Palestinians could then attempt to regain a larger portion of the Mandate of Palestine or could live side by side with the State of Israel. The PNC has stated that the latter is the intention of the secular leadership of the Palestinian national movement, although there is debate regarding how much territory must come under Palestinian control for mutual coexistence to be acceptable. If Israel does not withdraw from the Occupied Territories, Palestinians can either continue the *intifada* against Israel or end the *intifada* and accept the occupation. There is at present no evidence that Palestinians are willing to return to the pre-*intifada* situation or accept the continued control by Israel of the West Bank and Gaza Strip. Palestinians see their actions as a fight for independence, and nothing short of this will cause them to end the uprising.

Finally, there remains in theory the possibility of a single, unified but binational state with equal civil, political, economic, social, cultural, and national rights for all residents. This is the model proposed by the Mac-Donald White Paper in 1939 and by the PNC in its 1971 call for a "democratic secular state" in Palestine. The idea was rejected in 1939 by some Palestinians and in both 1939 and 1971 by Zionists. Given the present atmosphere of high tension and hostility, this model would likely be rejected again: Zionists and Palestinians want their *own* states.

Internationally, there is widespread consensus that some form of two-state model is the most appropriate solution to this enduring problem, with the exact boundaries to be worked out in negotiations. This consensus is reflected in the rapid diplomatic recognition given to the State of Palestine after its declaration of independence in November 1988. In the first year after the declaration, over 100 countries extended formal diplomatic relations to Palestine, and additional countries indicated approval for the principle of a Palestinian state but withheld formal recognition until borders had been set. A two-state solution is not ideal for either Israelis or Palestinians. It means Zionists must give up their dream of a modern State of Israel that includes "Judea and Samaria" and must accept a position as one state among many in the Levant, rather than attempting to dominate the region as they have done in the past. For Palestinians, it means accepting that ancient Palestinian cities such as Jaffa will not be part of the Palestinian state, and that the Palestinian nation will be split between two political entities: Israel and Palestine (whether as an independent state or linked to Jordan).

STAGES IN THE PEACE PROCESS

The exact form of an eventual solution to the Israeli-Palestinian conflict is a matter to be negotiated by the relevant parties. It is possible, however, to examine various aspects of the negotiation process and indicate the general and specific issues that will need to be addressed as part of that process. In the broadest sense, any peace plan must provide for Palestinian and Israeli self-determination and assure the legitimate security interests of Palestinians, Israelis, and all states in the region. For the plan to succeed, it must have the support of significant portions of the Palestinian and Jewish Israeli communities, as well as the tacit agreement of the United States, Russia, and the Arab states in the region. Any plan forced upon one party or another will ultimately fail to bring peace, for it will not be based on a shared commitment to that goal. After 100 years of conflict between Zionists and Palestinians, a just and stable peace will be difficult to achieve. But with the alternative of continued conflict, many believe working toward peace is the only choice.

Harold H. Saunders, who served in a variety of capacities as a member of the staff of the U.S. National Security Council and in the State Department, participated in the mediation of five Arab-Israeli agreements between 1973 and 1979. He has suggested that the peace process in the Middle East has five overlapping parts that must be worked through by the participants. Although he stresses that these are not discrete stages, each of which must be completed before the next one can commence, they do represent an unfolding process that occurs over a period of time. The parts of the Saunders outline are:

- □ defining the problem
- □ developing a commitment to negotiate
- □ arranging a negotiation
- □ the actual process of negotiation
- □ implementation of the agreements negotiated

Each is essential for successful completion of the peace process.[2]

Recognition and Commitment

The first step toward negotiation occurs when each party recognizes that a problem exists, defines precisely what the problem is, assesses how it feels about the situation, and acknowledges that the problem needs to be handled in cooperation with one or more other players. According to Saunders, "An early condition for negotiation is that each side must define the problem as being at least partly shared with another party. Each

These slogans on a door of the interreligious House of Hope in the Galilee village of Shafa 'Amr reflect members' hope for positive relations between Palestinians and Jews. The bumper stickers read No to Racism! in Arabic and Hebrew.

side's definition must somehow acknowledge the hopes and pain of the other side. Only when each side sees the other side's problems as part of the problem will the two definitions together suggest that a jointly attempted solution is worth considering."[3] Thus, formulating the problem in this way is a necessary precondition for negotiations to occur.

Intimately connected to a definition of the problem is the development of a commitment to negotiate. Saunders comments that this is often the most complex part of the whole peace process: "Before leaders will negotiate, they have to judge (1) whether a negotiated solution would be better or not better than continuing the present situation, (2) whether a fair settlement could be fashioned that would be politically manageable, (3) whether leaders on the other side could accept the settlement and survive politically, and (4) whether the balance of forces would permit agreement on such a settlement."[4] What is really involved is a judgment that the status quo is not in the best interest of the actor and that it is possible to achieve a fair settlement. Recall, however, that because of internal political dynamics, decisions about what constitutes the best interests of a state or other actor are not always straightforward. Once there is a recognition that the problem can be dealt with fairly through negotiation, it is possible to move on to the negotiation activity itself.

These first two parts of the negotiation process have proven difficult for Palestinians and Israelis in the past. Neither group has been willing or able to define the conflict between them as a joint issue in which the problems of the other party must be taken into account. In recent years this situation has begun to change, and there are now increasing numbers of individual Israelis and Palestinians who have made this psychological leap. In the post-Oslo period the leadership of Israel and the PLO appear to have concluded the Israeli-Palestinian conflict is an issue about which they must negotiate, as opposed to one about which they must, for political reasons, appear to negotiate while not actually doing so.

Preliminaries to Negotiation

Before substantive negotiations can begin, a set of procedural issues must first be resolved. These may appear trivial or the answers self-evident, but the manner in which these preliminary questions are dealt with can greatly influence the outcome of subsequent discussions:

- □ *Who* will be involved in the negotiations?
- □ *What* will the substantive agenda look like, and *how* will the negotiations be structured?
- □ *When* and *where* will the negotiations take place?
- □ *Why* are the negotiations occurring at this particular point in time?

Much of the debate over the 1991 Madrid conference and subsequent negotiations revolved around these types of issues. For instance, there was
disagreement about the composition of the Palestinian delegation. The official Israeli government position was that Israel would not negotiate with
a representative of the PLO under any circumstances. The Palestinian position was that the PLO is the sole legitimate representative of the Palestinian people and that Israel had no right to stipulate with whom it would
negotiate, any more than the PLO could decide they would refuse to negotiate with anyone who in the past was part of Irgun or the Stern Gang. For
both sides, this issue took on great symbolic importance. One of the significant elements of the process that led to the Oslo Accords was that Israel
recognized "the PLO as the representative of the Palestinian people and
[decided to] commence negotiations with the PLO" after the PLO reiterated its 1988 statement acknowledging "the right of the State of Israel to
exist in peace and security."[5]

The substantive agenda for negotiation was also controversial. Israel
preferred to delay discussion of the final form of a future peace agreement, the possibility of an independent Palestinian state, Jerusalem, Israeli settlers currently living in the Occupied Territories, and other difficult issues. Palestinians wanted a clear statement that the ultimate
resolution of the conflict would include an end to the Israeli occupation of
the West Bank (including East Jerusalem) and the Gaza Strip. Israel felt it
was premature to make such a commitment; the Palestinians believed
without agreement on this critical point there was little about which to negotiate. The inability to agree on preliminaries is not unique to Israelis and
Palestinians. Negotiators participating in the Paris peace talks on the U.S.
withdrawal from Vietnam debated endlessly about the shape of the table
at which the negotiators would sit. Arms control discussions between the
United States and the former Soviet Union routinely alternated between
embassies in U.S.- and Soviet-allied countries so neither side was given a
psychological edge.

Negotiation and Implementation

The fourth and fifth parts of the peace process as described by
Saunders are the ones on which most people focus their attention: the actual negotiation and the implementation of any agreements made. The latter is at least as important as the former, for if an agreement is reached that
for whatever reason cannot be implemented, it is meaningless. Furthermore, the peace process is just that, an ongoing process, not a one-time
event. This has been dramatically illustrated in the years after the Egyptian-Israeli Peace Treaty was signed. The treaty resolved certain issues between the two parties and set out ways in which additional issues could

be dealt with, but it did not mean that suddenly there was a completely free and friendly relationship between the two countries. This is likely to be the case with Israelis and Palestinians as well. The scars of a century of conflict will not be magically healed by a peace agreement.

ISSUES FOR NEGOTIATION

Once individuals representing Israelis and Palestinians have agreed to sit together and negotiate, with or without representatives from other state or nonstate actors, they will need to consider a number of issues. These include:

□ specific, fixed, agreed-upon boundaries for Israel and for the Arab states in the region
□ the status of Jerusalem
□ the political, civil, and national status of Jewish Israelis currently living within the West Bank, including East Jerusalem, and the Gaza Strip
□ the political, civil, and national status of Palestinians currently living within Israel
□ the political, civil, and national status of Palestinians and Jews currently living outside the borders of the British Mandate of Palestine
□ compensation for Palestinians and Israelis who were forced to leave their homes and property as a direct result of the Israeli-Palestinian conflict
□ the allocation of resources such as water among the states in the region
□ the economic viability of Israel, Palestine, and the other states in the region
□ the assurance of mutual security for all states and all peoples in the region
□ the role of the international community in supervising a negotiated settlement

Each of these points addresses a significant and controversial issue that must be resolved in order for the conflict between Israelis and Palestinians to be ended.

Borders and the Status of Jerusalem

One of the most obvious issues is that of establishing specific, fixed boundaries for Israel and for the Arab states in the region. Unlike virtually all other countries in the world, Israel has never officially indicated what it considers to be its legal boundaries, except for its border with Egypt, which was set as part of the 1979 Egyptian-Israeli Peace Treaty. Until 1967 the de facto borders of the state were the 1949 armistice lines with Egypt, Lebanon, Syria, and Jordan. Since 1967 the de facto territory of Israel has included East Jerusalem and the West Bank, the Golan Heights, the Gaza Strip, and, until the Camp David Accords, all or part of the Sinai Peninsula. These are the borders shown on official Israeli maps, with no indication of what areas were captured in the June 1967 War. Before a peace treaty can be concluded, these de facto boundaries will have to be replaced with de jure, agreed-upon borders between Israel and the surrounding states.

There are several starting places for the discussion on borders. In 1947 UN Resolution 181 proposed one set of boundaries between Israel and Palestine. These boundaries were never adhered to. Few people seriously suggest a complete return to the UN-mandated borders, but this does represent one option. The 1949 armistice lines suggest a second possible set of borders about which to begin discussions. Both of these proposals would require modification to avoid dividing towns in half, separating agricultural lands from the people who work them, or cutting a village off from its only source of water. Every effort should be made to establish reasonable borders that take practical concerns into account. Some consideration will also need to be given to making the territory of each state as contiguous as possible and providing access between parts of the state if it is not physically united. For example, if a Palestinian state is defined as encompassing the West Bank and the Gaza Strip, there will need to be provisions made for Palestinians to travel freely between the two areas.

The status of Jerusalem is in some ways the single most difficult question to resolve and will require tremendous creativity and flexibility on the part of negotiators. Neither Israelis nor Palestinians are willing to give up their access to Jerusalem; both believe Jerusalem should be the capital of their state. Several options have been proposed. One possibility is that East (Arab) Jerusalem could be made the capital of Palestine, with West (Jewish) Jerusalem serving as the capital of Israel. This would satisfy the desire of each party to claim the city but might mean redividing Jerusalem as was the situation prior to 1967. Few people want to see the return of the walls and the gates or to give up access to half of the city. Another proposal is to internationalize Jerusalem, so that it would be part of neither (or both) Palestine and Israel. This option has its own set of difficulties, however, including that of providing security and preventing citizens from one state from traveling through Jerusalem to gain access to the other state without permission. The large number of religious sites—Jewish, Christian, and Muslim—within the walled Old City area and immediately adjacent to it further compounds the problem. This means that addi-

Streets are crowded in one of the main shopping areas inside the walled Old City of Jerusalem. The Damascus Gate is in the background.

tional state and nonstate actors such as the Vatican (with interests in Christian shrines) and Saudi Arabia (as the protector of Muslim holy places) feel they have legitimate interests in the future of Jerusalem, which they would not have were Jerusalem a purely secular city such as Berlin or Hong Kong. The status of Jerusalem will not be quickly or easily determined.

Citizenship Rights

A third set of concerns has to do with the legal position of Palestinians and Israelis who are currently living in the territories to be included in the borders of the other group. For example, will Jewish Israelis living in settlements in the West Bank be allowed to remain in a Palestinian state? If yes, under what conditions? Will they be allowed to apply for citizenship in the State of Palestine? What if they want to remain citizens of Israel but live in Palestine? Similarly, will the status of Palestinians living within the boundaries of Israel change in any way? Will they be allowed to become citizens of the State of Palestine but remain in Israel? Will Palestinians and their descendants who fled or were forced to leave the area during the Palestine War or the June 1967 War be allowed to return to their homes in Israel? Will there be a Palestinian "right of return" to the West Bank and Gaza Strip comparable to the Israeli Law of Return for all Jews? A related

Women and men pray separately at the massive Western Wall, a remnant of the ancient Jewish temple complex that was destroyed by the Romans in 70 BCE and one of the most sacred Jewish sites. In the foreground, a group of men are celebrating a bar mitzvah ceremony.

matter is compensation for Palestinians forced to leave their homes, lands, and property as a direct result of the Israeli-Palestinian conflict who choose not to return at this point. On what basis would such compensation be determined and who would be responsible for paying for it?

Many people assume that the creation of a Palestinian state would lead to a mass movement of Palestinians from all over the world into that state. Although it is impossible to determine how many Palestinians would exercise the right to return to Palestine, two pieces of evidence are suggestive. First, a significant number of committed Zionists from the United States and elsewhere have not chosen to move to Israel. For them, knowing the State of Israel exists and supporting it politically and financially is a sufficient expression of their convictions. They do not wish to leave their homes to move there. This may well also be the case for Palestinians who have made lives for themselves outside of mandatory Palestine. The conditions are not fully comparable as the majority of Palestinians left the area no more than fifty years ago and still have family ties there. It does seem likely, however, that many Palestinians will choose to remain in their current homes and only visit, rather than permanently return to, the land of their birth or their parents' birth, much as Irish who immigrated to North America in the late nineteenth century remained there even after the creation of an independent Ireland in 1922.

An additional piece of evidence comes from a public opinion poll reported in the *Jerusalem Post* on 1 September 1989, although it dealt only with Palestinians currently living in Israel. When asked: "If a Palestinian State were established, would most Israeli Arabs be interested in joining?" 71 percent of Israeli Palestinians said they thought not. When asked specifically: "If the possibility presented itself to you, would you wish to live outside Israel?" 75 percent of Israeli Palestinians said they would remain in Israel, even though 69 percent believed Israeli Palestinians are discriminated against simply because they are Arab.

Economic Concerns

Thus far, the issues identified as requiring resolution have been primarily political in a narrow sense. In contrast, the allocation of water resources is a practical issue with widespread ramifications for the region. From Israel's establishment as a state in 1948, its intensive agriculture and settlement activities have required water gathered from outside its borders. As early as 1953, for example, Israel began construction of a canal at Banat Yacoub in the UN demilitarized zone near the Syrian border for the diversion of the waters of the Jordan River. U.S. pressure forced Israel to move the water diversion point to the Sea of Galilee, outside the demilitarized zone.

At present, per capita annual water consumption for each Israeli is more than 100,000 gallons, compared with 34,000 gallons for Palestinians from Gaza and less than 24,000 gallons for West Bank Palestinians.[6] Israel relies heavily on water from the Jordan River, the Sea of Galilee, the Yarmuk River, and the rain-fed aquifers located under the West Bank. According to a 1989 study by Israeli Professor Israel Shahak, approximately 213 billion gallons of water were expected to be drawn from West Bank sources in 1990, with 135 billion gallons to be allocated for use within pre-1967 Israel and 42 billion gallons to go to Jewish settlers in the West Bank. Only 36 billion gallons—about 17 percent of the water from the West Bank—was to be allocated for West Bank Palestinians,[7] hardly a sufficient quantity based on the relative populations.

Because of the importance Israel places on protecting its access to water, Palestinians in the West Bank and Gaza Strip are routinely forbidden to dig new wells, deepen existing wells, or put in water systems that might reduce the water available for Israel. In Gaza the situation has become critical. The drilling of deep wells by the Israeli settlers has caused sea water to get into the more shallow Palestinians wells. Water in the refugee camps frequently tastes of salt and is considered dangerously unhealthy. The salt also damages the agricultural produce of the Gazan Palestinians. In addition, there is the issue of shared underground aquifers, which do not conveniently follow artificially defined state boundaries. Any negotiated agreement between Israelis and Palestinians clearly will have to address water rights.

The question of water is only one of a number of related questions about the economic viability of two small states: Israel and Palestine. Israel is heavily dependent on foreign assistance from the United States and on individual contributions from U.S. Jews and others around the world. The possibility of reduced military expenditures may decrease this dependence, but it will be some time before Israel is economically viable without such assistance. At least initially a Palestinian state would also require extensive economic assistance from outside its borders in order to remain economically solvent. The World Bank estimates that the Occupied Territories will need at least $300–$500 million a year in the next decade for infrastructural development and other projects; the PLO has an economic growth plan that calls for $11.6 billion by the year 2000.[8] On the other hand, both Israel and Palestine have highly educated populations with supportive diaspora communities around the world. In the industrialized global economy of the 1990s these attributes may be more important than the size of their territories. After all, two of the major economic success stories in Asia in the 1980s were tiny Singapore and the city-state of Hong Kong.

In the long run, an independent State of Palestine and the Hashemite Kingdom of Jordan might agree to merge certain aspects of their economies. Or the State of Israel and the State of Palestine may conclude that some form of economic union would be to the benefit of both countries. The possibility of a joint Israeli-Palestinian state has been proposed periodically by Uri Avnery and was outlined in his 1968 book, reprinted in 1971 as *Israel Without Zionism: A Plan for Peace in the Middle East.*

In one version of his plan, Avnery suggests a Federation of the State of Israel (within the pre-1967 borders of Israel) and the Republic of Palestine (in the West Bank and Gaza Strip). Jerusalem would serve as the federal capital as well as the capital of both states and would remain a united city. Israel and Palestine would enter into an economic, military, and political pact specifying a unified economic system, some form of political coordination (particularly in terms of foreign policy), and security arrangements that would forbid foreign armies to enter the territory of either Israel or Palestine. In an extension of this idea, Avnery proposes a semitic union, involving a number of states in the Levant, which would be created only after the Federation of the State of Israel and the Republic of Palestine had been established and the issue of the Palestinian refugees had been addressed. His hope is that by stressing the historical heritage and common cultural and spiritual background of the peoples in the region, it would be possible to work together economically and politically to the benefit of all parties. For many years, Avnery's ideas were considered visionary at best. But in recent years they have begun to attract notice because they represent the kind of creative thinking necessary to build an enduring peace between Palestinians and Jewish Israelis.

Security and the International Community

Two critical concerns have been left to the end: the assurance of security for all states and peoples in the region and the role of the international community in supervising the negotiated settlement. The assurance of security is the bedrock of any peace agreement. Between 1947 and the present, the conflict over Palestine has directly generated a total of seven major wars, from the war that followed the UN decision to partition the territory to the *intifada*. In order to enter into a peace agreement, both Palestinians and Israelis must be reassured that they are not risking their very existence by doing so. This is where the involvement of the international community becomes essential.

Not every peace agreement requires international or superpower guarantees. But this is not just any conflict. The duration and intensity of disagreement over Palestine, as well as the central role played in the past by the European powers, the superpowers, and intergovernmental groups such as the United Nations, mean that any negotiated solution to the conflict must involve actors beyond the states of the Levant. First and foremost, any peace agreement must meet the needs of Palestinians and Israelis, but it is far more likely to succeed if it has the endorsement of the international community.

PEACE NEGOTIATIONS IN THE 1990S

In the aftermath of the U.S.-led war against Iraq, U.S. Secretary of State James Baker undertook a series of meetings with Arab and Israeli leaders that culminated in a regional peace conference, cosponsored by the United States and the former Soviet Union, in Madrid, Spain. Subsequent negotiations were held in Washington, D.C. (see Table 4.1). After an initial

TABLE 4.1 Bilateral Talks Between the Israeli and Palestinian-Jordanian Delegations

Madrid conference	30 October–1 November 1991
First round	3 November 1991
Second round	10–18 December 1991
Third round	13–16 January 1992
Fourth round	24 February–4 March 1992
Fifth round	27–30 April 1992
Sixth round	24 August–24 September 1992
Seventh round	21 October–20 November 1992
Eighth round	7–17 December 1992
Ninth round	27 April–13 May 1993
Tenth round	15 June–1 July 1993

burst of enthusiasm, Palestinian, and to some extent Israeli, popular support for the peace talks declined throughout the next twenty-two months, and at several points it appeared the negotiations would collapse entirely. Unexpectedly, at the end of August 1993, the Israeli government and the PLO announced they had been meeting secretly in Norway and had reached an interim agreement for Palestinian self-rule, beginning with the Gaza Strip and the West Bank town of Jericho. The Oslo Accords reinvigorated the negotiations but did not themselves constitute a final resolution to the conflict. Examination of the evolution of these negotiations, beginning with the months prior to the Madrid conference, illustrates the difficulties involved in even the most tentative moves toward conflict resolution.

The Madrid Conference

During the Gulf crisis, the Bush administration indicated repeatedly that once Iraq had withdrawn from Kuwait, the next priority for the United States was to address the Arab-Israeli conflict. Speaking before a joint session of Congress on 6 March 1991, Bush reaffirmed this position, stating that "a comprehensive peace must be grounded in UN Security Council resolutions 242 and 338 and the principle of territory for peace. This principle must be elaborated to provide for Israel's security and recognition, and at the same time for legitimate Palestinian political rights."[9]

Two days later, Baker began the first of eight trips to the Middle East to win support for a peace conference involving all relevant actors. Baker's goal was to make progress on the first three stages of negotiation discussed in the previous section: mutual recognition of a shared problem, development of a commitment to negotiate, and establishment of the procedural parameters for subsequent discussions. After numerous meetings throughout the Middle East, Baker developed his plan for a regional conference based on UN Security Council Resolutions 242 and 338. The conference would begin with a joint ceremonial opening before breaking up into bilateral talks between Israel, the Arab states bordering Israel, and the Palestinians. Palestinians would participate as part of a Palestinian-Jordanian delegation; the role of the United Nations would be limited to that of a silent observer.

Both Israel and Syria rejected the proposal. Syrian leaders felt they had already made significant compromises by agreeing to a regional rather than an international conference with only a very limited role for the United Nations. They also believed it was essential that the cosponsors be able to intervene in the negotiations when necessary to keep the process moving. Finally, Syria demanded that the conference be an ongoing multinational affair to prevent Israel from signing a separate peace agreement with one of the other Arab actors that did not address Israel's occupation of the Syrian Golan Heights.

Israel's position was that the United Nations was biased against Israel and should not be represented, even in an observer capacity, during the negotiations. Furthermore, Shamir insisted that Israel would only participate in direct negotiations; joint regional discussions were unacceptable. Israelis were divided over Soviet cosponsorship and over the possibility that the regional conference might be reconvened if direct negotiations stalled. Labor ministers criticized the Likud-led government for being inflexible. Leaders of the far-right parties threatened to withdraw from the coalition government if Shamir made any concessions. Even key members of the Israeli Cabinet disagreed openly. Israeli Foreign Minister David Levy made agreements with Baker that Shamir promptly disavowed. Defense Minister Sharon publicly endorsed increased settlements at a time when other Cabinet members were trying to downplay this sensitive activity.

There were also debates within the Palestinian community about whether to endorse the proposals presented by the United States. Many Palestinians, particularly supporters of Hamas, the PFLP, and the DFLP, felt the United States could not serve as a mediator for the conflict because it was unwilling to confront Israel on basic human rights issues, rejected discussion with the PLO, and refused to allow any official PLO role in the regional peace conference. Others, including most PPP, Fida, and Fateh supporters, believed Palestinians gained by having the opportunity to present their proposals, interpretations, and demands. They argued that if Palestinians refused to participate, the international community would view them as a "rejectionist" group that was unwilling to negotiate for peace.

Stalemated, Baker left the region. A frustrated President Bush mused publicly that he might simply issue invitations for a peace conference, under conditions he and Baker believed fair, and see who showed up. Bush and Baker believed this might force the parties to prove they were seriously interested in peace negotiations. Eventually, Syria and then Israel signed on to the U.S. proposal, and the twentieth session of the PNC, held in September 1991, also endorsed the conference and approved Palestinian participation in a U.S.- and Soviet-sponsored meeting.

The Madrid conference opened on 30 October 1991 with negotiators from Egypt, Israel, Lebanon, Syria, Jordan, and the Palestinians in attendance, along with representatives from the European Community and the Gulf Cooperation Council. It was a breakthrough for the Palestinians who, for the first time, were able to represent themselves in peace negotiations. Technically, the Palestinians were part of a joint delegation with the Jordanians, as Israel demanded, but the media and the other delegations treated them as an autonomous team. After three days, the opening phase of the conference ended, followed by a single day of bilateral discussions during which the Israeli and Palestinian-Jordanian delegations agreed to conduct negotiations along separate Palestinian-Israeli and Jordanian-Israeli "tracks." Then all progress halted. Israel argued that delegates should move the talks to the Middle East, but the Arab negotiators wanted to remain in Madrid. Israeli and Arab negotiators left Spain the following day with no agreement about where, when, or even whether further talks would occur.

Although the Madrid conference was not a complete failure, it could not be judged a great success either. In particular, Baker expressed his disappointment at the reluctance of the parties to take preliminary confidence-building measures. He wanted Israel to end its settlement activity in exchange for a suspension of the Arab economic boycott against Israel and a halt to the Palestinian *intifada*. Instead, in the weeks that followed, the Knesset passed a resolution declaring that Israel's control of the Golan Heights was not negotiable (while the Madrid conference was under way, Israel had established a new settlement there), and Shamir made public statements intended to emphasize that the land currently under Israeli control represented "an essential minimum of territory."[10]

Continuation of the Peace Process

To rejuvenate the peace process, the United States issued invitations to the Madrid conference delegations to continue their discussions in Washington, D.C. The Arab teams accepted and arrived for the scheduled opening of the second round of negotiations on 4 December 1991. Israel balked, however, insisting it needed until 9 December to prepare. The Arab delegations refused to meet on that date because it was the anniversary of the beginning of the *intifada*. Substantive negotiations between Israel and Syria and between Israel and Lebanon finally commenced on 10 Decem-

By Jeff Danziger in the *Christian Science Monitor* copyright © 1993 by TCSPS. Reprinted by permission.

ber and continued through 17 December, although the parties made little progress. The talks involving Israel, Jordan, and the Palestinians never advanced beyond procedural matters. The media labeled the discussions the "corridor talks" because the delegates spent the entire week arguing in the hallways and never even entered their assigned meeting rooms.

The negotiations reconvened on 13 January 1992, six days later than originally scheduled. This time the delay was due to Palestinian anger at Israeli settlers who had moved into Palestinian homes in Silwan (East Jerusalem) and at an Israeli expulsion order issued against twelve Palestinian activists accused of involvement in attacks against Jewish settlers. Residents of the Occupied Territories urged the Palestinian delegation to withdraw from the negotiations completely, arguing that Israel had been deliberately provocative by violating the Fourth Geneva Convention while conducting peace talks. After the UN Security Council voted unanimously to "strongly condemn" Israel's expulsion order (Resolution 726) and the EC formally protested Israel's actions, the Palestinian negotiators decided to continue with the bilateral talks.

During the third set of meetings, Palestinians and Israelis were able to move beyond the procedural issues that stymied them in December and turn to matters of substance. The Israeli delegation offered Palestinians an "interim self-governing authority" that would provide Palestinians with limited responsibility in areas such as agriculture, taxation, trade, and education but would maintain Israeli control over security, foreign affairs, and the Jewish settlers living in the Occupied Territories. The Palestinian delegation presented a series of ideas that Israel had already rejected, including self-rule for the residents of East Jerusalem; a freeze on all Jewish settlements; and an internationally supervised election for a parliament that would assume authority over the people, land, and resources of the Occupied Territories until the negotiation of their final status. The wide gap between the two proposals led to a standoff. Further complicating negotiations, two small right-wing parties that were essential to Likud's slim control of the Knesset withdrew from the coalition to express their opposition to the talks. As a result, Shamir no longer had a majority in the Knesset and was compelled to call early elections.

Shortly after the January bilateral meetings ended, many of the same delegations reconvened in Moscow for multilateral negotiations involving two dozen countries, including China, Turkey, Japan, and members of the Gulf Cooperation Council. The emphasis of the two-day meeting was on practical matters: economic development, water resources, arms control, refugees, and the environment. Five regional working groups were established to address these issues; each group has met separately on several subsequent occasions. By the end of 1993, the greatest progress had been made by the environment and water resources committees (which eventually merged) and by the economic development group.

During the fourth round of bilateral meetings that opened on 24 February 1992, both the Israeli and Palestinian delegations reiterated many of the same suggestions made during the January talks. The Israelis offered to give Palestinians greater control over civil services and regulatory agencies such as local transportation, culture, health, industry, and religious affairs but refused to consider any transfer to the Palestinians of control over land, water, or security and ignored the Palestinian proposal for elections. The Palestinian scheme was titled "Model of the Palestinian Interim Self-Governing Authority" (PISGA). It called for almost total Israeli withdrawal from the Occupied Territories and elections for legislative and judicial branches of a new Palestinian government. Analysts and politicians widely interpreted the document as a blueprint for the establishment of an independent Palestinian state, which at that point Israel considered totally unacceptable. The round ended inconclusively amid media speculation of a deadlock.

When the fifth set of talks began on 27 April 1992, the discussions focused on familiar topics raised during previous meetings, but the delegates made no significant progress. Negotiations were then suspended until after the Israeli elections in June. By this point, the Likud government was under criticism from all sides: from the Left for its failure to achieve significant progress after six months of discussion and from the Right for continuing to negotiate with a Palestinian team whose connection to the PLO was increasingly explicit.

After Labor's electoral victory, a new sense of optimism accompanied the two-stage sixth round when it opened on 24 August. Palestinians were disappointed, however, with Prime Minister Rabin's decision to maintain the original negotiating team, fearing this meant there would be little change in Israel's negotiating stance. It had become clear there were three main types of issues: "the terms of reference, including 242 and the idea of transitionality; territorial jurisdiction, including questions of land, water, settlements, and Jerusalem; and the powers of the Palestinian authority, including its structure, the question of legislative power, and the issue of elections."[11]

The seventh round of the talks ran from 21 October until 20 November, with a ten-day recess for the U.S. presidential elections. The talks again stalled, this time over whether to begin discussing details of limited Palestinian self-government before or after the Israeli and Palestinian delegations had reached a consensus on the basic terms of the negotiation. After a seemingly futile year, Palestinian support for the peace process had declined significantly. The PFLP and the DFLP joined with other resistance organizations concerned about the lack of progress to establish the Damascus-based "Group of Ten." They put intense pressure on the Palestinian team not to attend the eighth round of talks, scheduled to begin 7 December. As a compromise, the Palestinian team sent only a reduced delegation of four members.

The eighth round ended abruptly when Israel expelled more than 400 Palestinians accused of membership in Hamas or the Islamic Jihad to southern Lebanon for two years. The UN Security Council criticized the Israeli action and called for the immediate return of the deportees (Resolution 799). After Israel announced that 100 of the Palestinians could return and the rest might have their exile cut to one year, the United States pressured members of the UN Security Council to drop the issue. As a result, the floundering peace process lost whatever momentum still existed, and it appeared likely that talks could not be revived. A poll taken in February 1992 showed that 83 percent of West Bank and Gaza Palestinians surveyed opposed the return of the Palestinian delegation to the peace talks until Israel permitted the expelled Palestinians to return.[12]

Three months later, Israel sealed off the West Bank (excluding East Jerusalem) and the Gaza Strip from Israel and East Jerusalem indefinitely, indicating the move was in response to increased *intifada* violence against Israeli Jews. This action further reduced Palestinian support for renewed negotiations. Throughout the spring, the United States lobbied hard to bring the two parties back to the bargaining table. To the surprise of many, the Palestinian negotiating team agreed to resume discussions on 27 April 1993, after Israel made several symbolic concessions such as allowing thirty Palestinians exiled years earlier to return to the Occupied Territories and accepting the explicit involvement in the negotiations of Feisal Husseini, a newly designated member of the PLO Executive Committee from East Jerusalem. The Group of Ten strongly condemned the delegation's decision.

Israeli and Palestinian optimists anticipated significant progress in the long-delayed ninth round because so much was at stake; their hopes were dashed when the session ended without the anticipated breakthrough. Two days before the talks concluded, the United States—now under the Clinton administration—offered a two-stage draft of an "Israeli-Palestinian Joint Declaration of Principles" that was almost identical to a proposal already made by the Israeli team and rejected by the Palestinians. Palestinians refused to accept the U.S. document, and in the weeks that followed, Palestinian delegation head Haider Abd al-Shafi repeatedly called for suspension of Palestinian participation in the talks.

As the tenth round of talks opened on 15 June, the mood was listless and fatalistic. Everyone seemed to believe discussions would continue but that substantive progress was a long way off. On 30 June, the United States presented a new working paper to the participants. The document was generally satisfactory to the Israeli delegation except for a reference to allowing discussion of Jerusalem in the last stage of negotiations. Israeli leaders reiterated publicly that Israel would make no concessions on Jerusalem, which they said must remain the eternal and undivided capital of Israel.

The U.S. document angered the Palestinians. In it, the United States referred to the Occupied Territories as "disputed" rather than "occupied," implying that both Israel and the Palestinians had valid claims to the West Bank and Gaza Strip; made no mention of a "land for peace" formula; and described the Palestinians as the "inhabitants of the territories" rather than as a "people" or a "nation." These positions were consistent with past Israeli claims to the biblical Judea and Samaria but, particularly with respect to the status of the West Bank and Gaza Strip, represented a sharp deviation from the terms under which the bilateral peace process began at the Madrid conference during the Bush administration.

Following the tenth round, opposition parties in the Israeli Knesset (Likud, Tzomet, Moledet, and the National Religious party) proposed a vote of no-confidence in the government, citing, among other factors, an alleged secret Israeli-PLO dialogue. In August, two members of the PLO Executive Committee resigned, and three of the top Palestinian negotiators—Feisal Husseini, Hanan Ashrawi, and Saeb Erakat—unsuccessfully attempted to withdraw from the team.

For those people who believed that diplomats could quickly resolve the problems between Israel, the Palestinians, and the Arab states if all the parties would sit together and talk, the nearly two years of public negotiations were sobering. Saunders's framework provides some insight into why the negotiations had such difficulties. First, although the United States as an external power was able to facilitate the invitation and conduct of negotiations (stages three and four), significant problems relevant to stages one and two remained unresolved. Rhetoric and political posturing rather than serious discussion dominated the meetings, key definitional disputes and procedural issues remained important even after the negotiations began, and the most difficult substantive issues—such as Jerusalem and Israeli settlements—were completely ignored. Furthermore, significant political constituencies among Israelis and Palestinians opposed *any* negotiations, thus reducing the level of the leadership's commitment. In effect, the Madrid conference and subsequent rounds attempted to finesse the first two elements in the peace process. This approach was unsuccessful. The lack of rapid results illustrated yet again the complexity of this issue and the inability of any outside actor, even the United States as the world's superpower, to impose a solution on the conflicting parties. Yet, month after month, all the delegations returned to the bargaining table. They apparently concluded that talking, however ineffectively, was better than not talking at all, a perspective not universally shared by the communities they represented.

The Oslo Accords

Unknown to any of the delegates involved in the faltering bilateral talks, behind-the-scenes negotiations were taking place in Europe. In September 1992, a senior Norwegian diplomat suggested to Israeli deputy foreign minister Yossi Beilin that Norway could serve as a secret passage for direct talks between Israel and the PLO. After a brief conversation in December, Israeli history professor Yair Hirschfeld and senior PLO official Ahmed Suleiman Khoury (Abu Ala) began a series of top secret discussions on 20 January 1993, facilitated by Norwegian foreign minister Johan Jorgen Holst. Deliberately avoiding publicity, a small group held fourteen informal sessions in Norway over the next nine months. The Israeli participants reported to Beilin, who kept a skeptical Rabin and Israeli foreign minister Shimon Peres informed; Abu Ala maintained close contact with PLO official Mahmoud Abbas and with Arafat. Both sides agreed to keep the United States, as well as local Palestinian and Israeli leaders, out of the loop.[13]

There was a great deal of speculation about the factors leading to these back-channel negotiations. On the Israeli side, the government had lost faith in the Madrid peace process. Labor leaders became convinced that the only way to reduce violence between Israeli Jews and Palestinians was to deal directly with the PLO to achieve a meaningful peace agreement. It was also clear to the Israeli government that support among Palestinians for the Arafat's Fateh party was declining in response to political challenges from both Islamists and secular opposition groups. If Israel wanted to negotiate with Arafat rather than the leaders of Hamas or the PFLP, it had to move quickly. Furthermore, the economic situation in Israel was difficult and likely to worsen as pressures mounted in the United States to reduce foreign aid allocations to Israel.

The PLO also had reasons to pursue alternatives to the Washington-based bilateral talks. Palestinians in the Occupied Territories were angry that human rights violations had not declined during the negotiations and questioned the value of Arafat's diplomatic strategy. Arafat needed a concrete achievement to restore his credibility. Arafat was also worried that without an agreement, Israeli land confiscation and settlement activity would soon make the occupation irreversible.[14] In addition, the PLO, like Israel, had serious financial problems: The collapse of the Soviet Union and GCC anger over Arafat's support of Iraq during the 1990–1991 Gulf War resulted in the loss of significant sources of military and economic assistance. The status of the United States as the world's sole superpower was a new political reality to which Palestinians had to adjust. Finally, both Arafat and Rabin wanted to be remembered as leaders who brought peace to the region.

In August 1993, rumors began to spread about the European back-channel, and on 30 August, the Israeli newspaper *Yediot Ahronot* published the text of a draft Israeli-Palestinian agreement worked out by the Oslo negotiators. Less than two weeks later, on 9 September, Rabin and Arafat exchanged letters of mutual recognition. This cleared the way for Abbas and Peres to sign the "Declaration of Principles on Interim Self-Government Arrangements" on 13 September 1993 as Arafat, Rabin, and U.S. president Clinton looked on.

The Oslo Accords called for "a transitional period not exceeding five years, leading to a permanent settlement based on Security Council Resolutions 242 and 338." According to the agreement, during this period Israel would gradually withdraw its troops from major Palestinian population centers in the Occupied Territories, beginning in the Gaza Strip and the town of Jericho. Israel would retain control of East Jerusalem and Jewish settlements as well as roads near the settlements and external security; however, a "strong [Palestinian] police force" would take responsibility for "public order and internal security" in the rest of the West Bank and Gaza.

The Israeli troop redeployment was originally scheduled to be completed by the end of July 1994, prior to internationally supervised elections for a Palestinian Council to replace the Israeli civil administration. The Council would have authority over "education and culture, health,

Yitzhak Rabin and Yasir Arafat shake hands at the signing of the Oslo Accords in Washington, D.C., on 13 September 1993. Reprinted by permission of Reuters/Bettmann.

social welfare, direct taxation, and tourism." Within two years after the initial Israeli withdrawal from Gaza and Jericho, Israel and the PLO are to begin "permanent status negotiations ... [on] remaining issues, including Jerusalem, refugees, settlements, security arrangements, borders, relations and cooperation with other neighbors, and other issues of common interest." The parties agreed to establish an Israeli-Palestinian Liaison Committee and an Israeli-Palestinian Economic Cooperation Committee to address issues of common interest during the transition period.[15]

The initial response to the Oslo Accords was positive among the general Israeli and Palestinian populations, with a variety of polls reporting between 53 and 75 percent support.[16] Among political elites and activists, there was more dissension. In the Israeli Knesset, the 23 September vote on whether to endorse the Oslo Accords was close: 61 members in favor, 50 against, with 8 abstentions; one person was absent.

Those Israelis who supported a complete Israeli withdrawal from the Occupied Territories were enthusiastic about the agreement as a first step. Labor party leaders pointed out that the Declaration of Principles provided a means for Israel to withdraw from the troublesome Gaza Strip, which has no religious significance for Israel, and from densely populated Palestinian areas in the West Bank. At the same time, since the settlements would remain in place initially and the status of Jerusalem was not immediately under discussion, Israel would have the best of both worlds: control of the land on which Jews had settled without having to rule over a hostile Palestinian population.

Nonetheless, many Israelis had serious reservations about the agreement. Likud and Tzomet leaders agreed with the Israeli Left that the agreement provided the framework for a Palestinian state, an outcome they opposed on national security grounds. Benjamin Netanyahu called the Accords a historical blunder; others labeled Arafat a terrorist who could not be trusted and vowed to resist implementation of the Declaration of Principles. Although military officials were glad to relinquish responsibility for Palestinian security in the Occupied Territories, they were worried about protecting the Jewish settlers and unhappy that Rabin did not consult with the military during the secret negotiations.

Most settlers—particularly those who had moved to the West Bank or Gaza for ideological or religious rather than practical reasons—vehemently opposed the Accords and felt betrayed by the government. The comment of Rabbi Eliezer Melamed, secretary of the Rabbinical Forum of Rabbis in Judea, Samaria, and Gaza, was typical: "[The government leaders] have sinned against Zionism by turning the clock back 30 years, they have sinned against the people by ignoring their opinions, and they have sinned against democracy because such a fateful agreement needs a much larger majority."[17] Settlers wondered aloud what the long-term implications of the agreement were: Would the government force them to leave their homes? Would there be compensation? Some adamantly refused to consider relocating and predicted violence when the Palestinian self-governing authority took control. In the post-Oslo period, Rabin declined to discuss the future status of the settlements publicly; however, Labor politicians indicated Rabin was willing to give up Israeli control of about a hundred West Bank and Gaza settlements as part of the final arrangements with the Palestinians.[18]

There was a similar range of opinions within the Palestinian community. Acceptance of the agreement came mostly from the ranks of Fateh and Fida. Supporters believed that Palestinian civil authority over the Gaza Strip and Jericho was the first step toward an independent Palestinian state and peaceful coexistence with Israel. They also felt Israeli recognition of the PLO as the representative of the Palestinian people was significant because it acknowledged the Palestinians as a distinct group with legitimate political rights. The PPP's initial response was more muted: hopeful but worried. By February 1994 concerns about the direction of the negotiations led the PPP to withdraw its support of the Declaration of Principles.

Other Palestinians argued that the political process that led to the Oslo Accords was autocratic and that the Accords themselves were deeply flawed, involving wide-ranging and inappropriate concessions. Critics raised several concerns. First, they felt the Declaration of Principles was extremely vague, leaving wide room for interpretation. Second, the plan deferred discussion of several critical issues: creation of a Palestinian state, return of the Palestinian refugees expelled in 1948 and 1967, sovereignty over East Jerusalem, settlements, security arrangements, the release of Palestinian political prisoners, and permanent borders. Israeli soldiers were required only to redeploy, not withdraw, from the Occupied Territories and complete withdrawal was not specified as part of the final status negotiations. Furthermore, there were no plans for Israel to return any of the land it had confiscated, nor any promise by Israel to cease confiscation and settlement activities during the interim period.

Third, these critics believed Arafat was not serious about democracy. They worried that the Palestinian police and civil administration, including the committees that manage the international funds promised to Palestinians for economic development, would end up in the hands of Fateh supporters operating under Arafat's direct control. Drafts of a new Palestinian Constitution, which seemed to move away from the initial commitment to early national elections, were not encouraging:

> In general outline, the government [will be] organised around a powerful president, the chair of the PLO executive committee. A vaguely defined legislative authority is entrusted to a "Council of the National Authority," which is appointed by the PLO executive committee until replaced by a popularly elected Council. ... Although not popularly elected, the president of the National Authority controls the legislative and administrative process as well as the security forces. ...[19]

A number of Palestinian groups sharing these concerns—PFLP, DFLP, Hamas, Islamic Jihad, and others—joined together as the Democratic Nationalist-Islamic Front, which was committed to working against the Oslo Accords.

Perhaps in recognition of the deep divisions within the Palestinian community and his shaky base of support, Arafat did not convene the Palestine National Council to vote on whether to accept the signed Declaration of Principles, further fueling Palestinian anger at the nondemocratic nature of the decision-making process. Arafat did, however, call together the PNC Central Committee in October. Twenty-five members of the Central Council—mostly supporters of the PFLP and DFLP—boycotted the proceedings. In a contentious session, those attending endorsed the Oslo Accords 63 to 8, with 11 abstentions.

Despite Israeli and Palestinian political opposition, talks on the implementation of the Oslo Accords began almost immediately after the signing ceremony. Negotiators quickly encountered difficulties, however, and the deadline for beginning Israeli military withdrawal and Palestinian control of Gaza and Jericho, originally set for no later than 13 December 1993, had to be postponed. Throughout the fall and winter, sluggish progress on negotiations was accompanied by increasing Israeli-Palestinian violence, particularly between Israeli settlers and the military wing of Hamas. In addition, it appeared to many Palestinians that Israeli troops were targeting Hamas and Fateh military officers, although Israeli officials denied the charge.

Palestinians temporarily halted the talks in February 1994 after the Hebron massacre by an Israeli settler and subsequent Israeli military response left 40 Palestinians dead in a single day. Negotiations resumed after the UN Security Council passed Resolution 904 condemning the massacre and Israel outlawed membership in two small groups, Kach and Kahane Chai, that advocated the expulsion of Palestinians from the Occupied Territories. Israel also freed hundreds of Palestinian political prisoners in what it called a goodwill gesture; right-wing Israelies criticized the prisoner release, saying such actions should come only after the PLO had proven itself willing and able to control Palestinian violence against Israelis.

As negotiations dragged on, support for the agreement fell. In February 1994, a secret poll commissioned by Rabin's office showed Israeli public support for the peace deal had dropped to 34 percent, less than half of what it was immediately following the September signing ceremony. Enthusiasm for the Oslo Accords also declined among Palestinians. A survey conducted in January found only 45 percent supported the agreement, with 40 percent against, compared with 69 percent supporting and 28 percent opposing in September.[20] In a declaration issued in early May 1994, former head of the Palestinian peace delegation Haider abd al-Shafi and twenty-two other prominent Palestinians from the Occupied Territories spoke out strongly against the approach Arafat was taking: "We the undersigned hereby declare that any Israeli Palestinian agreement which … confers legitimacy to the illegal unilateral actions of the Israeli occupier … shall lack Palestinian and international legitimacy and shall therefore not be binding on the Palestinian people, its national institutions, public figures and political forces."[21]

Finally, nearly five months behind schedule, on 4 May 1994 Arafat and Rabin signed a 250-page Cairo Agreement on the Gaza Strip and the Jericho Area, intended to put into effect the Declaration of Principles. Within days, Palestinian police began to move into the newly autonomous areas, and on 13 May Israel turned over control of Jericho to them. Shortly thereafter, Israeli troops finished their redeployment in the Gaza Strip, completing the first stage of the Oslo Accords.

CONCLUSION

This book began with the underlying idea that the conflict over Palestine represents a clash of two national groups—Palestinians and Jews—attempting to achieve self-determination in the nineteenth and twentieth centuries. The conflict that developed over Zionist and Palestinian claims to the same part of the Levant is simultaneously rooted in its own reality and a highly internationalized conflict. The multiple actors involved—the European states and the League of Nations in the pre–World War II period; the United States, the Soviet Union/Russia, the United Nations, and European Community after 1945—have influenced how the conflict has evolved as each of these actors pursued its own interests in the region. This international involvement has increased the level of violence among Israelis, Palestinians, and the Arab states in a number of ways, most obviously through massive arms transfers. At the same time, international actors have also played constructive roles on occasion, through conflict mediation and peacekeeping activities. The international dimension of the conflict can also be seen in the increased instability within the surrounding states that have been drawn, willingly or not, into the conflict. Finally, the clash is made more complex by the tremendous range of opinions on foreign policy goals that exist within Israel and among Palestinians. It is clear from examining the internal political dynamics within these two nations that international actors cannot be accurately viewed as monolithic entities attempting to pursue an uncontestably defined national interest.

At present there is little goodwill between the general Jewish Israeli and Palestinian populations. Yet even if the two groups do not like each other or have confidence in one another, they must find a way to live together. This suggests a multitrack approach to the problem. On the one hand, there need to be opportunities for informal interaction between Israeli Jews and Palestinians so that prejudices and stereotypes can begin to be broken down. Confidence-building measures must be developed to allow Palestinians and Israeli Jews to learn to trust each other, and both groups will have to forgive and move beyond, if not forget, the wrongs they believe have been done to them by the other side. At the same time, it must be recognized that not all Israeli Jews or all Palestinians will be interested in peaceful coexistence, particularly initially. Thus, there must also be practical and hardheaded guarantees to protect the security of Palestinians and Israeli Jews.

Two national groups have fought over one small piece of land in the Levant for over 100 years. Palestinians and the Arab countries have been unable to defeat Israel militarily; Israel has been unable to eliminate Palestinian nationalism. Neither of these conditions is likely to change in the near future. Thus, the choice facing Israelis and Palestinians is whether to continue to fight indefinitely or to search for a just and equitable negotiated settlement to their conflict. With mutual recognition, mutual acknowledgment of the right of national self-determination, and mutual acceptance of fixed and secure boundaries for all states in the Levant, a way may be found to resolve this enduring and destructive dilemma in world politics.

□ □ □

Discussion Questions

These questions are designed to elicit thoughtful analysis and debate. In many cases there are no "right" answers; instead, responses will depend on an individual's political perspective and values.

CHAPTER ONE

1. What are the attributes of a nation? Is the division of the world into nation-states the best form of social and political organization? Is national self-determination a right of all national peoples? If yes, what are the challenges involved in realizing this objective?

2. Was it inevitable that Zionism and Palestinian nationalism clash?

3. What hampered a unified Palestinian response against Jewish immigration?

4. How did the pre-1948 period in the Middle East shape present-day realities? What impact did international perceptions have on policy decisions made about Palestine? What factors contributed to the internationalization of the Israeli-Palestinian conflict?

5. What other choices did the United Nations have in 1947 other than partition? Why do you think the countries of the United Nations voted the way they did?

CHAPTER TWO

1. How important are political leadership and ideology to the success of nationalism? What difficulties faced the Palestinian and Zionist/Israeli leaderships from the 1880s until the present?

2. How did the June 1967 War and the subsequent Israeli occupation of territories captured in the war influence the goals and aspirations of Israeli Jews? of Palestinians in Israel? of Palestinians in the West Bank and Gaza Strip?

3. What is the role of the Knesset in Israeli politics? How has this evolved over the past five decades? What are some key issues that divide Israeli political parties? Are there any issues on which they all agree? What impact, if any, did the 1992 election have on Israeli government policies toward the Israeli-Palestinian conflict?

4. What have been some significant turning points in the evolution of Palestinian politics? How have these critical events influenced the development of the groups that make up the Palestinian national movement? What are the principle issues on which these groups agree or disagree?

5. To what extent has the *intifada* changed the character of the conflict over Palestine?

CHAPTER THREE

1. How have regional actors been drawn into the Israeli-Palestinian conflict since 1948?

2. Both Israel and the Arab states claim that the other side has started most of the wars between them. What are the reasons each actor gives for making this claim? Do you find some arguments more compelling than others? What reasons might an international actor have for deliberately initiating a crisis?

3. Has U.S. policy toward Israel and the Palestinians been consistent over the past five decades? What are some important elements of that policy? How did it evolve? Can you identify any critical shifts in the U.S. approach to the Israeli-Palestinian conflict?

4. What role should a concern about human rights violations play in determining the foreign policy relations of a country such as the United States? What role should the United Nations have in addressing violations of human rights?

5. Should militarization in the Middle East concern the international community? What are the reasons for your answer?

6. Is terrorism ever justified? Is the use of an economic tool of foreign policy ever justified? Is civil or international war ever justified? What assumptions about the conduct of international relations underlie your response?

CHAPTER FOUR

1. What are the various types of violence in the Israeli-Palestinian conflict? What factors may lead to an escalation of the violence? What factors may decrease the violence?

2. What can individuals in the United States do to move forward the peace process between Israelis and Palestinians? Can individuals be more influential in some aspects of the process than in others? Is such involvement appropriate or inappropriate? Explain.

3. What state or nonstate actors need to be involved in the resolution of the Palestinian-Israeli conflict? What mechanisms can best allow all the significant voices to be heard?

4. How, if at all, have the Madrid conference, the subsequent peace negotiations, the 1993 Oslo Accords, and the 1994 Cairo Agreement changed the configuration of the Israeli-Palestinian conflict? What domestic, regional, and international factors led to the Oslo Accords? Will this agreement put an end to the *intifada*? Will it bring peace? Why or why not?

5. If you were a Palestinian, what would you consider the essential elements of a peace agreement with Israel? How would you respond if you were an Israeli? Is there any room for negotiation between the two positions you have outlined?

6. If you were an adviser to the president of the United States, what would you suggest U.S. policy toward Israel, Palestinians, and the Arab world should be? Would your advice change if you were an adviser to the leadership of the European Parliament or the United Nations?

□ □ □

Notes

INTRODUCTION

1. Feisal Husseini, quoted in "15,000 Jews and Palestinians Join in Jerusalem Peace Rally," *New York Times,* 31 December 1989.

2. "Text of Leaders' Statements at the Signing of the Mideast Pacts," *New York Times,* 14 September 1993.

CHAPTER ONE

1. Janet L. Abu-Lughod, "The Demographic Transformation of Palestine," in *The Transformation of Palestine,* ed. Ibrahim Abu-Lughod (Evanston, Ill.: Northwestern University Press, 1971), p. 142.

2. Uriah Zevi Engelman, "Sources of Jewish Statistics," in *The Jews: Their History, Culture and Religion,* vol. 2, ed. Louis Finkelstein (London: Peter Owen, 1961), p. 1520.

3. Dates and description of *aliyot* are taken from *Encyclopedia Judaica,* vol. 20. (Jerusalem: Kerr Publishing, 1971). Although there is a high degree of consensus on the years of the first three *aliyot,* scholars disagree on the dates they assign to the fourth and fifth *aliyot.*

4. *The Complete Diaries of Theodor Herzl,* vol. I (New York: Herzl Press and Thomas Yoseloff, 1960), p. 88; quoted in David Hirst, *The Gun and the Olive Branch: The Roots of Violence in the Middle East,* 2d ed. (London: Faber and Faber, 1984), p. 20.

5. Uri Avnery, *Israel Without Zionists* (New York: Macmillan, 1968); reprinted as *Israel Without Zionism: A Plan for Peace in the Middle East* (New York: Collier Books, 1971), p. 50.

6. Jewish immigration figures are taken from Dan Horowitz and Moshe Lissak, *Origins of the Israeli Polity: Palestine under the Mandate* (Chicago: University of Chicago Press, 1978), appendix 1; Walid Khalidi, ed., *From Haven to Conquest: Readings in Zionism and the Palestine Problem Until 1948* (Beirut: Institute for Palestine Studies, 1971; reprint, Washington, D.C.: Institute for Palestine Studies, 1987), p. 841; Ann Mosely Lesch, *Arab Politics in Palestine, 1917–1939* (Ithaca: Cornell University Press, 1979), p. 27; and Jacob Lestchinsky, "Jewish Migrations, 1840–1956," in *The Jews: Their History, Culture and Religion,* vol. 2, ed. Louis Finkelstein (London: Peter Owen, 1961). Horowitz and Lissak are citing A. Gertz, ed., *Statistical Handbook of Jewish Palestine, 1947* (Jerusalem: Jewish Agency, Department of Statistics, 1947).

7. Brith Shalom's founding document is quoted in *A Land of Two Peoples: Martin Buber on Jews and Arabs*, ed. Paul R. Mendes-Flohr (New York: Oxford University Press, 1982), pp. 74–75.

8. George Antonius, *The Arab Awakening: The Story of the Arab National Movement* (G. P. Putnam's Sons, 1946; reprint, New York: Capricorn Books, 1965), pp. 83–84.

9. Hirst, *The Gun and the Olive Branch*, p. 70.

10. Hirst, *The Gun and the Olive Branch*, p. 93; Khalidi, *From Haven to Conquest*, pp. 846–849.

11. "The Balfour Declaration, November 2, 1917," in *The Arab-Israeli Conflict*, vol. 3, *Documents*, ed. John Norton Moore (Princeton: Princeton University Press, 1974), p. 34.

12. "Excerpt from the Report of the American Section of the International Commission on Mandates in Turkey (The King-Crane Commission), August 28, 1919," in *The Arab-Israeli Conflict*, vol. 3, *Documents*, ed. John Norton Moore (Princeton: Princeton University Press, 1974), pp. 56–57, 59.

13. Neville Barbour, *Nisi Dominus: A Survey of the Palestine Controversy* (London: George G. Harrap, 1946), p. 103.

14. Chaim Weizmann, *Trial and Error* (London: Hamish Hamilton, 1949), p. 305.

15. Quoted in Doreen Ingrams, *Palestine Papers, 1917–1922: Seeds of Conflict* (London: John Murray, 1972), p. 93.

16. "Statement of British Policy in Palestine from Mr. Churchill to the Zionist Organization (The Churchill White Paper), June 3, 1922," in *The Arab-Israeli Conflict*, vol. 3, *Documents*, ed. John Norton Moore (Princeton: Princeton University Press, 1974), pp. 67–68.

17. "Report of the Palestine Royal Commission (Peel Commission)—1937," in *The Israel-Arab Reader: A Documentary History of the Middle East Conflict*, rev. ed., ed. Walter Laqueur and Barry Rubin (New York: Penguin, 1984), pp. 57–58.

18. Barbour, *Nisi Dominus*, p. 201.

19. See *Palestine Post*, 19 May 1939.

20. Avnery, *Israel Without Zionism*, p. 102.

CHAPTER TWO

1. James McDonald, *My Mission to Israel* (New York: Simon and Schuster, 1952), p. 176.

2. Benny Morris, *The Birth of the Palestinian Refugee Problem, 1947–1949* (New York: Cambridge University Press, 1987).

3. Simha Flapan, *The Birth of Israel: Myths and Realities* (New York: Pantheon Books, 1987), p. 42. Flapan is citing Michael Bar-Zohar, *Ben Gurion: A Political Biography* (Tel Aviv, 1977), p. 704.

4. Laurie A. Brand, *Palestinians in the Arab World: Institution Building and the Search for State* (New York: Columbia University Press, 1988), p. 9.

5. Yosef Weitz, *Yomani Ve'igrotai Labanim* (My Diary and Letters to the Children), vol. 2, p. 181; cited in Morris, *Birth of the Palestinian Refugee Problem*, p. 27; and David Hirst, *The Gun and the Olive Branch: The Roots of Violence in the Middle East*, 2d ed. (London: Faber and Faber, 1984), p. 130.

6. Israel Central Bureau of Statistics, *Statistical Abstract of Israel 1987*, no. 34 (Jerusalem, 1987), pp. 154–155.

7. Abbas Shiblak, *The Lure of Zion: The Case of the Iraqi Jews* (London: Al Saqi Books, 1986).

8. Maxim Ghailan, "Letters," *New Outlook*, November/December 1989, 4.

9. Meron Benvenisti, *1987 Report: Demographic, Economic, Legal, Social and Political Developments in the West Bank* (Jerusalem: West Bank Data Base Project, 1987), pp. 70–71.

10. Scott Reese and Jan Abu-Shakrah, *Colonial Pursuits: Settler Violence During the Uprising in the Occupied Territories* (Chicago: DataBase Project on Palestinian Human Rights, 1989), p. 23.

11. Peace Now, Settlement Watch Team, *The Real Map: A Demographic and Geographic Analysis of the Population of the West Bank and the Gaza Strip* (Jerusalem: Peace Now, November 1992), p. 15. Data on Jerusalem are from Palestine Human Rights Information Center (PHRIC), *From the Field* (Jerusalem: PHRIC, January 1992), p. 1.

12. Reese and Abu-Shakrah, *Colonial Pursuits*, p. 5.

13. Jamal R. Nassar, *The Palestine Liberation Organization: From Armed Struggle to the Declaration of Independence* (New York: Praeger, 1991), p. 92. Nassar is citing Ghazi Khurshid, *Dalil Harakat al-Mukawamah al-Filastiniyah* (A Handbook of the Palestinian Resistance Movement) (Beirut: PLO Research Center, 1971), p. 16.

14. Palestine National Council, "Political Communiqué, Algiers, 15 November 1988," *Journal of Palestine Studies* 70 (Winter 1988), pp. 216–223.

15. Ziad Abu-Amr, "Hamas: A Historical and Political Background," *Journal of Palestine Studies* 88 (Summer 1993), p. 5.

16. *Jerusalem Post*, 14 December 1987.

17. A more detailed discussion of these events is contained in Deborah J. Gerner, "Palestinians, Israelis, and the *Intifada:* The Third Year and Beyond," *Arab Studies Quarterly* 13:3-4 (Summer/Fall 1991), pp. 19–59.

18. B'Tselem, *Activity of the Undercover Units in the Occupied Territories* (Jerusalem: B'Tselem, May 1992); PHRIC, *Targeting to Kill: Israel's Undercover Units* (Jerusalem: PHRIC, May 1992).

19. PHRIC, "Human Rights Violations Under Israeli Rule During the Uprising," in *Uprising Update* (Washington, D.C.: PHRIC, April 1994).

20. PHRIC, "Human Rights Violations Under Israeli Rule During the Uprising," in *Uprising Update* (Washington, D.C.: PHRIC, December 1993).

CHAPTER THREE

1. See Geoffrey Blainey, *The Causes of War* (New York: Free Press, 1988); Greg Cashman, *What Causes War? An Introduction to Theories of International Conflict* (New York: Lexington Books, 1993); and John A. Vasquez, *The War Puzzle* (Cambridge: Cambridge University Press, 1993).

2. Richard Ned Lebow, *Between Peace and War: The Nature of International Crisis* (Baltimore: Johns Hopkins University Press, 1981), p. 25.

3. David Hirst, *The Gun and the Olive Branch: The Roots of Violence in the Middle East*, 2d ed. (London: Faber and Faber, 1984), p. 211, citing *Le Monde*, 29 February 1968.

4. Lyndon B. Johnson, *The Vantage Point: Perspectives of the Presidency, 1963–1969* (New York: Holt, Rinehart, and Winston, 1971), p. 293; and Stephen Green, *Taking Sides: America's Secret Relations with a Militant Israel* (New York: William Morrow, 1984), pp. 199–200.

5. "Excerpts from [Prime Minister Menachem] Begin Speech at National Defense College," *New York Times*, 21 August 1982, p. 4.

6. Kennett Love, *Suez: The Twice-Fought War* (New York: McGraw-Hill, 1969), p. 677.

7. This sociopsychological phenomenon has been analyzed extensively by Irving L. Janis in his book *Groupthink: Psychological Studies of Policy Decisions and Fiascoes* (Boston: Houghton Mifflin, 1982). As Janis explains, "groupthink refers to a deterioration of mental efficiency, reality testing, and moral judgment that results from in-group pressures" (p. 9). The symptoms include overestimation of the group's power and morality, various forms of closed-mindedness, and diverse pressures toward uniformity.

8. Quoted by David Holden and Richard Johns, *The House of Saud: The Rise and Rule of the Most Powerful Dynasty in the Arab World* (New York: Holt, Rinehart, and Winston, 1981), p. 332.

9. Quoted by Henry Kissinger, *Years of Upheaval* (Boston: Little, Brown, 1982), p. 536.

10. Hirst, *The Gun and the Olive Branch*, pp. 405–406.

11. Seán MacBride, *Israel in Lebanon: The Report of the International Commission to Enquire into Reported Violations of International Law by Israel During Its Invasion of the Lebanon* (London: Ithaca Press, 1983), pp. 190–191.

12. Jim Muir, "Rabin's Revenge Exacts an Appalling Toll," *Middle East International* (London), no. 456 (6 August 1993), pp. 3–4; Haim Baram, "The Crime and Its Reward," *Middle East International* (London), no. 456 (6 August 1993), p. 4.

13. For an analysis of the roots of the Gulf War and its future implications regionally and internationally, see Phyllis Bennis and Michel Moushabeck, eds., *Beyond the Storm: A Gulf Crisis Reader* (New York: Olive Branch Press, 1991); and Micah L. Sifry and Christopher Cerf, eds., *The Gulf War Reader* (New York: Times Books/Random House, 1991).

14. In February 1991, the United States rewarded Israel for this restraint with a one-year supplemental financial package that included $650 million in aid to reimburse Israel for economic losses sustained during the Gulf War, $1.1 billion for defense-related equipment, and other military assistance. This allocation was in addition to the $3 billion in economic and military aid that Israel receives from the United States each year. Richard H. Curtiss, "After Baker's Fourth Shuttle, Next Move Is Up to Bush," *Washington Report on Middle East Affairs* 10:1 (May/June 1991), p. 89.

15. "Baker's Tone on Jerusalem Softens," *New York Times*, 31 March 1990.

16. Henry Cabot Lodge, "Security Council Condemns Israel for Action Against

Syria." Statement made in the UN Security Council, 12 January 1956, *Department of State Bulletin*, vol. 34, 30 January 1956, pp. 182–184. The attacks on Qibya, Nahalin, Gaza, and Tiberias to which Lodge referred all resulted in a significant number of deaths and heightened the insecurity Palestinians felt.

17. Cheryl A. Rubenberg, *Israel and the American National Interest: A Critical Examination* (Chicago: University of Illinois Press, 1986), p. 188.

18. *New York Times*, 15 December 1988.

19. Ibid.

20. "A Gallup/IPS Survey Regarding the Conflict Between Israel and the Palestinians," *Journal of Palestine Studies* 74 (Winter 1990), pp. 75–86.

21. Steven Erlanger, "In a Less Arid Russia, Jewish Life Flowers Again," *New York Times*, 19 September 1993. Immigration figures for the last five months of 1993 are estimated based on previous months.

22. Thomas L. Friedman, "Baker Chides Israel on New Settlements," *New York Times*, 23 May 1991, p. A4.

23. Thomas L. Friedman, "Bush Backs Baker's Criticism of Israeli Settlements," *New York Times*, 24 May 1991. A chronology of U.S. settlement policy is provided in Donald Neff, "Settlements and Guarantees: The US Threatens Linkage," *Middle East International* (London), no. 409 (27 September 1991), pp. 3–4.

24. Richard H. Curtiss, "An Autopsy Report on the Death of the Middle East Peace Process," *Washington Report on Middle East Affairs* 12:1 (June 1993), p. 43.

25. Peretz Kidron, "Partial Settlement Freeze," *Middle East International* (London), no. 431 (7 August 1992), p. 5.

26. Alan Cowell, "Soviets Seeking to Become a Team Player in the Mideast Diplomatic Game," *New York Times*, 12 December 1989, p. 4.

27. U.S. Arms Control and Disarmament Agency, *World Military Expenditures and Arms Transfers 1991–1992* (Washington, D.C.: U.S. Government Printing Office, March 1994), table 3.

28. John Herz, "Idealist Internationalism and the Security Dilemma," *World Politics* 2 (1950), p. 157. Also see Robert Jervis, "Cooperation Under the Security Dilemma," *World Politics* 30:2 (January 1978), pp. 167–214.

29. Daniel P. Hewitt, *Military Expenditure: International Comparison of Trends* (Washington, D.C.: International Monetary Fund, May 1991), table 3.

30. Yahya Sadowski, "Scuds Versus Butter: The Political Economy of Arms Control in the Arab World," *Middle East Report* (July-August 1992), pp. 3–4.

31. Michael Stohl and George Lopez, "Introduction," in *The State as Terrorist*, ed. Michael Stohl and George Lopez (Westport, Conn.: Greenwood Press, 1984), p. 7.

CHAPTER FOUR

1. The average total fertility rate for women in Israel is 2.9 children, whereas for West Bank women it is 5.7 children and for Gazan women the figure is 7.9 children. Abdel R. Omran and Garzaneh Roudi, "The Middle East Population Puzzle," *Population Bulletin* 48:1 (July 1993), p. 13. Basic population figures are from David Newman, *Population, Settlement, and Conflict: Israel and the West Bank* (Cambridge: Cambridge University Press, 1991), p. 20. The issue of population parity is dis-

cussed by James W. Moore, "Immigration and the Demographic Balance in Israel and the Occupied Territories," *Middle East Policy* 1:3 (Fall 1992), pp. 88–105.

2. Harold H. Saunders, *The Other Walls: The Politics of the Arab-Israeli Peace Process*, rev. ed. (Princeton: Princeton University Press, 1991), chapter 2. Also see Janice Gross Stein, ed., *Getting to the Table: The Process of International Prenegotiation* (Baltimore: Johns Hopkins University Press, 1989).

3. Saunders, *The Other Walls*, pp. 23–24.

4. Ibid., p. 24.

5. "The Letters by Arafat and Rabin," *New York Times*, 10 September 1993.

6. Alan Cowell, "Hurdle to Peace: Parting the Mideast's Waters," *New York Times*, 10 September 1993.

7. Israel Shahak, "Diplomacy Must Not Obscure the Realities of Israeli Occupation," *Middle East International* (London), no. 351 (26 May 1989), p. 16.

8. Elaine Sciolino, "U.S. to Contribute $250 Million in Aid for Palestinians," *New York Times*, 21 September 1993. The six-volume World Bank report, *Developing the Occupied Territories: An Investment in Peace*, was published in September 1993. Another often cited study is by the Institute for Social and Economic Policy in the Middle East of the John F. Kennedy School of Government, Harvard University: *Securing Peace in the Middle East: Project on Economic Transition* (Cambridge: Harvard University, June 1993).

9. Donald Neff, "The Empty Ring to Bush's 'New World Order,'" *Middle East International* (London), no. 396 (22 March 1991), p. 3.

10. Clyde Haberman, "Israel Re-emphasizes Hard-Line Stance on Talks," *New York Times*, 14 November 1991.

11. Camille Mansour, "The Palestinian-Israeli Peace Negotiations: An Overview and Assessment," *Journal of Palestine Studies* 87 (Spring 1993), p. 23.

12. The poll was conducted by the Jerusalem Media and Communications Centre 18–20 February. Maxim Ghilan, "Road to Disaster," *Israel and Palestine Political Report* (Paris), no. 181 (February/March 1993), p. 6.

13. Clyde Haberman, "How the Oslo Connection Led to the Mideast Pact," *New York Times*, 5 September 1993, p. 1.

14. Despite the 1992 Rabin-Bush agreement on a partial settlement freeze, systematic land confiscation, selective annexation, and settlement development continued under the Sheves plan that was approved by the Israeli cabinet on 24 February 1993. Awad Mansour and Sharif Jaradat, *Clever Concealment: Jewish Settlement in the Occupied Territories Under the Rabin Government, August 1992–September 1993* (Jerusalem: PHRIC, February 1994); and "Acceleration of Land Confiscation and Settlement Building Since the Signing of the Agreement," *News From Within* 10:2 (February 1994), pp. 2–3.

15. Quotes taken from a photocopy of the signed draft of the "Declaration of Principles," dated 19 August 1993. Minor changes between this version and the document signed in Washington, D.C., did not affect the quoted sections.

16. Russell Watson, "Peace At Last?" *Newsweek*, 13 September 1993, p. 26; Center for Palestine Research and Studies, "Israeli Palestinian Agreement 'Gaza-Jericho First'—Results of Poll" (Nablus, West Bank, n.d.), photocopy.

17. Herb Keinon, "Protesters' cacophony 'to blot out Arafat's name,'" *Jerusalem Post*, 10 September 1993, p. 2.

18. Leslie Susser, "Goodbye to 100 Settlements?" *Jerusalem Report*, 18 November 1993, p. 16.

19. Naseer Aruri and John Carroll, "The Palestinian 'Constitution' and the 'old regime,'" *Middle East International* 473 (15 April 1994), p. 16.

20. "Secret government poll shows big drop in support for PLO deal," *The Jerusalem Report*, 10 February 1994, p. 4.

21. Haider Abd al-Shafi et al., "Declaration," *Palestine Report*, 1 May 1994, p. 9.

□ □ □

Suggested Readings

Abboushi, W. F. *The Unmaking of Palestine*. Brattleboro, Vt.: Amana, 1990.

Abed-Rabbo, Samir, and Doris Safie, eds. *The Palestinian Uprising*. Belmont, Mass.: AAUG Press, 1990.

Abu-Lughod, Ibrahim, ed. *The Transformation of Palestine*. Evanston, Ill.: Northwestern University Press, 1971; reprint, 1987.

_____, ed. *Palestinian Rights: Affirmation and Denial*. Wilmette, Ill.: Medina Press, 1982.

Alternative Information Centre. *Three Years of Intifada*. Jerusalem: AIC, 1991.

Amirahmadi, Hooshang, ed. *The United States and the Middle East: A Search for New Perspectives*. Albany: State University of New York Press, 1993.

Antonius, George. *The Arab Awakening: The Story of the Arab National Movement*. G. P. Putnam's Sons, 1946; reprint, New York: Capricorn Books, 1965.

Arian, Asher. *Politics in Israel: The Second Generation*, rev. ed. Chatham, N.J.: Chatham House Publishers, Inc., 1989.

Arian, Asher, Ilan Talmud, and Tamar Hermann. *National Security and Public Opinion in Israel*. Tel Aviv: Jerusalem Post Press, 1988.

Aronoff, Muron J. *Israeli Visions and Divisions: Cultural Change and Political Conflict*. New Brunswick, N.J.: Transaction Publishers, 1989.

Aronson, Geoffrey. *Israel, Palestinians, and the Intifada: Creating Facts on the West Bank*. London: Keagan Paul International and the Institute for Palestine Studies (Washington, D.C.) 1990.

Aruri, Naseer H., ed. *Occupation: Israel over Palestine*. 2d ed. Belmont, Mass.: Association of Arab-American University Graduates, 1989.

Ateek, Naim S., Marc H. Ellis, and Rosemary Radford Ruether, eds. *Faith and the Intifada: Palestinian Christian Voices*. Maryknoll, N.Y.: Orbis Books, 1992.

Avineri, Shlomo. *The Making of Modern Zionism: The Intellectual Origins of the Jewish State*. New York: Basic Books, 1981.

Avishai, Bernard. *The Tragedy of Zionism: Revolution and Democracy in the Land of Israel*. New York: Farrar, Straus and Giroux, 1985.

Avnery, Uri. *My Friend, the Enemy*. Westport, Conn.: Lawrence Hill, 1986.

Barbour, Neville. *Nisi Dominus: A Survey of the Palestine Controversy*. London: George G. Harrap, 1946.

Beit-Hallahmi, Benjamin. *Original Sins: Reflections on the History of Zionism and Israel*. Concord, Mass.: Pluto Press, 1992.

Benvenisti, Meron. *1987 Report: Demographic, Economic, Legal, Social and Political Developments in the West Bank*. Jerusalem: West Bank Data Base Project, 1987.

205

Benvenisti, Méron, and Shlomo Khayat. *The West Bank and Gaza Atlas*. Jerusalem: The West Bank Data Base Project, 1988.

Berger, Elmer. *Peace for Palestine: First Lost Opportunity*. Gainsville: University Press of Florida, 1993.

Bing, Anthony G. *Israeli Pacifist: The Life of Joseph Abileah*. Syracuse, N.Y.: Syracuse University Press, 1990.

Boulding, Elise, ed. *Building Peace in the Middle East: Challenges for States and Civil Society*. Boulder: Lynne Rienner Publishers, 1994.

Brand, Laurie A. *Palestinians in the Arab World: Institution Building and the Search for State*. New York: Columbia University Press, 1988.

Brecher, Michael. *Decisions in Israel's Foreign Policy*. New Haven: Yale University Press, 1975.

Brynen, Rex, ed. *Echoes of the Intifada: Regional Repercussions of the Palestinian-Israeli Conflict*. Boulder: Westview Press, 1991.

Buehrig, Edward Henry. *The UN and the Palestinian Refugees: A Study in Nonterritorial Administration*. Bloomington: Indiana University Press, 1971.

Cobban, Helena. *The Palestinian Liberation Organisation: People, Power and Politics*. Cambridge: Cambridge University Press, 1984.

Cohen, Michael J. *Palestine and the Great Powers, 1945–1948*. Princeton: Princeton University Press, 1982.

Cohen, Mitchell. *Zion and State: Nation, Class and the Shaping of Modern Israel*. New York: Columbia University Press, 1987; Columbia University Press Morningside Edition, 1992 (with new preface).

Cossali, Paul, and Clive Robson. *Stateless in Gaza*. London: Zed Books, 1986.

Curtiss, Richard H. *A Changing Image: American Perceptions of the Arab-Israeli Dispute*. 2d ed. Washington, D.C.: American Educational Trust, 1986.

Dajani, Burhan. "The September 1993 Israeli-Palestinian Documents: A Textual Analysis." *Journal of Palestine Studies* 91 (Spring 1994), pp. 5–23.

Drysdale, Alasdair, and Raymond A. Hinnebusch. *Syria and the Middle East Peace Process*. New York: Council of Foreign Relations Press, 1991.

Fernea, Elizabeth Warnock, and Mary Evelyn Hocking, eds. *The Struggle for Peace: Israelis and Palestinians*. Austin: University of Texas Press, 1992.

Flapan, Simha. *The Birth of Israel: Myths and Realities*. New York: Pantheon Books, 1987.

Freedman, Robert O., ed. *The Intifada: Its Impact on Israel, the Arab World, and the Superpowers*. Miami: Florida International University Press, 1991.

Friedman, Robert I. *Zealots for Zion: Inside Israel's West Bank Settlement Movement*. New York: Random House, 1992.

Green, Stephen. *Taking Sides: America's Secret Relations with a Militant Israel*. New York: William Morrow, 1984.

————. *Living by the Sword: America and Israel in the Middle East, 1968–87*. Brattleboro, Vt.: Amana Books, 1988.

Gresh, Alain. *The PLO: The Struggle Within*. Translated by A. M. Berrett. London: Zed Books, 1985.

Grossman, David. *Sleeping on a Wire: Conversations with Palestinians in Israel*. Translated by Haim Watzman. New York: Farrar, Straus and Giroux, 1993.

Halsell, Grace. *Journey to Jerusalem*. New York: Macmillan, 1981.

Harkabi, Yehoshafat. *Hachroat Goraliot*. Tel Aviv: Am Oved, 1966; reprinted in revised form as *Israel's Fateful Hour*. Translated by Lenn Schramm. New York: Harper & Row, 1988.

Heller, Mark A. *A Palestinian State: The Implications for Israel*. Cambridge: Harvard University Press, 1982.

Hertzburg, Arthur, ed. *The Zionist Idea: A Historical Analysis and Reader*. New York: Atheneum, 1959.

Hirst, David. *The Gun and the Olive Branch: The Roots of Violence in the Middle East*. 2d ed. London: Faber and Faber, 1984.

Horowitz, Dan, and Moshe Lissak. *Origins of the Israeli Polity: Palestine Under the Mandate*. Chicago: University of Chicago Press, 1987.

Hourani, Albert, et al. *The Modern Middle East*. London: I. B. Tauris, 1993.

Hunter, F. Robert. *The Palestinian Uprising: A War by Other Means*. 2d ed. Berkeley: University of California Press, 1993.

Hurewitz, J. C. *The Struggle for Palestine*. New York: W. W. Norton, 1950.

Hurwitz, Deena, ed. *Walking the Red Line: Israelis in Search of Justice for Palestine*. Philadelphia: New Society Publishers, 1992.

Ingrams, Doreen. *Palestine Papers 1917–1922: Seeds of Conflict*. London: John Murray, 1972.

Israel and the Occupied Territories: Administrative Detention During the Palestinian Intifada. New York: Amnesty International, 1989.

Jansen, Michael. *Dissonance in Zion*. London: Zed Books, 1987.

Jerusalem Media and Communication Centre. *Israeli Obstacles to Economic Development in the Occupied Palestinian Territories*. Jerusalem: JMCC, 1992.

Kaufman, Edy, Shukri B. Abed, and Robert L. Rothstein, eds. *Democracy, Peace, and the Israeli-Palestinian Conflict*. Boulder: Lynne Rienner Publishers, 1993.

Kedourie, Elie, and Sylvia G. Haim, eds. *Zionism and Arabism in Palestine and Israel*. London: Frank Cass, 1982.

Keller, Adam. *Terrible Days: Social Divisions and Political Paradoxes in Israel*. Amstelveen, Holland: Cypres, 1987.

Khalaf, Issa. *Politics in Palestine: Arab Factionalism and Social Disintegration, 1939–1948*. Albany: State University of New York Press, 1991.

Khalidi, Rashid. *Under Siege: PLO Decisionmaking During the 1982 War*. New York: Columbia University Press, 1986.

Khalidi, Walid. "The Gulf Crisis: Origins and Consequences." *Journal of Palestine Studies* 78 (Winter 1991), pp. 5–29.

_____, ed. *From Haven to Conquest: Readings in Zionism and the Palestine Problem Until 1948*. Beirut: Institute for Palestine Studies, 1971; reprint, Washington, D.C.: Institute for Palestine Studies, 1987.

Khouri, Fred J. *The Arab-Israeli Dilemma*. 3d ed. Syracuse, N.Y.: Syracuse University Press, 1985.

Kimmerling, Baruch, and Joel S. Migdal. *Palestinians: The Making of a People*. New York: Free Press, 1993.

Kushner, David, ed. *Palestine in the Late Ottoman Period: Political, Social, and Economic Transformation*. Jerusalem: Yad Izhak Ben-Zvi Press, 1986.

Kyle, Keith. *Suez*. New York: St. Martin's Press, 1991.

Lesch, Ann Mosely. *Arab Politics in Palestine, 1917–1939*. Ithaca: Cornell University Press, 1979.

Lesch, Ann Mosely, and Mark Tessler. *Israel, Egypt, and the Palestinians: From Camp David to Intifada*. Bloomington: Indiana University Press, 1989.

Lockman, Zachary, and Joel Beinin, eds. *Intifada: The Palestinian Uprising Against Israeli Occupation*. Boston: South End Press, 1989.

Louis, William Roger, and Robert W. Stookey, eds. *The End of the Palestine Mandate*. Austin: University of Texas Press, 1986.

Lukacs, Yehuda, ed. *The Israeli-Palestinian Conflict: A Documentary Record*. 2d ed. New York: Cambridge University Press, 1991.

Lukacs, Yehuda, and Abdalla M. Battah, eds. *The Arab-Israeli Conflict: Two Decades of Change*. Boulder: Westview Press, 1988.

Lustick, Ian S. *Arabs in the Jewish State: Israel's Control of a National Minority*. Austin: University of Texas Press, 1980.

———. *For the Land and the Lord: Jewish Fundamentalism in Israel*. New York: Council on Foreign Relations, 1988.

———, ed. *Arab-Israeli Relations: A Collection of Contending Perspectives and Recent Research*. 10 vols. New York: Garland Publishing, Inc., 1994.

Mandel, Neville. *The Arabs and Zionism Before World War I*. Berkeley: University of California Press, 1976.

Marlowe, John. *Rebellion in Palestine*. London: Cresset Press, 1946.

Mattar, Philip. "The PLO and the Gulf Crisis." *Middle East Journal* 48:1 (Winter 1994), pp. 31–46.

Mendelsohn, Everett. *A Compassionate Peace: A Future for Israel, Palestine, and the Middle East*. New York: Farrar, Straus and Giroux, 1989.

Moore, John Norton, ed. *The Arab-Israeli Conflict*. Vol. 3, *Documents*. Princeton: Princeton University Press, 1974.

Morris, Benny. *The Birth of the Palestinian Refugee Problem, 1947–1949*. Cambridge: Cambridge University Press, 1987.

———. *1948 and After: Israel and the Palestinians*. Oxford: Clarendon Press, 1990.

Muslih, Muhammad Y. *The Origins of Palestinian Nationalism*. New York: Columbia University Press, 1988.

Najjar, Orayb Aref, with Kitty Warnock. *Portraits of Palestinian Women*. Salt Lake City: University of Utah Press, 1992.

Nakhleh, Khalil, and Elia Zureik, eds. *The Sociology of the Palestinians*. New York: St. Martin's Press, 1980.

Nassar, Jamal R. *The Palestine Liberation Organization: From Armed Struggle to the Declaration of Independence*. New York: Praeger, 1991.

Nassar, Jamal R., and Roger Heacock, eds. *Intifada: Palestine at the Crossroads*. New York: Praeger, 1990.

Neff, Donald. *Warriors at Suez: Eisenhower Takes America into the Middle East*. New York: Simon and Schuster, 1981.

———. *Warriors for Jerusalem: The Six Days That Changed the Middle East*. Brattleboro, Vt.: Amana Books, 1988.

_____. *Warriors Against Israel: America Comes to the Rescue*. Brattleboro, Vt.: Amana Books, 1988.

Neuman, David, ed. *The Impact of Gush Emunim Politics and Settlement in the West Bank*. London: Croom Helm, 1985.

Ovendale, Ritchie. *The Origins of the Arab-Israeli Wars*. 2d ed. New York: Longman, 1992.

Owen, Roger, ed. *Studies in the Economic and Social History of Palestine in the Nineteenth and Twentieth Centuries*. Carbondale and Edwardsville: Southern Illinois University Press, 1982.

Pappe, Ilan. *The Making of the Arab-Israeli Conflict, 1947–1959*. London: I. B. Tauris, 1992.

Parfitt, Tudor. *The Jews in Palestine, 1800–1882*. Woodbridge, Suffolk: Boydell Press, 1987.

Parker, Richard B. *The Politics of Miscalculation in the Middle East*. Bloomington: Indiana University Press, 1993.

Peretz, Don. *Intifada: The Palestinian Uprising*. Boulder: Westview Press, 1990.

Punishing a Nation: Human Rights Violations During the Palestinian Uprising. Washington, D.C.: Al-Haq/Law in the Service of Man, 1988.

Quandt, William B. *Peace Process: American Diplomacy and the Arab-Israeli Conflict Since 1967*. Washington, D.C.: The Brookings Institution; Berkeley and Los Angeles: University of California Press, 1993.

_____, ed. *The Middle East: Ten Years After Camp David*. Washington, D.C.: The Brookings Institution, 1988.

Quigley, John. *Palestine and Israel: A Challenge to Justice*. Durham, N.C.: Duke University Press, 1990.

Rabinovich, Itamar, and Jehuda Reinharz, eds. *Israel in the Middle East: Documents and Readings on Society, Politics and Foreign Relations, 1948–Present*. New York: Oxford University Press, 1984.

Randal, Jonathan. *The Tragedy of Lebanon: Christian Warlords, Israeli Adventurers, and American Bunglers*. London: Hogarth Press, 1990.

Reese, Scott, and Jan Abu-Shakrah. *Colonial Pursuits: Settler Violence During the Uprising in the Occupied Territories*. Chicago: DataBase Project on Palestinian Human Rights, 1989.

Rigby, Andrew. *Living the Intifada*. London: Zed Books, Ltd., 1991.

Rosenwasser, Penny. *Voices from a "Promised Land": Palestinian and Israeli Peace Activists Speak Their Hearts*. Willimantic, Conn.: Curbstone Press, 1992.

Roy, Sara. *The Gaza Strip*. Jerusalem: West Bank Data Base Project, 1986.

Rubenberg, Cheryl A. *Israel and the American National Interest: A Critical Examination*. Urbana: University of Illinois Press, 1986.

Ruether, Rosemary Radford, and Marc H. Ellis, eds. *Beyond Occupation: American Jewish, Christian, and Palestinian Voices for Peace*. Boston: Beacon Press, 1990.

Ruether, Rosemary Radford, and Herman J. Ruether. *The Wrath of Jonah: The Crisis of Religious Nationalism in the Israeli-Palestinian Conflict*. New York: Harper and Row, 1989.

Sacher, Howard M., ed. *The Rise of Israel: A Documentary Record from the Nineteenth Century to 1948*. 38 vols. New York: Garland Publishing, 1987.

Sahliyeh, Emile. *In Search of Leadership: West Bank Politics Since 1967.* Washington, D.C.: The Brookings Institution, 1988.

Said, Edward. *The Question of Palestine.* New York: Vintage, 1980.

————. "The Morning After." *The London Review of Books,* 21 October 1993, pp. 3–7.

Said, Edward, and Christopher Hitchens, eds. *Blaming the Victims: Spurious Scholarship and the Palestinian Question.* London: Verso, 1988.

Saunders, Harold H. *The Other Walls: The Politics of the Arab-Israeli Peace Process.* Rev. ed. Princeton: Princeton University Press, 1991.

Schiff, Ze'ev, and Ehud Ya'ari. *Israel's Lebanon War.* Translated by Ina Friedman. New York: Simon and Schuster, 1984.

————. *Intifada: The Palestinian Uprising—Israel's Third Front.* Translated by Ina Friedman. New York: Simon and Schuster, 1989.

Schölch, Alexander. *Palestine in Transformation, 1856–1882: Studies in Social, Economic, and Political Development.* Washington, D.C.: Institute for Palestine Studies, 1993.

Segal, Jerome M. *Creating the Palestinian State: A Strategy for Peace.* Chicago: Lawrence Hill Books, 1989.

Segev, Tom. *1949: The First Israelis.* New York: Free Press, 1986.

Shafir, Gershon. *Land, Labor and the Origins of the Israeli-Palestinian Conflict, 1882–1914.* Cambridge: Cambridge University Press, 1989.

Shehadeh, Raja. *Occupier's Law: Israel and the West Bank.* Rev. ed. Washington, D.C.: Institute for Palestine Studies, 1988.

Shlaim, Avi. *Collusion Across the Jordan: King Abdullah, the Zionist Movement, and the Partition of Palestine.* New York: Columbia University Press, 1988.

————. "Prelude to the Accord: Likud, Labor, and the Palestinians." *Journal of Palestine Studies* 90 (Winter 1994), pp. 5–20.

Slapikoff, Saul A. *Consider and Hear Me: Voices from Palestine and Israel.* Philadelphia: Temple University Press, 1993.

Smith, Charles D. *Palestine and the Arab-Israeli Conflict.* 2d ed. New York: St. Martin's Press, 1992.

Smooha, Sammy. *Arabs and Jews in Israel.* Vol. 1, *Conflicting and Shared Attitudes in a Divided Society.* Boulder, Westview Press, 1989.

————. *Arabs and Jews in Israel.* Vol. 2, *Change and Continuity in Mutual Intolerance.* Boulder: Westview Press, 1992.

Spiegel, Steven L. *The Other Arab-Israeli Conflict: Making America's Middle East Policy, from Truman to Reagan.* Chicago: University of Chicago Press, 1985.

Spinzak, Ehud. *The Ascendance of Israel's Radical Right.* New York: Oxford University Press, 1991.

Strum, Philippa. *The Women Are Marching: The Second Sex and the Palestinian Revolution.* Brooklyn, N.Y.: Lawrence Hill Books, 1992.

Suleiman, Michael W. *The Arabs in the Mind of America.* Brattleboro, Vt.: Amana Books, 1988.

————, ed. *U.S. Policy on Palestine.* Normal, Ill.: AAUG Press, 1994.

Swirski, Shlomo. *Israel: The Oriental Majority.* Translated by Barbara Swirski. London: Zed Books, 1989.

Viorst, Milton. *Sands of Sorrow: Israel's Journey from Independence.* New York: Harper and Row, 1987.

Vital, David. *Zionism: The Origins of Zionism.* Oxford: Clarendon Press, 1975.

_____. *Zionism: The Formative Years.* Oxford: Clarendon Press, 1982.

_____. *Zionism:The Crucial Phase.* Oxford: Clarendon Press, 1987.

Wallach, John, and Janet Wallach. *The New Palestinians: The Emerging Generation of Leaders.* Rocklin, Calif.: Prima Publishing, 1992.

Wilson, Mary C. *King Abdullah, Britain and the Making of Jordan.* Cambridge: Cambridge University Press, 1987.

Zureik, Elia. *The Palestinians in Israel: A Study in Internal Colonialism.* London: Routledge and Kegan Paul, 1979.

Zureik, Elia, and Fouad Moughrabi, eds. *Public Opinion and the Palestine Question.* New York: St. Martin's Press, 1987.

□   □   □

Recommended Resources

These films have been chosen to illustrate a variety of viewpoints on the Israeli-Palestinian conflict. Some are too long to be shown in a regular class meeting, but could be used in a special evening session.

Beyond the Green Line. 67 minutes, 1993.
This is a powerful investigation of the effects of the *intifada* on Jews and Palestinians, including the ways it has challenged traditional self-images of both peoples. The film includes interviews with extremists and moderates, liberals and fundamentalists; it also shows army activities in Gaza, illegal patrols by Israeli settlers on the West Bank, and the dynamiting of Arab houses. Directed by Mili Gottlieb for Amadeus Film Productions Ltd. Distributed by Filmmakers Library.

Courage Along the Divide. 75 minutes, 1987.
A documentary by Victor Schonfeld, this film presents haunting images of the wretched living conditions and brutality experienced by Palestinian Arabs as everyday occurrence. It includes a fascinating debate among Israeli soldiers about whether or not they should serve in the West Bank and Gaza and an interview with U.S.-Palestinian peace activist Mubarak Awad. Each of the three parts of this film could be used separately. Arabic, Hebrew, and English with English subtitles. Produced for Central Independent Television/SPI and distributed by Filmmakers Library.

Gaza Ghetto. 82 minutes, 1984.
This film by PeA Holmquist, Joan Mandell, and Pierre Bjorklund focuses on the daily lives of three generations of a Palestinian family and their neighbors living in Jabalia refugee camp in the Gaza Strip. Interviews with Israeli general Ariel Sharon and former military coordinator for the West Bank and Gaza Binyamin Ben Eliezar are included, as is archival footage of Sharon's "pacification" program in Gaza. Distributed by First Run/Icarus Films.

On Our Land. 55 minutes, 1983.
Filmed by Antonia Caccia, this is a portrayal of daily life in 1981 in Umm el-Fahm, the largest Palestinian village inside Israel. A traditional farming community, its members now participate in the Israeli wage economy. The film

discusses the discrimination in housing and employment these Palestinian Israeli citizens experience and compares their situation with that of the residents of Israeli settlements built on land that used to belong to Umm el-Fahm. Distributed by First Run/Icarus Films.

Palestine: Promises, Rebellion, Abdication. 10-part series of varying lengths, 17 to 36 minutes, 1980.
This British analysis of the history of the conflict over Palestine through the establishment of the State of Israel was originally produced for Thames Television. It features interviews with Israeli and Palestinian historians, British statespersons, and military officers and includes archival footage. The first three sections ("Promises") cover the period from 1914, when Palestine came under British control, until 1935. The next four parts ("Rebellion") examine the Arab Revolt of 1936–1939, Hitler's rise to power and the Nuremberg laws in Germany, the Anglo-American Commission's recommendations, and the British withdrawal from Palestine. The final three films ("Abdication") begin with the United Nations' involvement in the issue and deal with 1947 and 1948. Distributed by Heritage Visual Sales.

Palestinian Portraits. 22 minutes, 1987.
In this documentary, a diverse group of U.S.-Palestinian women and men in all walks of life from the Catholic priesthood to neurosurgery to ballet talk about their deep-rooted identification with the culture, landscape, history, and future of their homeland. It breaks down stereotypes and gives audiences a more rounded perspective on the Palestinian people. Produced by the United Nations and distributed by First Run/Icarus Films.

The Shadow of the West. 50 minutes, 1986.
Focusing on the plight of the Palestinians as the most enduring residue of the modern encounter between the Arabs and the West, Edward Said traces the course of European involvement with the Near East via the Crusades to Napoleon's campaign in Egypt and the French and English entrepreneurs, adventurers, and empire builders who came in his wake. Part of "The Arabs: A Living History," a documentary series by Landmark Films.

Shoot and Cry. 51 minutes, 1988.
Through the eyes of two men—an eighteen-year-old Israeli conscript and a Palestinian working illegally in Tel Aviv—this film shows the effect of the Israeli occupation of the West Bank and Gaza Strip on Israeli society. Israelis representing a diversity of viewpoints argue among themselves over the dilemma, cast as a choice between morality and security, which in this context means settlement. The phrase "shoot and cry" was first used during the 1982 War in Lebanon to describe Israeli soldiers who, torn between patriotism and conscience, would shoot first, then cry later. Produced by the National Film Board of Canada, directed by Helen Kladawsky and Miguel Merkin, and distributed by First Run/Icarus Films.

Stranger at Home. 93 minutes, 1985.
Palestinian artist Kamal Boullata, exiled for twenty years, returns to Jerusalem with his friend, Jewish Dutch filmmaker and director Rudolf van den Berg. Both confront dreams and apprehensions. In an especially interesting scene, the two discuss immigration policies and learn that Boullata, born in the West Bank, would not be allowed to immigrate, whereas his Jewish Dutch friend, with no ties to Israel, could be immediately granted residency. Arabic, English, and Hebrew with English subtitles. Distributed by Ben van Meerendonk.

The Struggle for Peace. 57 minutes, 1991.
Filmed by a crew made up of Israelis, Palestinians, and Americans, this well-written video examines the efforts of several grassroots organizations trying to bring about a peaceful settlement to Israeli-Palestinian strife. Israeli soldiers who refuse to serve in the Occupied Territories, "Women in Black," the tax resistance of the Palestinian village of Beit Sahour, and an Israeli-Palestinian dialogue group that began during the *intifada* and continued after the Gulf War are among those featured. Produced by Elizabeth Fernea, directed by Steven Talley, and distributed by First Run/Icarus Films.

Voices from Gaza. 51 minutes, 1989.
With a minimum of commentary, this film lets the voices of the Palestinians in the Gaza Strip, particularly the 70 percent who are refugees, speak for themselves of life under Israeli occupation and the enormous social changes brought about by the *intifada.* The film, which is directed by Antonia Caccia and produced by Maysoon Pachachi, provides a description of the work of the underground popular committees responsible for health, education, and welfare services as well as a discussion of the conditions in the camps since the uprising began. Distributed by First Run/Icarus Films.

We Are God's Soldiers. 52 minutes, 1993.
This study of Islamic movements in the Gaza Strip was filmed in 1992. It includes interviews with some of the Hamas leaders expelled later that year as well as a discussion of the role of women. The story of two brothers, one a supporter of Fateh, the other favoring Hamas, illustrates internal Palestinian debate. Arabic with English subtitles. Produced by AlQuds Television Productions for Channel 4, United Kingdom, and available from AlQuds Distributions.

Wedding in Galilee. 110 minutes, 1986.
Both a strong sense of Palestinian national cultural identity and deep historical attachment to the land are communicated in this drama of a Muslim marriage ceremony that takes place in a Palestinian village in the Galilee, under the watchful eyes of the Israeli authorities. This beautiful, award-winning film was directed by Israeli-Palestinian Michael Khleifi and produced by Jacqueline Louis and Bernard Lorain. Arabic and Hebrew with English subtitles. Distributed by Kino International Corporation.

The Women Next Door. 80 minutes, 1992.

This thought-provoking documentary explores the ways the occupation has affected the roles and lives of Palestinian and Israeli women, particularly since the *intifada.* It examines the meaning of femininity, motherhood, birth, violence, compassion, and female solidarity in the context of the ongoing political conflict. Directed and filmed by three women: two Israeli, one Palestinian. Distributed by Women Make Movies.

□ □ □

Glossary

Aliyah (pl. *Aliyot*) literally means "going up"; the word refers to a wave of immigration to Israel.

Arab Revolt of 1936–1939 was a massive and sustained violent and nonviolent protest against Zionist immigration to Palestine that was brutally suppressed by Britain.

Ashkenazi (n. pl. Ashkenazim) are Jews of German and East European descent.

Balfour Declaration was the 1917 statement issued by the British foreign secretary and approved by the British government that called for the establishment of a Jewish homeland in Palestine with protection for the "civil and religious rights of existing non-Jewish communities in Palestine," which were 90 percent of the population at the time.

Brinkmanship is a strategy of risking confrontation by challenging an adversary's important commitment in the hope that the adversary will back down rather than fight.

Camp David Accords refer to the 17 September 1978 agreement made by Egypt, Israel, and the United States that provided a framework for an Egyptian-Israeli Peace Treaty (signed in 1979) and proposed that a self-governing Palestinian authority be established for the West Bank and Gaza Strip.

Churchill White Paper indicated in 1922 that it was not Britain's intention that an exclusively Jewish state be created in Palestine, nor was there to be any subordination of Arab population, language, or culture to Jewish nationalist aspirations.

Diaspora, meaning dispersion, originally referred to Jews who were scattered after the Babylonian captivity and now describes the exile situation of any national group of people.

Gush Emunim (literally, Bloc of the Faithful) is a religious-nationalist Jewish Israeli settlement movement.

Haganah, Zionist paramilitary force of the Jewish settlers in Palestine, became the Israeli Defense Forces in 1948.

Histadrut is Israel's General Federation of Jewish Labor and a key nongovernmental player in Israeli politics.

Hussein-McMahon correspondence, letters written in 1915 and 1916 between Sharif Hussein of Mecca and the British High Commissioner of Egypt Henry McMahon, set out the terms under which Hussein's family would lead an Arab revolt against Ottoman rule in exchange for British promises of independence after the end of the war.

Idealism, describing the political orientation that holds that human nature is essentially good and that wars occur because of bad institutional structures rather than evil people, focuses on international law and international organizations as tools to manage international interactions.

Imperialism is the establishment of political and economic control by a state or empire over foreign territories.

Intifada is the Palestinian uprising in the West Bank and Gaza Strip that began in December 1987.

Irgun Zvai Leumi was an underground Zionist paramilitary group established by the Revisionists in the pre-1948 period.

Jewish Agency, established in 1929 to support the Yishuv through raising funds for Jewish immigration to Palestine, is closely affiliated with the World Zionist Organization.

Jewish National Fund is an organization responsible for the purchase and development of land that then becomes the inalienable property of the Jewish people.

Justification of hostility refers to an actor's deliberately promoting a crisis situation in order to provide a public excuse to go to war.

Kibbutz (pl. *kibbutzim*) refers to a Jewish settlement with collective ownership and communal living that was, initially, almost entirely agricultural.

King-Crane Commission was appointed by U.S. President Wilson in 1919 to determine the political preferences of the people of Greater Syria, Palestine, and Mesopotamia and report to the Paris Peace Conference.

Knesset is Israel's single-chamber legislative body, that is, the Parliament.

Labor party is the socialist group dominant in the Knesset from 1948 until 1977, which was part of two Unity governments between 1984 and 1990 and returned to power in 1992.

Labor Zionism was the mainstream Zionist-socialist movement in the prestate period as represented by the World Zionist Organization.

Levant refers to the eastern Mediterranean region, including Lebanon, Syria, Jordan, and the Mandate of Palestine.

Likud coalition is the right-wing nationalist political bloc with roots in the Revisionist movement that was a part of, or in control of, every Israeli government between 1977 and 1992.

MacDonald White Paper was the 1939 British report that concluded the Peel Commission's partition proposal was unworkable and a binational state should be created in Palestine.

Mandate describes a commission granted to a country to administer the political affairs of an area and prepare it for independence.

Millet **system** of governance used by the Ottoman Empire placed Jews and Christians under the jurisdiction of their own religious authorities for most legal, social, cultural, and religious affairs.

Moshav (pl. *moshavim*) refers to an Israeli cooperative agricultural settlement on government land with some private economic activities.

Nation designates a group of people with a shared history and culture and corporate sense of common identity.

Peel Commission report contained the 1937 British proposal to partition Palestine into Jewish and Arab states.

Plan Dalet was a military blueprint for the defense of Jewish settlements in predominantly Arab areas; it called for the expulsion of Palestinians who resisted Zionist attacks and the destruction of their homes.

Pogrom is the organized massacre or persecution of a minority group, especially used to refer to the nineteenth-century Russian persecution of Jews.

Rational actor model assumes international actors are monolithic entities that operate as rational, efficient decisionmakers.

Realism characterizes the political approach that views humans as flawed and power-seeking and believes international relations is a struggle between nation-states for security in a hostile environment.

Revisionist movement is an ultranationalist, nonsocialist form of Zionism, established by Vladimir Jabotinsky in the 1920s and a precursor of Likud, that advocated Jewish settlement on both sides of the Jordan River and the use of force to create the state of Israel.

Security dilemma refers to the difficulty one actor has in providing for its legitimate security without appearing to threaten the security of its opponents, thus setting off a power competition.

Sephardic (n. pl. Sephardim) originally referred to Jews of Spanish descent but is now used to identify Jews from Arab countries as well.

Shiite Muslims make up the second-largest group of Muslims and are found primarily in Iraq, Iran, and Lebanon.

Sovereignty emphasizes the territorial integrity of states and their claim of the right to conduct their domestic and foreign affairs without external interference as long as they do not challenge the sovereignty of other states.

Spinoff crises result from an actor's involvement in a primary conflict; these secondary crises are not desired by the originator of the original crisis but may be difficult to avoid.

State is a centralized political unit with sovereignty over a fixed territory and population.

Stern Gang, named after its founder, Avraham Stern, is the Zionist underground paramilitary group that split off from Irgun in 1940 and was opposed to cooperation with the British. It is also known by the acronym Lehi, for Lohamei Herut Israeli (Fighters for the Freedom of Israel).

Sunni Islam is the main, orthodox form of Islam as practiced by the majority of Muslims.

Sykes-Picot Agreement between Britain and France in 1916 arranged for the division of the Levant into areas of colonial influence after the end of World War I.

Taif Accord of 1989 brokered an agreement between warring factions in Lebanon and eventually ended the fifteen-year war; it also redistributed power in the government to reflect more accurately the composition of the population.

UN Resolution 181 was passed by the General Assembly on 29 November 1947 and called for the partition of Palestine into Jewish and Palestinian states.

UN Resolution 242, passed by the Security Council on 22 November 1967, called on Israel to withdraw from territories occupied in the June 1967 War.

UN Resolution 338 was passed by the Security Council on 22 October 1973 and called for a cease-fire-in-place to halt the October 1973 War and the implementation of UN Resolution 242.

Yishuv refers to the Jewish community in Palestine in the pre-1948 period.

Zionism is nineteenth- and twentieth-century Jewish nationalism, generally but not exclusively taking the form of support for Israel as a Jewish state.

Chronology

1516–1918	Ottoman (Turkish) Empire controls most of the Middle East, including the Levant region
1880s	Beginning of Arab movement for independence from the Ottoman Empire
1881–1903	Beginning of Russian pogroms against Jews; first wave (*aliyah*) of Jewish immigration to Palestine; Dreyfus affair in France
1896	Publication of Theodor Herzl's *The State of the Jews*
1897	First Zionist Congress meets at Basel, Switzerland
1904–1914	Second *aliyah*
1914–1918	Word War I
1915–1916	Hussein-McMahon correspondence
1916	Sykes-Picot Agreement
1917	Balfour Declaration
1919	King-Crane Commission report to the Paris Peace Conference; creation of the League of Nations
1919–1923	Third *aliyah*
1920	Britain sets up Civil Administration for Palestine
1922	Churchill White Paper indicates Britain does not intend Palestine to become a Jewish state
1924–1928	Fourth *aliyah*
1929	Western Wall riots between Palestinians and Zionists
1929–1939	Fifth *aliyah*
1933	Hitler comes to power in Germany
1935	Passage in Germany of the Nuremberg Laws directed against Jews
1936–1939	Arab Revolt; Britain crushes rebellion, expels its leaders
1937	Peel Commission report recommends partition of Palestine
1938	Germany annexes Austria; Munich Pact allows Germany to occupy the Sudetenland of Czechoslovakia
1939	MacDonald White Paper recommends immigration restrictions and the establishment within ten years of an independent, binational state in Palestine; Germany invades Poland; official beginning of World War II in Europe
1945	United Nations established; World War II ends
1946	Anglo-American Commission of Inquiry recommends UN trusteeship over Palestine; Irgun militia blows up the King David Hotel in Jerusalem

1947	Great Britain requests that the United Nations deal with the question of Palestine; UN General Assembly Resolution 181 on the partition of Palestine
1948–1949	Internal war in Palestine followed by internal and international war after Israel declares independence; Israel, Egypt, and Jordan take over land designated for Palestinian state, displacing approximately 750,000 Palestinians
1948–1958	Massive Jewish immigration to Israel from Europe, North Africa, and Asia
1956	Suez War begins when Israel, supported by Britain and France, attacks Egypt
1957	Israel evacuates the Sinai and the Gaza Strip; United Nations Emergency Force established to protect Israeli-Egyptian border
1964	Egypt and other Arab states establish PLO
1965	First Fateh guerrilla action against Israel
1967	June War initiated by Israeli attack on Egypt: Israel occupies the Sinai, the Gaza Strip, the Golan Heights, and the West Bank, extends Israeli law over East Jerusalem; UN Security Council Resolution 242
1968–1970	War of Attrition between Israel and Egypt, Israel and Syria
1969	PLO incorporates the goal of a democratic secular state in Palestine; Cairo Agreement legitimates PLO armed presence in Lebanon
1970	Rogers Plan; civil war between Jordan and the Palestinians following airplane hijackings by the PFLP
1971	"Pacification" of Gaza by Ariel Sharon
1972	Soviet military advisers expelled from Egypt
1973	October War begins when Egypt attacks Israel to regain the territories Israel captured in 1967; UN Security Council Resolution 338; OAPEC oil embargo; Non-Aligned Movement recognizes PLO as the representative of the Palestinian people
1974	Sinai I Accord between Egypt and Israel; Arab League conference at Rabat, Morocco, passes resolution declaring PLO the sole legitimate representative of the Palestinian people; Arafat addresses United Nations; PLO granted observer status at the UN
1975	Civil war in Lebanon begins; U.S.-Israeli memorandum commits the United States not to talk with the PLO until, among other requirements, the PLO accepts UN Resolutions 242 and 338; Sinai II Accords between Egypt and Israel
1976	Pro-PLO candidates sweep municipal elections in the West Bank
1977	Likud wins Israeli elections, Menachem Begin becomes prime minister; Sadat visits Jerusalem and addresses the Israeli Knesset; negotiations begin between Israel and Egypt
1978	Israeli invasion of southern Lebanon; Begin, Sadat, and Carter meet for thirteen days, sign the Camp David Accords
1979	Begin and Sadat sign Israeli-Egyptian Peace Treaty in Washington, D.C.

1980	Israel officially annexes all of East Jerusalem, UN Security Council condemns action; Venice Declaration adopted by EC
1981	Israeli attack against Iraqi nuclear reactor; U.S.-sponsored cease-fire between Israel and the PLO that lasts until June 1982; establishment of Israeli civil administration in West Bank and Gaza Strip; Israeli annexation of the Syrian Golan Heights
1982	Massive Palestinian protests against civil administration; Israel completes evacuation of the Sinai; Israeli invasion of Lebanon; Reagan peace plan; massacre at Sabra and Shatilla refugee camps
1983	Beginning of the War of the Camps in Lebanon
1984	Early elections in Israel result in creation of Labor-Likud Unity government
1985	Israel withdraws from most of Lebanon, leaving an Israeli-allied Lebanese force in control of the southern areas; PLO pledges to restrict its attacks to Israel and the Israeli-occupied Palestinian territories; Israel bombs Tunisian headquarters of the PLO
1986	Israel and Soviet Union hold discussions on establishment of consulates; Iran-Contra affair revealed in United States
1987	Emergency meeting of the League of Arab States focuses primarily on the Iran-Iraq War, virtually ignoring Palestinian-Israeli conflict; beginning of the Palestinian *intifada*
1988	King Hussein announces Jordan will disengage legally and administratively from the West Bank; Israeli national election results in a badly divided Knesset and a second Unity government; declaration of the State of Palestine at the Palestine National Council meeting in Algiers; Yasir Arafat satisfies the United States that he has met their conditions for a "substantive dialogue"
1989	U.S. State Department publishes highly critical report on Israeli human rights practices; Shamir plan calling for limited Palestinian elections; international peace demonstration in Jerusalem
1990	Israeli National Unity government collapses over proposed negotiations with Palestinians; massive influx of Soviet Jews to Israel; President Bush reaffirms U.S. policy on East Jerusalem as occupied; Yitzhak Shamir forms a narrow, right-wing government headed by Likud; United States suspends dialogue with PLO; Iraq invades Kuwait
1991	U.S.-led coalition defeats Iraq; international Arab-Israeli peace conference in Madrid
1992	Ongoing bilateral and multilateral peace talks; Labor party wins plurality in Israeli elections, Yitzhak Rabin becomes prime minister; Israel deports 400 alleged Hamas supporters to southern Lebanon
1993	Israel seals off Occupied Territories (except East Jerusalem) from Israel indefinitely; massive Israeli attack on Lebanon; Israel and

the PLO sign Oslo Accords on interim self-government
arrangements; Israel misses December deadline for initial
withdrawal of troops

1994   Massacre of Palestinians in Hebron damages peace process; Cairo
Agreement on implementation of the Oslo Accords; Palestinian
police force arrives in Jericho and Gaza Strip

□   □   □

About the Book and Author

The Israeli-Palestinian conflict has once again captured world attention—this time because of the coming together of Arafat and Rabin as a result of the secret Oslo Accords and the reactions ensuing from this historic—and challenging—event. *One Land, Two Peoples,* originally published in the throes of the *intifada,* now brings its wide readership up to date on progress in the peace negotiations, beginning with their breakdown and subsequent stalemate following the Gulf War and the ensuing renaissance stimulated by the Oslo Accords. *One Land, Two Peoples* describes the Israeli-Palestinian dynamic as a conflict "rooted in its own reality"—a struggle that, despite its international dimensions, must be resolved by the principals themselves. Throughout, Deborah Gerner shows how what is happening today is steeped in the history of the region and illustrates ways that theories of international relations can help address questions about the politics of national identity and the roles of economics, culture, religion, and outside actors in fueling or quelling the conflict.

In its first edition, this text was commended for its clarity, conciseness, and balanced viewpoint. It has been used in college classrooms ranging from international relations and foreign policy to Middle East studies, religious studies, peace studies, history, English, and many more. This new and fully revised second edition includes updated maps, tables, photos, illustrations, media resources, chronology, and glossary, all of which add to the superb text presentation.

Deborah J. Gerner is associate professor of political science at the University of Kansas.

BOOKS IN THIS SERIES

Index

Abbas, Mahmoud, 1, 187
Abd al-Shafi, Haider, 186, 192
Abdullah, King of Jordan, 44
Achille Lauro hijacking, 160
ADP. *See* Arab Democratic party
Afghanistan, 151
Africa. *See* Third World states
Afro-Asian states. *See* Third World states
Agudat Yisrael, 21, 67–68, 70
AHC. *See* Arab Higher Committee for
    Palestine
AIPAC. *See* American-Israel Public Affairs
    Committee
Ala, Abu, 187
Alexander II, Tsar of Russia, 12
ALF. *See* Arab Liberation Front
Algeria, 84, 127, 149
Algiers Declaration, 94–95, 96
Aliyah. See Jewish immigration
Allon, Yigal, 80
Amal, 128
American-Israel Public Affairs Committee
    (AIPAC), 146
Amnesty International, 82
Anglo-American Commission of Inquiry, 41
ANM. *See* Arab National Movement
Anti-Semitism, 12, 15, 21
Arab Congress, 24
Arab Democratic party (ADP), 69, 71
Arab Executive, 24
Arab Higher Committee for Palestine (AHC),
    27, 28, 42, 51, 85
Arab League, 42, 97, 129
    and peace process, 140, 141
    and PLO, 85, 90–91, 103
    See also Arab states
Arab Liberation Front (ALF), 89
Arab nationalism, 21–22, 23
Arab National Movement (ANM), 86, 87
Arab Revolt (1936–1939), 26–28, 38
Arab states
    boycott of Israel, 182

and British mandate, 38
and Camp David Accords, 138, 139, 140
importance of, 47, 49, 103
Jews in, 11–12, 53
Palestinian isolation from, 48, 58
Palestinian mistrust of, 84, 97, 120–121, 124
Palestinian refugees in, 48, 52, 133
and petroleum embargo, 120
and PLO, 84, 86, 90–91, 103
role in Palestinian dispersion, 50–51
Soviet relations with, 108, 119, 149–151, 153
U.S. relations with, 110, 117, 132, 149
See also Arab League; June 1967 War;
    October 1973 War; Organization of
    Petroleum Exporting Countries; Palestine
    War
Arafat, Yasir, 85, 88(photo), 96, 157
    and DFLP, 88
    and Gulf War, 129, 188
    and Israeli peace movement, 73
    and 1982 War in Lebanon, 93, 125–126, 127
    and Oslo Accords, 1, 2, 89, 187, 188, 191, 192
    Stockholm Declaration, 142–143
al-Ard, 59
Arens, Moshe, 99, 100
Ashkenazi-Sephardic division, 57, 63, 68, 73
Ashrawi, Hanan, 186
Aspin, Les, 147
Assad, Hafez, 121–122, 138, 151
Aswan Dam project (Egypt), 108, 150
Austro-Hungarian Empire, 32
Auto-Emancipation! (Pinsker), 13
Avnery, Uri, 15, 39, 178–179

Baghdad Pact (1955), 108, 149
Baker, James, 144, 145–146
    and Madrid Conference, 179, 180, 181, 182
Balfour, Arthur James, 23, 30. *See also* Balfour
    Declaration
Balfour Declaration, 23–24, 26, 29–32, 33, 42,
    89
Banat Yacoub, 177

Palestinian federation proposals, 94, 144,
168, 178
and Palestinian national movement, 28, 93,
94
Palestinians in, 52, 122
Jordan Valley Development Plan. *See* United
Plan for Jordan Valley Development
Judea. *See* East Jerusalem
June 1967 War, 47, 110–115
and crisis theory, 107
refugees from, 113, 122, 133
and Soviet Union, 149–150
and U.S. policy, 135, 136
See also Occupied Territories
Justification of hostility crisis, 107, 112–113,
126

Kahan, Yitzhak, 127
Karameh, Battle of, 121
Karp Report, 78
Kennedy, John F., 131, 135
Kenya, 108
Keren Hayesod (Jewish Foundation Fund), 17
Khalaf, Salah. *See* Iyad, Abu
Khalidi, Husseini, 26
Khoury, Ahmed Suleiman. *See* Ala, Abu
Khrushchev, Nikita, 149
Kibbutzim, 16, 19, 65, 72
King-Crane Commission (1919), 33–34
Kissinger, Henry, 117, 118, 119, 137, 138, 142,
150
Klinghoffer, Leon, 160
Knesset, 56, 61, 83
Kuwait. *See* Gulf War

Labor party (Israel), 61, 63, 65–66
and Histadrut, 72
and Madrid Conference, 185
and October 1973 War, 116
and Oslo Accords, 187, 189–190
and peace movement, 73
and PLO negotiations, 65
recent elections, 69, 70, 71, 147, 185
Labor Zionism, 19–20
Lake Tiberias attack, 134–135
"Land-for-peace" proposals, 63, 65, 80
Law for the Acquisition of Absentee Property
(1950), 58
Laws of Return, 56
League of Nations, 28, 31, 33, 34, 36, 46, 122
Lebanese Forces, 128
Lebanese Front (LF), 123
Lebanese National Movement (LNM), 123

Lebanon
border incidents, 90, 125, 128
Israeli invasion (1978), 73, 124
and June 1967 War, 113
and 1956 Suez War, 109
1958 crisis, 135
1975–1976 Civil War, 122–124
Palestinians in, 52, 122–123
and United States, 124, 128, 140–142
War of the Camps, 128
See also Arab states; 1982 War in Lebanon
Lebow, Richard Ned, 106–107
Lehi. *See* Stern Gang
Levant, 21
Levinger, Moshe, 72
Levy, David, 66, 181
Lewis, Samuel, 147
LF. *See* Lebanese Front
Liberal party (Israel), 66
Libya, 89, 149, 152
Likud coalition (Israel), 61, 63, 66–67
and Madrid Conference, 184, 186
and Occupied Territories, 80, 91
and October 1973 War, 116
and Oslo Accords, 66, 190
and peace process, 137
and PLO negotiations, 65
recent elections, 69, 70, 71, 184
LNM. *See* Lebanese National Movement
Lodge, Henry Cabot, 135, 202(n16)
Lohamei Herut Israeli. *See* Stern Gang
Lopez, George, 160–161
Lovers of Zion (Hovevei Tsion), 13–14

Maastricht Treaty, 157
MacBride, Seán, 127
MacDonald, J. Ramsay, 37
MacDonald White Paper (1939), 38–39, 41, 168
McMahon, Sir Henry, 28–29, 38
Madrid Conference (1991), 104, 148, 172, 179–
182, 180(table)
and Israeli internal politics, 71, 181, 184, 185,
186
Washington rounds, 182–187
Magnes, Judah L., 20
Malik, Charles, 109
Malta, 157
Mapai party (Israel), 63
Mapam (Israel), 65–66
Maronite Christians (Lebanon), 122, 123, 124,
128
Meir, Golda, 116
Melamed, Eliezer, 190
Meretz (Energy) party (Israel), 65–66, 71, 73